Yes Gawd!

In the series *Religious Engagement in Democratic Politics*,
edited by PAUL A. DJUPE

ROYAL G. CRAVENS III

Yes Gawd!

How Faith Shapes LGBT Identity and
Politics in the United States

TEMPLE UNIVERSITY PRESS
Philadelphia • Rome • Tokyo

TEMPLE UNIVERSITY PRESS
Philadelphia, Pennsylvania 19122
tupress.temple.edu

Library of Congress Cataloging-in-Publication Data

Names: Cravens, Royal G., III, 1986– author.
Title: Yes Gawd! : how faith shapes LGBT identity and politics in the
    United States / Royal G. Cravens III.
Other titles: Religious engagement in democratic politics.
Description: Philadelphia : Temple University Press, 2024. | Series:
    Religious Engagement in Democratic Politics | An online supplemental
    appendix containing a methodological appendix, data files, and graphics
    is available through the Harvard Dataverse. | Includes bibliographical
    references and index. | Summary: "Systematically examines how religious
    development affects LGBT identity, political attitudes, and political
    behaviors in the United States"— Provided by publisher.
Identifiers: LCCN 2023020547 (print) | LCCN 2023020548 (ebook) | ISBN
    9781439924426 (cloth) | ISBN 9781439924433 (paperback) | ISBN
    9781439924440 (pdf)
Subjects: LCSH: Sexual minorities—Political activity—United States. |
    Sexual minorities—Religious life—United States. | Religion and
    politics—United States.
Classification: LCC HQ73.73.U6 C73 2024 (print) | LCC HQ73.73.U6 (ebook)
    | DDC 306.760973—dc23/eng/20230807
LC record available at https://lccn.loc.gov/2023020547
LC ebook record available at https://lccn.loc.gov/2023020548

Printed in the United States of America

9 8 7 6 5 4 3 2 1

To Darren, Mom (Barbara), and Dad (Gene)

Contents

Accessing the Online Supplemental Materials

An online supplemental appendix containing a methodological appendix, data files, and graphics is available through the Harvard Dataverse at the following web address: https://doi.org/10.7910/DVN/M87Q1V.

Yes Gawd!

Introduction

We pray, we pray
We pray the gay away!
'Cause boys like girls and girls like boys
And that's what God done say.

—ROBERTA AND REGGIE (SINGING), *WILL & GRACE*,
SEASON 9, EPISODE 4: "GRANDPA JACK"

Dominant (read: stereotypical) representations of lesbian, gay, bisexual, and transgender (LGBT) people in society operate on what I refer to as the *Will & Grace* paradigm. By that, I mean LGBT identity has generally been constructed in popular culture, and to a great extent in the scientific literature, as predominantly gay or lesbian, cisgender, white, middle or upper-middle class, and metropolitan. While *Will & Grace* was groundbreaking—the program featured two gay lead characters, was one of the first network television programs to air a kiss between two men, depicted LGBT people and families in sympathetic circumstances, and led then–vice president Joseph Biden to declare the show "did more to educate the American public than almost anybody's ever done so far" (Little 2012)—it still followed a familiar trope: an educated, white, gay professional navigating life on the Upper West Side of Manhattan. When religion was broached as a subject on the show, it was largely used as a foil to the happiness of the characters or their families. In fact, the chapter-opening quote is from a scene in which two camp counselors at a "conversion camp" (played by Jane Lynch and Andrew Rannells) sing about religiously inspired heteronormativity. The duet occurs before a group of young people, including Jack's (a lead character played by Sean Hayes) grandson, who were sent to the camp by their parents, who feared their children might be LGBT.

Although just one example, as I describe in this text, it is consistent with the dominant cognitive, affective, and behavioral paradigms in American society that incorrectly construct religion as anathema to the LGBT experience. While contemporary social scientific research disputes the economic, racial, and gendered constructions traditionally relied on in popular and scientific depictions of LGBT people, the effects of religion on the lived experiences of LGBT people is often relegated to the realm of the "epiphenomenal," "exotic," or solely theological among social and political scientists (see Boykin 1998; Comstock 1996; Fassinger and Arseneau 2007; Garcia 1998; Johnson and Henderson 2005; Movement Advancement Project et al. 2013; Parent, DeBlaere, and Moradi 2013; Sears and Badgett 2012; Wald et al. 2005).

This text diverges from this paradigm in several important ways. Namely, this project was undertaken with the assumption that LGBT people of faith exist and that LGBT people have agency in their own religious development, rather than operating on the heterosexist assumption that faith is only a foil to LGBT identity. In this text, I show that religious affiliation and spirituality are common experiences among LGBT people, albeit less common than among non-LGBT people. More importantly, when it comes to faith, LGBT people are not simply the product of negative experiences with "organized religion." LGBT people have struggled for representation and acceptance in America's faith communities; however, LGBT spirituality is not only resilient but it is also an animating and creative force. LGBT people have embraced the American pluralist tradition and created cosmologies, spiritual communities, and religious institutions that provide spiritual affirmation. This text contributes much-needed detail to our understanding of how LGBT people create, define, and experience spirituality and spiritual affirmation and its consequences for their identity and political development.

Another divergence from scholarly and popular conceptions of LGBT people that emerges from this text is that faith affects the politics of LGBT people—which, in turn, potentially drives broader political priorities and mobilizations for the LGBT movement. The movement has largely been reactive to the countermovement tactics of the Religious Right (see Fetner 2008). Consequently, many non-LGBT people and even some LGBT people have internalized the notion that to be faithful and LGBT is an aberration. However, from the earliest days of the modern LGBT movement, LGBT people of faith led political mobilization efforts. This text is not a history of those events, but it does demonstrate the mobilizing power of faith for LGBT people by contrasting the effects of participation in faith and secular communities on political activism. While the political effects of faith are similar between LGBT and non-LGBT people, this text shows the importance of accounting for affirming faith experiences when studying LGBT populations. While I show that faith can be a political resource for LGBT people, religious affirmation offers its own unique contribution to the social milieu by stimulating political mobilization and, in some cases, moderating political attitudes.

There can be no doubt that certain religious beliefs influence negative attitudes toward LGBT people, and conservative religious groups have subjected LGBT people to experiences like those satirized by *Will & Grace*. Importantly, however, this does not preclude the existence of religious LGBT people (Hinrichs and Rosenberg 2002; Negy and Eisnmann 2005; Norton and Herek 2013; Selzer 1992). In fact, in both random and nonrandom samples of LGBT people in the United States, most survey participants express some religious affiliation (Cravens 2017; 2018; Herek et al. 2010; Sherkat 2016)—a point I address in Chapter 2. Furthermore, numerous qualitative studies have analyzed the psychological and sociological mechanisms that religious LGBT people adopt to integrate their sexual and religious identities (see Barton 2010; 2011; 2012; Boykin 1998; Coley 2020; Comstock 1996, especially chapter 2; Griffin 2006; Mahaffy 1996; McQueeney 2009; Minwalla, Rosser, Feldman, and Varga 2005; O'Brien 2004; Rahman 2010; Rodriguez and Ouellette 2000; Schnoor 2006; Walton 2006; Wilcox 2003; Wolkomir 2006; Yip 1997).

Of primary concern to the present study is the apparent duality of LGBT religious experience. Social and political scientists have observed an association between coming out—that is, openly identifying as LGBT—and religious nonaffiliation (Comstock 1996). Specifically, using a national probability sample of LGBT adults, Egan, Edelman, and Sherrill (2008) observe more than one-quarter of survey participants report becoming less religious after coming out; while, Lewis, Rogers, and Sherrill (2011, 671), using a subsample of the thirteen thousand American adults who responded to a Harris Interactive Poll to study the political behavior of LGBT people in the 2000 presidential election, note "outness" is more prevalent among "non-Judeo Christians" and nonreligious gays and lesbians than among Christian LGBT people.

The perception, then, is that LGBT people who are religious are closeted, likely because they experience oppression on the basis of sexual orientation or gender identity from religious institutions.[1] For some LGBT people, this is an accurate characterization, and religious stigma is so pervasive they choose (some are forced) to undergo "reparative" or "conversion therapy" programs like the one led by Roberta and Reggie, which are designed to suppress homosexuality and reinforce heterosexist gender roles often based on fundamentalist interpretations of scripture (For the Bible Tells Me So 2007; Gerber 2008; Robinson and Spivey 2007; Wolkmir 2006). These individuals may identify as "ex-gay" or, despite strong feelings of same-sex attraction, may not identify as a sexual minority at all (Wolkmir 2006). To others, the liberation of coming out extends into religious belief. Some LGBT people, notably those observed by Egan, Edelman, and Sherrill (2008) and Lewis et al. (2011), no longer feel connected to the oppressive religious identity that constrained their sexuality and/or gender identity and disassociate with organized religious traditions or give up their faith altogether.

However, other LGBT people seek to adapt their understanding of faith from hostile to affirming. Those whom Comstock (1996) refers to as "switchers" seek out denominations affirming of their sexual and/or gender identity (see also Coley 2020). Still others, especially since the founding of "gay churches" such as the Metropolitan Community Church in 1968 (Perry and Lucas 1987), may have been socialized into a religious community that is affirming of their sexual and/or gender identity. These LGBT people may rarely, if ever, experience stigmatization from their faith tradition. Despite this variation in experience, religion and sexuality are often characterized solely as conflictual, and there is little research to explain how religiosity among LGBT people influences political attitudes and behavior.

Overview of Religious Affiliation among LGBT People

While I describe the trends from large-sample surveys of LGBT people and data sets that include substantial subsamples of LGBT people over time in Chapter 2, it is important to my argument (that faith and religious practice are relatively common experiences among LGBT people and that these experiences affect their political development) to briefly review some descriptive data from a few instrumental surveys of LGBT people in the United States. Contemporary survey data lends evidence to the hypothesis that LGBT people are less likely to report a religious affiliation than non-LGBT people, yet the little-publicized fact is that religious affiliation is a common experience among this group (Murphy 2015; Sherkat 2016). Figure I.1 graphically depicts responses to questions of religious affiliation among samples and subsamples of LGBT adults in the United States. The bar chart in Figure I.1a displays the denominational distribution among respondents to a 2013 Pew Research Center study using a self-administered online survey instrument. The probability sample consists of 1,190 self-identified lesbian, gay, and bisexual respondents (one of the largest sexual minority–focused data collection projects using probability sampling techniques to date). As the figure shows, in response to the question, "What is your present religion, if any?" even when agnosticism and atheism are combined, a not altogether congruent combination, the category does not represent even a plurality of respondents. Instead, nearly 70% of the sample indicate affiliation with some religious tradition.

The bar chart in Figure I.1b displays the denominational distribution among the small number ($n = 102$) of lesbian, gay, and bisexual respondents to the 2016 General Social Survey—one of the longest-running surveys of social and political behavior in the United States, which only started asking respondents' sexual orientation in 2008. While a plurality (42.1%) of respondents in this case indicate no religious affiliation (i.e., "none"), the majority of respondents, again, indicate some religious affiliation. Of course, generalizations based on this particular case are not possible. The data do, however, lend evidence to support the conclusion that a majority of LGBT people in the United States affiliate with a religious tradition.

Similarly, the bar chart in Figure I.1c displays the denominational distribution among the large number (n = 4,737) of lesbian, gay, bisexual, and "other" sexual identity respondents to the 2016 Cooperative Congressional Election Study. This data represents one of the largest subsamples of sexual minority people with one of the most comprehensive denominational questions available (similar surveys were fielded in 2018 and 2020 and include transgender respondents, which I review in Chapters 1 and 2). As the chart shows, roughly one-quarter (27.4%) of the subsample identify as either atheist or agnostic, while the majority of the subsample identify with one of a wide variety of religious denominations.

Finally, a similar pattern emerges in the graphic depiction of responses to the 2010 Social Justice Survey question "What religion do you currently practice?" (see the bar chart in Figure I.1d). While this data has limited generalizability because the data were collected using snowball sampling techniques, and many responses were collected at LGBT political or social events, the data represent one of the largest data collection efforts focused on the lived experiences of LGBT People of Color (POC) to date. While there appears to be an outsized "other" category, again, the majority of respondents identify with some religious tradition, while only about one in ten (10.8%) identify as either atheist or agnostic.

Across the surveys represented in Figure I.1a–d, the data are also consistent in describing the dominant religious experiences of LGBT people. That is, the majority of religious respondents identify with either Protestant Christianity or Roman Catholicism, not unlike the general population of heterosexuals in the United States. Whereas smaller proportions of white respondents report affiliation with minority faith traditions, among the predominantly LGBT POC sample, minority religious traditions are much better represented. Regardless, from a social scientific perspective, it is important to not only recognize the existence of these experiences but also accurately conceptualize and measure them.

To this point, the data represented in Figure I.1 also demonstrate the limitations to our knowledge of LGBT religious affiliation. For example, while making a distinction in the published report, in the public data release, the Pew (2013a) study classifies "other" religious traditions as both Christian and non-Christian minority faiths. For example, the "other" category represents

(a)

(b)

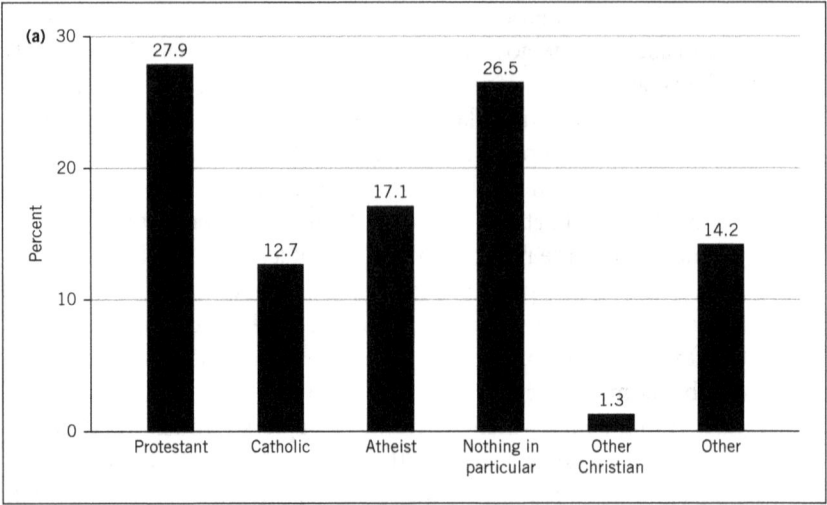

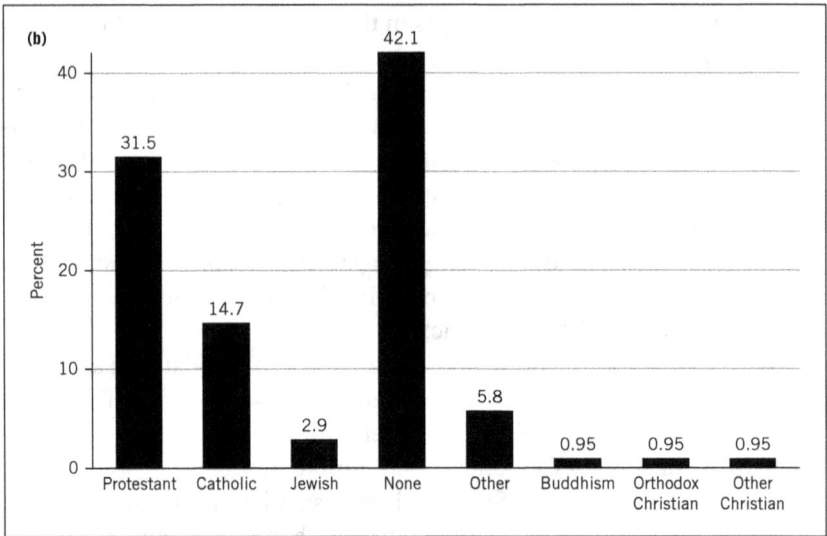

Figure I.1 Distribution of Religious Affiliation among LGBT Adults in the United States. A. "What is your present religion, if any?"; *n* = 1,190; data obtained using probability sampling. (*Pew Research Center [2013a]*). B. "What is your religious preference?"; *n* = 102; data obtained using probability sampling; see Smith et al. (2016). (*General Social Survey [2016]*). C. "What is your present religion, if any?"; *n* = 4,737; data obtained using probability sampling; see Ansolabehere and Schaffner (2017). (*Cooperative Congressional Election Study [2016]*). D. "What religion do you currently practice?"; *n* = 4,665; data obtained using probability sampling; see Battle, Pastrana, and Daniels (2010). (*Social Justice Survey [2016]*)

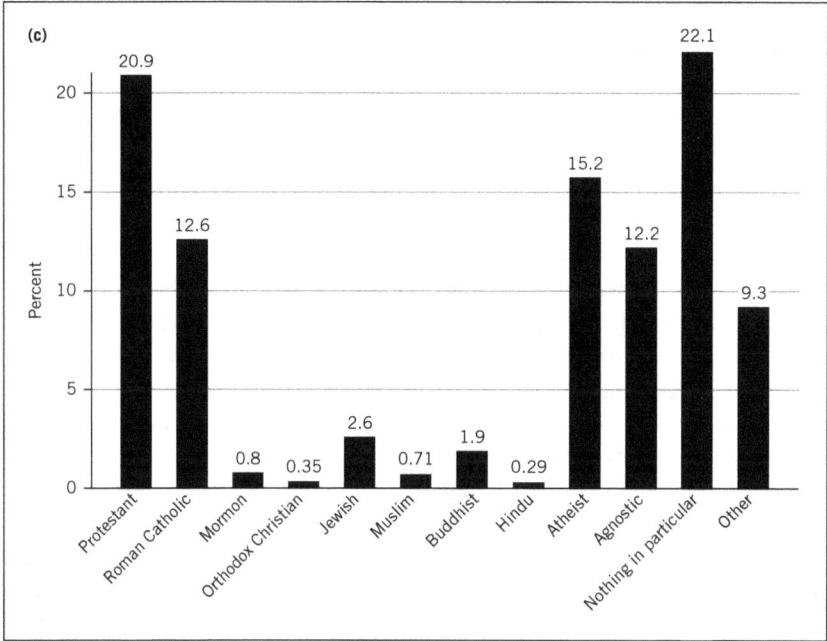

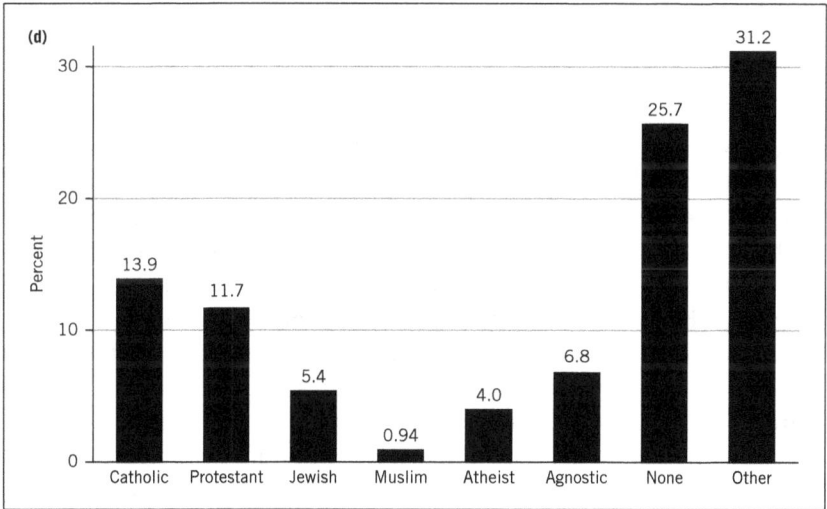

Figure I.1 (*continued*)

Mormon, Greek Orthodox, Hindu, Jewish, and Muslim LGBT people. The conflation of these traditions severely limits the predictive power of the data and is emblematic of the problems with quantitative research, especially survey research, observed by Comstock (1996), Wald and Wilcox (2006), Wald, Silverman, and Fridy (2005), Woodberry and Smith (1998), and others.

Data limitations are further evinced by the confusion about the meaning of categories such as "unaffiliated," "nothing particular," or "other." For example, in the report accompanying their 2013 survey, Pew (2013a, 91) classifies respondents who indicate "no particular" religious affiliation as nonreligious for the purposes of data analysis, even though the respondents did not specifically identify as agnostic or atheist.[2] Their interpretation of the data, therefore, suggest only about half (51%) of LGBT respondents identify as religious. The ambiguity of conceptualization and measurement of religious and nonreligious identities and experiences has serious implications for the attribution of social scientific phenomena, a topic to which I return in Chapter 2 (Woodberry and Smith 1998).

In addition, the hegemony of Christianity is often reflected in survey methodologies that measure religious affiliations and practices. Assumptions about *how* people practice faith through scripture reading or even attending religious services, for example, generally assume a Christian orthodoxy that is applicable to all other religious practices. This is obviously a fallacy, but the confluence of these biases—heterosexism, cisnormativity, and Christian religiocentrism—contributes to our general lack of understanding of LGBT people of faith.[3]

Regardless of the limitations, Figure I.1 makes clear that even though a number of LGBT people may reject religion after coming out, religious affiliation is a common experience among the majority of LGBT people in the United States. As with any social identity, however, affiliation alone is often not enough to motivate political participation, a phenomenon especially true of sexual minority identities (Duncan, Mincer, and Dunn 2017).

Of the four previously mentioned studies, only one analyzes the results and attempts to provide context to the findings. In its report, the Pew Research Center (2013a, 90), while noting that roughly one-third of LGBT respondents indicate conflict between their religious and sexual identities, also observes that "LGBT adults who do have a religious affiliation generally attend worship services less frequently and attach less importance to religion in their lives than do religiously affiliated adults in the general public" (i.e., heterosexuals).

While reporting similar associational findings as these studies, Herek et al. (2010, 189) observe that about one-quarter (23.3%) of their probability sample of 662 lesbian, gay, and bisexual adults in the United States indicate they "attend religious services" either "weekly" or "at least monthly." In the same study, Herek et al. (2010, 190) also note a similar proportion (27.8%) receive either "quite a bit" or "a great deal" of "daily guidance from religion." In both instances, majorities of respondents report affective or behavioral responses that suggest religion may only amount to a minor concern in their daily experience.

The political effects of religious association, however, are more complex than measures of religious affiliation or attendance alone (Driskell, Embry, and Lyon 2008). One goal of this study is to more fully interrogate how LGBT people participate in religious activities and the extent to which these activities influence their political behavior. This study will also interrogate when and how religious and sexual identities conflict or when one's religious experiences affirm one's sexuality and the repercussions for political attitudes and activism.

Why Study Religion among LGBT People?

In their synopsis of religious studies within the discipline of political science, Kenneth Wald, Adam Silverman, and Kevin Fridy (2005) observe that until the 1980s, religion and its effect on political outcomes was largely unstudied or ignored by Americanists within the discipline. Wald and Clyde Wilcox (2006) make a similar observation. Apart from historical and comparative studies, political scientists largely viewed religion as "too epiphenomenal" or "exotic" rather than as an indicator with significant predictive power (Wald and Wilcox 2006; Wald, Silverman, and Fridy 2005, 122–23). The rapid political ascendency of Jerry Falwell, Pat Robertson, the Moral Majority, and the Religious Right led many political scientists to reexamine dominant theories of religion and politics, especially focusing on conservative Christianity (Wald and Wilcox 2006). Even then, it was not until the 1990s that political science began regarding religious movements as "legitimate political participants with reasonable perspectives" as opposed to earlier assumptions that labeled religion as a "mystical" and "irrational" influence on political outcomes (Wald, Silverman, and Fridy 2005, 124; see also Wald, Kellstedt, and Legge 1993, 121). Despite these early hostilities, the study of religion in political science has produced a substantial and distinguished body of literature.

The study of LGBT people and their politics, as with many marginalized groups, exhibits a similar trajectory within academe. Despite growing acceptance, attitudes about LGBT people and LGBT research within the discipline of political science largely mirror those of the broader heterosexist society (Mucciaroni 2011; Novkov and Barclay 2010). The long history of LGBT political organizing in the United States notwithstanding, it was not until the 1980s and 1990s that the discipline began to recognize the important contributions of LGBT scholars as well as the subject matter of their research agendas. The recalcitrance of the discipline combined with the obstreperous nature of many LGBT scholars has led to intradisciplinary controversy as the study of LGBT politics, along with LGBT political scientists, continues to be marginalized (Burgess and Sampaio 2017).

Despite recent efforts at inclusiveness, as Mucciaroni (2011) notes, one primary objection to LGBT political research among political scientists is the fear that social scientific standards will be compromised in the pursuit of a biased social or political agenda. The study of religion in American politics has endured similar criticism; however, Wald and Wilcox (2006, 523) recognize the unique contributions to the study of religion and politics by those social scientists who were personally familiar with the interaction between the two phenomena, people who "were often themselves clergy or children of clergymen." Similarly, the sociologists Robert Woodberry and Christian Smith (1998) note that an underlying unfamiliarity with religious doctrines and practices hindered early efforts to apply scientific methodologies to the study of religious groups and their politics. "Few social scientists," they quipped, "are religiously active," which contributes not only to a lack of understanding but also to poor conceptualization, mismeasurement, and potential misattribution of social scientific phenomena (Woodberry and Smith 1998, 33).

Religious affiliation is not a prerequisite to the scientific study of religion, just as identifying as LGBT is not a prerequisite to the scientific study of LGBT people. The point that Mucciaroni (2011), Wald and Wilcox (2006), and Woodberry and Smith (1998) make is that the experiences and identity of social scientists often influence the research questions they pose. The assumption that their research is skewed because of their familiarity with the subject matter or concern that their work is "political advocacy masquerading as scholarship" ignores the fact that "all decisions that we make about what to study are political because they reveal the topics that we consider most legitimate and important to warrant examination" (Mucciaroni 2011, 17). Moreover, the privileged position of most academics constrains their ability and willingness to "learn from those who are socially marginalized," even though there is an "advantage" to "understanding and solving social problems" by examining "those who experience and suffer from those problems" (Comstock 1996, 25). Indeed, as Mucciaroni (2011, 17) succinctly notes, "if our decision to study LGBT politics is a political one, so too was our neglect of it for many years."

These observations are certainly true of the present study. As an openly gay political scientist with a background in political advocacy, I am often queried regarding my research agenda. It is, however, as the aforementioned scholars adeptly conclude, my familiarity with an understudied aspect of the

LGBT political experience that leads me to an empirical scientific inquiry, specifically using primary and secondary survey data, into the political effects of religious belief and practice among LGBT people.

Theoretical Overview

That religion is a common feature of the LGBT experience raises questions about its influence on the political behavior of LGBT people. Two of the most popular social scientific theories characterize religion as (1) an agent of political socialization that transmits values, beliefs, and behaviors that inform one's political development (Erikson and Tedin 2015; Harris 1994; 1999; Neundorf and Smets 2017; Wolkomir 2006); and, (2) a political resource that allows adherents to accrue civic and organizational skills, such as public speaking, event organizing, and persuasiveness, which are then translated into secular political action (Verba, Schlozman, and Brady 1995; Brady, Verba, and Schlozman 1995).

In their analysis of American civic engagement, Verba, Schlozman, and Brady (1995, 196–97) observe that religious participation is far less stratified than political participation. While "the affluent are more likely to take part in non-political activity," they also note that the "gap in activity between income groups is reduced to the point of insignificance with respect to giving time to religious activity." They also observe women are more likely to participate in religious activity than men and that African Americans are more likely than whites to participate in religious activity. Across the various identity characteristics in their models, Verba, Schlozman, and Brady (1995, 320) conclude, "the church" is "the domain of equal access to opportunities to learn civic skills," skills that are important determinants of political participation.

To be clear, however, more recent research shows that much of the resource mobilization associated with religious participation comes from recruitment (see Djupe and Gilbert 2006; Djupe and Grant 2001; McClerking and McDaniel 2005; McDaniel 2008), and an egalitarian distribution of civic skills is not always achieved (Djupe, Anand, and Gilbert 2007; Friesen and Djupe 2017; Robnett and Bany 2011). I return to this debate in Chapter 6. For now, it is apparent that our understanding of the mechanisms involved have evolved as the study of religion and politics has progressed, especially when focused on the experiences of marginalized groups in religious spaces including Black, Indigenous, and People of Color; women; and LGBT people. Furthermore, beyond religious affiliation, religious participation is associated with political activity.

Religious experiences can also be formative life events, while religious institutions, communities, and leaders can act as agents of socialization (Erikson and Tedin 2015). Any of these agents can impart values, beliefs, and behaviors that are consistent with an underlying religious "cosmology" that helps believers find their place in the spiritual and political realms (see Thumma and Gray 2005). Consistent with both political resource and political socialization theories, studies of LGBT politics suggest "coming out" (i.e., openly identifying as LGBT) represents an inflection point in LGBT social and political development (Egan 2012; Egan, Edelman, and Sherrill 2008). That is, like religion, coming out is an agent of socialization that offers opportunities to accrue cognitive resources as LGBT people embed within supportive social networks. Specifically, after coming out, LGBT people often undergo socializing experiences that require them to "update" their political attitudes and behavior (see Alwin and Krosnick 1991).

Important to the theoretical context of LGBT religion and politics, denominationalism in the United States and the democratizing efforts of the LGBT movement contributed to the development of non-native religious traditions that affirm, rather than theologically condemn, LGBT identities and participation (see Thumma and Gray 2005). Since the 1970s, a growing number of religious denominations explicitly affirm LGBT identities and experiences, opening their fellowships to LGBT people and allowing them to benefit from a relatively new form of political socialization (see McQueeney 2009; Moon and Tobin 2018; Moon, Tobin, and Sumerau 2019).

Like other agents of political socialization, religious agents transmit values, beliefs, and behaviors that augment political attitudes and participation (Putnam and Campbell 2010). Religious socialization can develop civic duty and political efficacy, among other cognitive and behavioral skills that contribute to political attitudinal and behavioral development (e.g., Schwadel et al. 2016). The LGBT socioreligious experience is also consistent with recent political theorizing about the "life-cycle" effects of politics on religious choices. That is, LGBT-affirming religious traditions may present political socializing opportunities for LGBT people or allow the development of different resources at different points throughout their lives, depending on the dictates of their politics (see Margolis 2018a).

While religion is largely considered to have positive repercussions for political participation and while religious belief is a common feature of the LGBT experience, the hostility of some religious denominations and the spiritual transformation associated with the coming out process pose several questions with implications for American democracy. First, is religiosity associated with political participation among LGBT people? Self-identified LGBT people are more likely to engage in political action on behalf of LGBT-specific policy priorities such as same-sex marriage (Egan 2012), but does religiosity extend into the sphere of non-LGBT-specific political activity? Similarly, as Verba, Schlozman, and Brady (1995) suggest, do all religious LGBT people accrue civic, organizational, and cognitive resources equally, or as others (see Djupe and Gilbert 2006) have shown with regard to the limitations of political resource theory, do resources only accrue to those who either attend an affirming denomination or who have completely reconciled their faith and sexuality?

Because there are few quantitative studies that interrogate denominational differences among LGBT people, and even fewer that examine political correlates, questions about denominational effects also arise. Are LGBT people within certain denominations more politically active than others? Similarly, are there denominational influences on political attitudes? Finally, what life-cycle effects may be at play when LGBT people form their religious identities or choose which religious traditions to adopt, adapt, or leave?

In addition, given the breadth of scholarship noting distinctions in politico-religious experiences across racial and ethnic groups and the lack of quantitative analysis of the religious experiences of LGBT POC, intersectional queries emerge (Djupe and Neiheisel 2012; Griffin 2006; Harris 1999). For example, while some Black religious LGBT people seek out new spiritual homes, many remain in predominantly Black congregations after coming out, largely due to racism in gay-affirming white congregations (Griffin 2006). In such cases, how does the politico-religious experience differ when one's sexuality is affirmed but not one's racial identity or vice versa? Recent research posits middle-class economic indicators are likely to be associated with homophobia among Black Protestants, leading to questions about the interaction of racial, economic, sexual, and religious characteristics (Irizarry and Perry 2017). In this text, I address these questions, and others, in order to develop a cohesive account of LGBT religion and politics in the United States.

Organization of the Book

This book is not an exploration of the theological differences in the interpretation of homosexuality. Rather, it is an exploration of the effects of religious belief and practice on political behavior among a population long persecuted by religious institutions and generally considered to be nonreligious. Despite this history, there are LGBT people of faith. In fact, a majority of LGBT people likely characterize themselves as such.

In Chapter 1, I review the construction of LGBT identity undertaken by conservative religious groups and the politico-religious efforts of LGBT people to confront this narrative and democratize both religion and politics in the United States. I use historiographic accounts focusing on conservative Evangelical Protestantism in the mid-twentieth century to demonstrate how conservative religious activists constructed LGBT identity as unreligious and secondary data analysis from surveys conducted by the Public Religion Research Institute and the General Social Survey to demonstrate how these frames resonate with a select group of Americans but potentially alienate younger generations. I then review the development of LGBT politico-religious activism, focusing on LGBT religious denominations and congregations that allow full participation for LGBT congregants and how these developments opened new opportunities for LGBT people to organize politically. I also highlight the importance of race and ethnicity to understanding both religious and LGBT identity development.

In Chapter 2, I provide an overview of religiosity among lesbian, gay, and bisexual people (including religious affiliation and public and private devotion) based on secondary data analysis of surveys conducted by the Cooperative Congressional Election Study (CCES) and the Pew Research Center. The CCES data from 2016–2020 offer a robust sample of sexual minority and transgender respondents and provide detailed trends in religious affiliation and religious participation over time.

In Chapter 3, I review the literature on political socialization theory and the transmission of religious and political identities and values through social interaction, focusing on the concept of framing. Using the "conversion" theory of LGBT political liberalism, I situate LGBT people and their experiences within the socialization paradigm. In this chapter, coming out serves as the key mechanism for understanding LGBT politico-religious distinctiveness. I analyze data collected from a representative sample of LGBT people (of my own design) to describe the religious and political socialization of LGBT people.

Descriptive analyses highlight the nature of the socializing experiences, including the sources (e.g., family, friends, media, church) and tone (i.e., positive, negative, or neutral) of information about LGBT people and identity and the religiosity of respondents before coming out. Statistical models demonstrate how specific religious experiences before coming out affect the importance of survey participants' LGBT identity and their decision to change their faith tradition after coming out.

In Chapter 4, I focus on post–coming out religious socialization among the group and pay specific attention to the relationship between affirming religious experiences and the importance of LGBT identity, religious and LGBT identity conflict, and the likelihood that survey participants change their faith tradition after coming out. I end this chapter by describing a model of LGBT religious development, based on observations in Chapters 3 and 4, and hypothesized relationships with political behavior.

In Chapter 5, I address several key questions in religious and political studies. Namely, how do LGBT people characterize the relationships among religion, politics, and LGBT culture? Also, why do LGBT people participate in religious, social, and political groups? I find that most LGBT people participate in religious and secular organizations for similar reasons. Based on a content analysis of open-ended survey responses, I describe dominant schemas or ways of understanding how religion affects politics and culture among the LGBT people I surveyed. For politics, religion can act as a catalyst and/or a facilitator. I demonstrate that some LGBT people hold activism (both religious and political) to be a component of their LGBT identity and that religion motivates them to engage in politics, often to address LGBT inequality. For others, such as those who experience conflict between their religious and LGBT identities, religion is a first step into political activism, where they first accrue resources (including the ability to integrate their religious and LGBT identities) before engaging in secular political activism. For still others, negative experiences with religious conservatives motivates political activism to keep religious conservatives from accruing political power.

In Chapter 6, I examine political activism and political attitudes. I first review the literature on political resource theory and the accrual of civic and cognitive resources among people who participate in voluntary social organizations (e.g., churches). I use data from the same survey introduced in Chapter 3 in descriptive analyses of solidary political activism (e.g., activism on behalf of LGBT people) and electoral activism (e.g., electoral behaviors like voting, volunteering, writing letters, and running for office). I then follow the same outline as Chapter 3 to describe how pre–coming out and post–coming out religious socialization affects (or does not affect) both forms of activism. I find that positive socialization does affect participation in later life, especially with regard to LGBT activism. I also find that post–coming out religious affirmation is especially important for solidary activism but has a multiplicative effect on electoral activism.

In Chapter 7, I review the literature on LGBT political distinctiveness and how socialization is thought to affect development of liberal political attitudes among LGBT people. I note religious socialization represents a potential cross-pressure with competing value frames. I outline responses to survey questions about a variety of political attitudes, including the role of government, egalitarianism, LGBT rights, gun control, abortion, partisanship, and 2020 vote choice. I then describe how pre–coming out and post–coming out religious socialization affects these attitudes. I find pre–coming out denominational affiliations are important predictors of attitudes later in life. I also find that post–coming out religious affirmation is indirectly related to political attitudes, in that the effect is transmitted through specific beliefs about the compatibility of LGBT identity and faith. I also find that religious and secular participation have different effects (one related to liberalism and one to conservatism) on political attitudes and that beliefs about the authority of religious institutions over one's life predict political conservatism.

In the final chapter, I summarize the findings and discuss the implications for LGBT political activism, American religious pluralism, and American politics. Namely, affirming religiosity is good for American democracy because it improves political engagement, but it does not guarantee a single political outcome (i.e., some religious beliefs are associated with conservatism among both LGBT and non-LGBT people). The results also support my argument that faith should be recognized as a legitimate component of the LGBT experience by social science, popular culture, *and* LGBT people. While religion/spirituality is a contested cultural feature for LGBT people, most understand that faith is a personal decision. Forcing religious beliefs on others (e.g., forcing LGBT people to attend religious schools or undergo religious rites, or forcing religion on LGBT Pride attendees) is generally the source of animosity that nonreligious LGBT people have toward organized religion, but LGBT people are discerning enough to locate their displeasure in organized religion rather than in individual religious LGBT people. Taken together, this book shows there is room for religion in LGBT communities and there is room for LGBT people in religious communities.

1

Making Room for LGBT People in American Religion and Politics

Rainbow Christ, you embody all the colors of the world.
Rainbows serve as bridges between different realms: Heaven
and Earth, east and west, queer and non-queer. Inspire us
to remember the values expressed in the rainbow flag of the
lesbian, gay, bisexual, transgender, and queer community.

—From *Rainbow Christ Prayer*
by Kittredge Cherry and Patrick Cheng

On January 4, 2020, the United Methodist Church (UMC), a Protestant Christian denomination with more than twelve million members worldwide, announced a proposal to split the denomination (M. Anderson 2020). The split was necessary, the proposal read, because the UMC and its members "have fundamental differences regarding their understanding and interpretation of Scripture, theology, and practice" as it relates to the "full participation" of LGBT people in the denomination (United Methodist Church 2019). The tensions between church members over the inclusion of LGBT people have long been simmering, and the proposal was the culmination of nearly half a century of debate.

In 1975, LGBT Methodists, first under the appellation Gay United Methodists, then Affirmation, began their efforts to pressure church leadership for doctrinal changes to affirm the identities and lives of LGBT Methodists through grassroots organization (see Cadge 2005). Between 1975 and 2020, numerous Methodist churches took public positions as "reconciling" congregations—a process that often requires periods of spiritual education, congregational outreach, and eventually a vote of the local membership—that welcome LGBT people in fellowship and allow them to occupy positions of authority within the church (Cadge 2005). Over fifty years, these congregation-level activities placed upward pressure on the denominational hierarchy, which often responded with intransigence. In 2017, for example, the church's judicial council (the supreme court of the church) ruled the ordination of

Karen P. Oliveto, a married lesbian woman, as a bishop violated church law. However, the council refused to rescind the ordination, leaving that decision to the regional jurisdiction that consecrated the bishop (Goodstein 2017).

The 2020 protocol, known formally as the Protocol of Reconciliation and Grace Through Separation, was scheduled for a vote at the annual general conference in May[1] and came after a contentious special session of the general conference the year before, in which a majority of the delegates voted down a proposal to bless same-sex unions and ordain LGBT ministers but instead strengthened bans on such practices (Chappell 2019). The 2020 proposal would allow conservative congregations to separate from the UMC, ostensibly allowing the remaining membership to formally adopt the LGBT-affirming policies that were defeated in 2019. The experiences of Bishop Oliveto and the 2020 protocol highlight both American regional and international conflicts over the religiosity of LGBT people. The case against Bishop Oliveto, for example, who was consecrated in the church's western jurisdiction (whose constituents live in more politically liberal states), was brought by the church's south-central jurisdiction (whose constituents live in more politically conservative states), while much of the opposition at the 2019 general conference came from congregations outside of the United States whose laws and societies, shaped by European colonialism and proselytization, remain overtly hostile to LGBT people.

The UMC is only one of the latest denominations to confront heterosexism within their faith tradition. As an undergraduate student at The University of the South (an Episcopal University in Tennessee colloquially known as Sewanee), I recall several conversations about Bishop V. Gene Robinson, the first openly gay man elected bishop in the Episcopal Church and an alumnus, and how the bishop's ordination fueled a schism that, like the one at UMC, witnessed conservative congregations form their own denomination rather than consent to alter church doctrines to explicitly affirm LGBT congregants' identities, lives, and positions in the church (Goodstein 2008). Other large Christian denominations, including Presbyterians, Lutherans, and the Church of Christ, have also experienced schisms over the affirmation of LGBT congregants. In addition, in 2021, the Southern Baptist Convention made headlines when its executive committee voted to expel two congregations because they allowed LGBT people to join as members (Crary 2021).

Due to internal and external influences, religious institutions are increasingly sorting into two camps depending on their doctrinal acceptance of LGBT people. This is primarily true of Christian traditions that have long been bastions for heterosexist theology; however, many religious traditions and sects across the world are experiencing pressure to specify their theological position on LGBT identity and rights (see Taylor and Snowdon 2014; Thumma and Gray 2005). Since the 1970s, the number of religious congregations in the United States that explicitly affirm the sexual and gender identities of their LGBT congregants has dramatically increased (see Moon and Tobin 2018). Moreover, rather than disassociating with religion, as is the popular stereotype, LGBT people have found new and creative ways to integrate their spirituality and LGBT identity (e.g., Wolkomir 2006).

LGBT and religious identities are not incompatible. Yet, the "culture war" narrative (i.e., LGBT people represent an attack on "traditional" social and family institutions), perpetuated by conservative religious groups, reifies a false dichotomy among religious LGBT people (and the general public) that they must choose between their faith and their truth. As evidence of the divide, a 2011 Public Religion Research Institute study, for example, finds more than one-third (38%) of Americans say allowing openly gay and lesbian people to become clergy is a bad thing for society. However, the findings are tempered by youth, denominational affiliation, and level of religious commitment, which I discuss later in the text (Cox and Jones 2011).

Religious LGBT people also experience pressure from within the LGBT community. Namely, due to anti-LGBT bigotry from conservative religious groups, the LGBT community is generally depicted as antireligious. Religious LGBT people, then, are viewed as an aberration by other (nonreligious) LGBT people (see Cravens 2018). While some LGBT people alter their religious affiliation after coming out, many do not. The underlying faith traditions in which LGBT people were raised, the faith traditions they engage with after coming out, and the cross-pressures from their religious and LGBT social networks have important implications for identity and political development among the group.

Yet, because LGBT-affirming religious traditions represent a relatively new development in the epic of American religious pluralism, we are still learning about how these social institutions affect LGBT politics (see Coley 2020). It is my contention that religion is an important component of the LGBT sociopolitical experience that influences the politics of LGBT people. In this chapter, I analyze the contentious relationship between LGBT identity and the dominant religious traditions in the United States, focusing on the construction of LGBT people as an antireligious "other" and the movement-countermovement politics of conservative religiosity and LGBT rights in the United States. I also briefly chronicle the development of supportive LGBT religious communities and institutions in the United States. In the next chapter, I examine the extent to which LGBT people actually participate in the myriad religious and spiritual traditions in the United States.

Constructing the "Other": Religious Attitudes and Political Behavior toward LGBT People

Attitudes toward gay and lesbian people in the United States have steadily improved since the 1970s, when attitudinal measurements began. While positive attitudinal change toward transgender people lags behind gays and lesbians, a combination of visibility, contact, sympathetic portrayals in popular culture, and elite attitude change has meant, overall, LGBT people are viewed more positively now than in previous decades across almost every demographic (Garrettson 2018). Even among religious Americans, attitudes toward LGBT people and rights trend positively (see Public Religion Research Institute 2020). However, research also shows religiosity remains one of the primary sources of negative affect toward LGBT people and rights (Cragun and Sumerau 2015).

Several factors contribute to faith-based variation in attitudes toward LGBT people, including denomination or faith tradition, individual religiosity, and racial or ethnic identity at the intersection of religious identity and practice (Vegter and Haider-Markel 2020). Monotheistic, and especially Abrahamic, traditions like Christianity, Islam, and Judaism are considered the most opposed to LGBT identity, same-sex sexual attraction or behavior, and/or gender diverse behavior (see Vegter and Haider-Markel 2020). While significant inter- and intragroup theological variation exists, these traditions share several characteristics that research has shown to be significant contributors to negative affect toward LGBT people and rights.

For example, using data from the 2007 Baylor Religion Survey, Whitehead (2012) demonstrates having a masculine conceptualization of God (i.e., viewing God as "he") is associated with heteronormative views about the place of women and men in society (i.e., belief that women should care for children, men are better suited for politics, and "husbands" should earn more money than "wives"). Taken together, Whitehead (2012, 150) concludes viewing God as a "he" contributes to beliefs in the "underlying gendered nature of reality" and that violations of that reality go against the will of God. In addition, literalist interpretations of sacred texts, a view of God as a disciplinarian (e.g., responsible for punishing sin), and a belief that LGBT people can "change" sinful behavior are correlated with negative or intolerant attitudes toward LGBT people and rights (Vegter and Haider-Markel 2020).

Individual religiosity, too, is a strong predictor of attitudes toward LGBT people. Although the concept is inconsistently measured, there are several facets of religiosity, including both public and private expressions of religious devotion (see Legge and Kellstedt 1993). Related to attitudes toward LGBT people, research suggests people who frequently attend religious services, for example, are less supportive of same-sex marriage across denominations (see

Vegter and Haider-Markel 2020). In an analysis of data from the World Values Survey, a globally administered survey with cases from over forty societies and a sample size of more than sixty thousand respondents, Adamczyk and Pitt (2009) find increasing religious importance among survey respondents is associated with disapproval of homosexuality. Among Christians specifically, Whitley's (2009, 22) meta-analysis also finds strong relationships between multiple measures of public and private religious devotion, including church attendance, self-reported religiosity, and the "extent to which people truly believe their religions' teachings and try to live their lives according to them" and negative attitudes toward gays and lesbians.

Similar relationships have been observed between religiosity and attitudes toward transgender people. While research is still emerging on the role of psychological indicators, such as disgust, and political orientations, such as authoritarianism, on attitudes toward transgender people and rights (see Miller et al. 2017), public and private religious devotion remain significant predictors of negative attitudes toward transgender people even after controlling for these other factors (see Castle 2019; Flores et al. 2018).

In addition to specific beliefs and religiosity, certain denominational associations are also correlated with negative attitudes or intolerance toward LGBT people, although recent research suggests political and social contexts and especially individual religiosity nuance these relationships (see Finke and Adamczyk 2008; Read 2003). For example, although communities of LGBT Muslims have developed in the United States, survey data suggests Muslims demonstrate the most negative affect toward LGBT people and rights of any U.S. faith tradition (see Adamczyk and Pitt 2009). Orthodox Judaism, too, is generally associated with negative attitudes toward same-sex sexual attraction or behavior and/or gender diverse behavior (see Vegter and Haider-Markel 2020). In the United States, however, no denomination has contributed to the negative construction of LGBT people or mobilized politically against LGBT rights more than conservative Evangelical Protestants (Fetner 2008; Oldfield 1996). Numerous studies demonstrate a relationship between Evangelical affiliation and intolerance of same-sex sexual attraction and behavior (Whitehead and Baker 2012), opposition to same-sex marriage and other civil rights (Whitehead 2010), and transgender identity, civil rights protections, and even political candidates (Haider-Markel et al. 2019; Vegter and Haider-Markel 2020).

Research indicates attitudes toward LGBT people among religious groups vary along racial cleavages as well; yet, the commonality of conservative or Evangelical Protestantism remains. For example, more than Muslims, white Evangelicals express the most negative affect toward LGBT people and rights of any religious group in the United States (see Jones 2020; Vegter and Haider-Markel 2020). The combination of Christian nationalism—that is, the belief that the power of government should be utilized to establish Christian religious beliefs as legal standards—and whiteness evidences especially toxic attitudes toward LGBT rights and the rights of most religious, racial, and ethnic minority groups (see Cravens 2022a; R. Jones 2020; Whitehead and Perry 2020). Latinx Evangelicals, too, express more negative attitudes toward same-sex marriage than Latinx Catholics, for example (Ellison, Acevedo, and Ramos-Wada 2011). Similarly, Black Protestants in the Evangelical tradition and those who regularly attend religious services are less likely to support same-sex marriage than non-Evangelical whites (Griffin 2006; Sherkat, de Vries, and Creek 2010).

To understand how LGBT religiosity and political activism developed throughout the twentieth century, it is necessary to review the political mobilization efforts of conservative Evangelicalism during the same period. LGBT political and religious development did not take place in a vacuum, and the mobilization of conservative Evangelicals was in response to many social, scientific, and religious developments. Yet, the conservative religious focus on sexuality and reliance on heteronormativity as a key component of their own identity meant the LGBT movement, with its focus on visibility and coming out, became a target for conservative religious jeremiads declaring LGBT identity and behavior "unnatural" and "immoral." That the HIV/AIDS epidemic disproportionately affected LGBT people and men who have sex with men was weaponized by conservative Protestants to advocate exclusionary public policy responses that constrained the activist strategies of the LGBT movement and largely led to further clashes between the groups over family, health care, education, immigration, and civil rights policy, among others. In the following, I review the political mobilization of Evangelical Protestants, focusing on the ways in which religion is used as a political resource and agent of socialization to construct both a conservative religious identity and an unreligious LGBT "other."

Evangelical Protestantism and the Politics of Sex(uality)

Similar social, political, and economic conditions that catalyzed the Prohibition movement also contributed to the formation of a politicized Evangelical identity in the mid-twentieth century (for a review, see Morone 2003). The increased role of government as part of the New Deal and Great Society, desegregation, feminism, conflict in Korea and Vietnam, Watergate, and mass communication, all influenced the development of an Evangelicalism unwed from separatists and fundamentalists (FitzGerald 2017). For some, religion compelled a conservative defense of sacred values, including family autonomy and individualism. For others, religion compelled defiant challenges to the status quo that perpetuated egregious violations of equally sacred values, including social welfare and selflessness. The direction (left or right) of politicized Evangelicalism has been hotly contested with theologians, philosophers, preachers, and political organizations advocating on both sides of the debate. Shared beliefs such as inerrancy, biblical literalism, millenarianism, dispensationalism, and so on motivated liberal political activism against war, American imperialism, environmental degradation, poverty, segregation, and sexism, as much as it did retrenchment and reactionism (see Swartz 2012). Although Evangelicals were later to the political arena than mainline Protestants and Catholics of the same era, by the 1970s both liberal and conservative Evangelicals adopted the belief that "social work and politics" were "legitimate, even divinely appointed, vocations" (Swartz 2012, 152).

The election of the nation's first Catholic president, Supreme Court cases such as *Engel v. Vitale* (1962) and *Abbington Township v. Schempp* (1963)—which outlawed mandatory prayer and Bible study in public schools, respectively—as well as the progression of civil rights legislation are just some of the examples of the perceived secularization of American society that troubled conservative Evangelical Protestants in the middle of the twentieth century (FitzGerald 2017). Spearheaded by southern ministers schooled in the revivalist style of their fathers, by the mid-1970s Evangelicalism became a major mobilizer of conservative political sentiment (FitzGerald 2017; Guth 1996; Oldfield 1996). Although Evangelical forays into Democratic political organization included the formation of the first postwar Evangelical organization to issue a presidential endorsement, Evangelicals for McGovern (Swartz 2012, 171), liberal Evangelical groups did not fare as well, likely because the people who responded to liberal political messages were usually younger, had less money, and exerted less influence over government officials than conservative Evangelicals like Billy Graham, Harold Ockenga, and Harold Lindsell.

In the 1970s, a number of Protestant Christian organizations galvanized around resistance to cultural changes stemming from the previous decade's social movement activism and conservative interpretations of theology to form a political countermovement known as the Religious Right (Fetner 2008; Layman 1997). In true pluralist fashion, most of the congregations that made up this countermovement had no formal denominational ties but were rather a patchwork of independent congregations loosely held together by what Stone (2012, 4) calls an "obsession with doctrinal purity." Because of the intimate connection between conservative Evangelicalism and the LGBT movement, the remainder of this section will focus on conservative Evangelical political mobilization.

In the middle of the twentieth century, a new crop of revivalists emerged ready to spread the gospel with the help of mass communication methods. Rather than eschewing political involvement, it was the contention of the

Evangelicals, including Pentecostals, charismatics, and Holiness denominations, that fervent political action was necessary to turn back the tide on what was quickly becoming a godless society. However, as Oldfield (1996) argues, the rise of conservative Evangelicalism represents more than just a reactionary countermovement. Although Evangelicals perceived their "subcultural values" as under attack, their theological underpinnings seemingly demanded social and political action. In describing the logic of political action among Evangelicals, Oldfield (1996, 55) reasons, "If I insist that I am in possession of the one true faith, capable of providing an overarching system of meaning in the face of death, misfortune, and evil, it is hard to simply 'switch off' that faith when I step out of the private realm. If the Bible is the inerrant word of God, then its authority should extend to all reams of life." Primed with this foundation, perceived attacks on religion emanating from the public sphere provoked Evangelicals to "fight back" and to "do so in the public domain of politics" (Oldfield 1996, 55).

Reminiscent of Prohibitionist preachers, the nature of the social issues concerning to the group led to their characterization by the conservative politician Pat Buchanan as cultural warriors, defending "traditional" (e.g., heteronormative) values against a liberal revolution at the 1992 Republican National Convention (Oldfield 1996; see Fiorina, Abrams, and Pope 2011). The work of this countermovement and its later iterations achieved substantial political success largely because of its ability to mobilize members of conservative religious congregations across the United States (Domke and Coe 2008; Green et al. 1996; Rozell and Wilcox 1995). Prominent national figures such as ministers Jerry Falwell, Pat Robertson, and James Dobson, and lay activists Anita Bryant and Phyllis Schlafly (a conservative Catholic), emerged leading national political organizations such as Focus on the Family, the Eagle Forum, and Protect America's Children. These organizations and personalities leveraged mass communication strategies such as direct mail and popular radio and television programs, including *The 700 Club* and *The Old Time Gospel Hour*. The strength of this loose web of believers, however, lay in its ability to activate networks of grassroots congregants who contributed money, recruited political candidates, and helped spread their shared values and philosophy (Fetner 2008). More than any other, the development of a political consciousness among these traditionally disengaged groups constructed largely in opposition to wicked "others" had lasting implications on LGBT identity development, including the actual and perceived religiosity of LGBT people.

As Fetner (2008) observes, the Religious Right primarily focused its political machinations on direct democracy in the 1970s. Their first success came in 1977, when a popular singer and Florida orange juice spokesperson named

Anita Bryant led an effort to repeal a civil rights ordinance adopted by Dade County, Florida, that protected people from discrimination on the basis of sexual orientation. Before the ordinance was adopted, Bryant was reportedly approached by leaders of her local Evangelical congregation to "use her powers of celebrity" to convince the board of commissioners to abandon the measure (Fetner 2008, 24). When the measure passed, Bryant organized what would be the first anti-LGBT movement organization, Save Our Children, to lead a formal campaign to repeal the ordinance. The group was successful, and the referendum was supported by nearly 70% of Dade County voters in 1977 (Stone 2012). Drawing on her own celebrity and the emerging networks of the Religious Right, two new groups, Anita Bryant Ministries and Protect America's Children, mounted a national public relations campaign to repeal similar laws across the United States, beginning a streak of successful repeal efforts that lasted into the twenty-first century (Stone 2012).

From these victories, new religious and political personalities emerged, such as Jerry Falwell and Pat Robertson. They saw an opportunity to ingratiate the Religious Right with conservative political activists within the Republican Party (Oldfield 1996). Along with deep pockets (raised through direct-mail campaigns) and a readymade grassroots network of culture warriors, the political incentive to capture Evangelical voters by opposing LGBT rights fit well with the exclusionary message the Religious Right constructed of the LGBT movement as reprobate and godless.

As mentioned previously, the social construction of LGBT people as incompatible with Evangelical orthodoxy is a function of several beliefs. One is inerrancy combined with a literalist interpretation of scripture. A second is the primacy of "the family" as a foundation for society. Relatedly, a third is described by social scientists as the disbelief in "attribution"—which fits well in the individualistic ethos of conservative Christianity.[2] Inerrancy, or the view that the Bible is the infallible word of God, indirectly compels action both to save souls and to remake society through political action. The Evangelical belief that "family" is the foundational unit of society is often attributed to the perceived attacks on the private sphere of religious belief throughout the mid-twentieth century. Government intrusions that dictate a community's religious traditions (e.g., forbidding prayer in public school and even mandating civil rights and abortion), it has been argued, reinforce Evangelical separatism and reliance on patriarchal heteronormative family structures as the paradigm of virtue and private autonomy. The ideal is so pervasive among premillenarians[3] that some argue "it has come to replace expectations of the Second Coming as a source of hope in a hopeless world" (Oldfield 1996, 56). Under such a regime, gender and sexual norms are highly policed. Undermining these foundational values risks societal collapse. This is why the last value, denial of attribution, is key to understanding the political mobilization of the Religious Right against LGBT rights.

Attribution theory has been used to explain the positive trend in public opinion toward LGBT people in the twentieth and twenty-first centuries (Garretson 2018; Vegter and Haider-Markel 2020). The theory suggests that people who believe sexual orientation and/or gender identity to be the result of genetic or biological processes, rather than an individual choice, are more likely to view LGBT people favorably and support LGBT civil rights. Consistent with individualistic theologies, the belief that sexual orientation and gender identity are not inherent characteristics, rather LGBT people choose to act in a manner inconsistent with inerrant biblical precepts, is common among Evangelicals.

Like the Prohibitionists before them, many Evangelicals believe physical and economic hardship are the result of individual moral failure. Indeed, many Evangelical leaders often compare "homosexuality" to drug and alcohol abuse (Erzen 2006). These themes—inerrancy, the family, and individual responsibility—converged with a lack of representation of LGBT people in popular culture in the 1970s to 1990s and a media narrative dominated by conservative Christians during the HIV/AIDS epidemic to the detriment of LGBT religious identity development. The resultant caricature of LGBT people fuels stereotypes across social groups that LGBT people cannot be religious. Two examples from Religious Right leaders illustrate these points.

First, in an interview recorded for an episode of the PBS news program *Frontline*, titled "Assault on Gay America," Jerry Falwell, pastor of the 22,000-member Thomas Road Baptist Church, expresses each of these themes. When asked, "Is it possible that you could be mistaken" that gays and lesbians are not "violating God's law on the Bible?" Falwell replied, "Only if God's mistaken" (Frontline 2000). As Falwell later explained, "I believe with all my heart that the Bible is the infallible word of God. I therefore believe that, whatever it says, is so."

Although Evangelicals broke with Christian fundamentalists over political mobilization, they shared the beliefs in inerrancy and conversion (i.e., being "born again"). The literalist interpretation of scripture, largely but not exclusively derived from the King James Version of the Bible, that informed Falwell's views on LGBT people has been used to support the belief that homosexuality is a sin that cuts believers off from fellowship with the body of Christ (see Thumma and Gray 2005). It may not always be sinful to be "tempted" (although admitting susceptibility to such temptations might prove disastrous to one's personal standing in the church), but acting on same-sex desires is forbidden (Erzen 2006). Indeed, Falwell expressed this view using a popular axiom: "We hate the sin, but we love the sinner, and likewise with gay [sic] and lesbians." He continues, "We counsel and minister to them. We do all we can to help. But we could never condone the lifestyle" (Frontline 2000). Along with the axiom, this view perpetuated the use of pseudo-psychological treatment programs dating to the Victorian era coupled with contemporary Evangelical theology to "repair" LGBT people (i.e., aversion-based therapy programs that promised to help those "struggling" with same-sex desires to become heterosexual; see Erzen 2006).

Second, in the 1980s, the HIV/AIDS epidemic and its disproportionate effect on gay men and intravenous drug users was the basis for polemical policy positions espoused by Evangelical preachers that also resonated with the burgeoning neoconservative movement in the United States (Fetner 2008). After ignoring the effects of the epidemic for most of the decade, Evangelicals eventually characterized AIDS as the consequence of moral failure and, more directly, God's punishment for sinful behavior. The National Research Council's report, "The Social Impact of AIDS in the United States," for example, quotes a May 1987 sermon from Jerry Falwell, broadcast on the *Old Time Gospel Hour*, titled "How Many Roads to Heaven." In it, the preacher says, "They [gay men] are scared to walk near one of their own kind right now. And what we [preachers] have been unable to do with our preaching, a God who hates sin has stopped dead in its tracks by saying 'do it and die.' 'Do it and die'" (Jonsen and Stryker 1993).

Similarly, in a 1993 speech to the National Association of Religious Broadcasters, Pat Robertson, host of the popular television program *The 700 Club* and 1988 Republican presidential candidate, addressed "a new plague stalking our land," in reference to AIDS (first identified in 1982). It was Robertson's contention, and that of many Evangelicals, that the 235,000 worldwide deaths attributable to AIDS to that point occurred "because the people have cast aside the sexual morals of The Holy Bible" (Robertson 1993). This scarlet *A* became synonymous with impurity, lack of self-control, and nonprocreational (gay) sex in the minds of Evangelicals—all violations of scripture and powerful constructions that further reified the belief that LGBT people cannot be religious.

In a clear contrast to the Social Gospel of the New Deal era, Evangelical political mobilization turned on the idea that because those infected with the disease rejected personal responsibility and godliness, nonheterosexual relationships should never be legally recognized nor was it appropriate to use government resources to assist them (e.g., use public funds to invest in medical research). Indeed, federal HIV/AIDS policy only viewed sympathetically those who were "unknowing victims" of the virus, such as children and hemophiliacs, and attitudes toward people with AIDS only changed after sympathetic cases—such as Ryan White, a cismale teenager from Indiana who contracted AIDS from a blood transfusion and was expelled from school—were widely publicized (see Donovan 1997).

Evangelical Attitudes about LGBT People and Rights

Contemporary survey data also suggest these values (and the relationships between them) are not characteristic of only Evangelical thought leaders. In 1994, the General Social Survey polled respondents on their feelings about the Bible as well as their feelings on homosexuality and shifting gender roles (the question on homosexuality appeared on only two of the three ballots administered in 1994). The survey did not ask respondents to self-identify as "Evangelical"; however, it did ask respondents to identify whether they believed the Bible was the "word of God," the "inspired word of God," or a "book of fables." These conceptualizations intimate belief in the Bible as the "word of God" equates to literalism whereas believing the Bible to be "inspired" suggests the text includes some amount of human interpretation in its moral judgments and should not be taken literally. In addition, the survey asked respondents if "homosexuality" is "something people choose" or "something they cannot change." Table 1.1 shows the results of a cross-tabulation of responses to the two questions.

Responses to the attribution question are almost evenly split among the respondents in the sample ($n = 958$), with 41% believing homosexuality is a choice and 44.2% believing homosexuality is innate. As Table 1.1 shows, however, of the respondents who answered both questions in 1994 ($n = 920$), more than half (56.8%, $n = 175$) of those who believed the Bible is the word of God also reported the belief that homosexuality is something people choose. Slightly more than one-third (35.8%, $n = 169$) of respondents who believe the Bible is inspired and slightly more than one-quarter (27.6%, $n = 39$) of respondents who believe the Bible is a book of fables also believed homosexuality is a choice. On the other hand, a majority of respondents who believed the Bible is a book of fables (60.9%, $n = 86$) and a plurality of those who believed the Bible is inspired (48.3%, $n = 230$) also report the belief that homosexuality is an innate characteristic, while fewer than one-third (31.8%, $n = 98$) of respondents who believe the Bible is the word of God also reported believing homosexuality is innate. These findings are also consistent with

TABLE 1.1 CROSS-TABULATION OF INERRANCY AND ATTRIBUTION					
Feelings about the Bible	Choice	Inherent	Don't Know	No Answer	Total
Word of God	175 (56.8%)[a]	98 (31.8%)	35 (11.3%)	0 (0.0%)	308 (100%)
Inspired Word	169 (35.8)	230 (48.8%)	65 (13.8%)	7 (1.49%)	471 (100%)
Book of Fables	39 (27.6%)	86 (60.9%)	16 (11.3%)	0 (0.0%)	141 (100%)
Total	383 (41.6%)	414 (45.0%)	116 (12.6%)	7 (.76%)	920 (100%)

Source: Data from the 1994 General Social Survey, row variable (*bible*), column variable (*homochng*).
Notes: $\chi^2 = 56.6$, p = .000; Cramer's V = .175.
[a] Row percent.

social scientific literature showing a negative relationship between biblical literalism and attribution (see Burdette, Ellison, and Hill 2005; Whitehead 2010).

In addition to measuring attribution, the 1994 General Social Survey also included an item measuring (dis)agreement with the statement, "It is not good if the man stays at home and cares for the children and the woman goes out to work." Table 1.2 shows a cross-tabulation of responses to this question and the inerrancy item. Note the original response set measured (dis)agreement on a five-point scale, but Table 1.2 collapses "strongly agree" and "agree" as well as "strongly disagree" and "disagree." The distribution is more negatively skewed than responses to the previous question. That is, the majority of responses, 57.2%, are concentrated around strongly/disagree. Still, about one-third (33.6%, $n = 96$) of respondents who report believing in inerrancy also report (strong) agreement with the statement that implies women working outside the home causes injury to the family—significantly more than those who believed in an inspired word or a book of fables.

These tables, of course, only offer a snapshot of attitudes and correlations between inerrancy, attribution, and gender roles that developed throughout the end of the twentieth century. Although statistically significant, the relationships are marginal in this sample. However, the survey data suggests a sizable proportion of Americans (about one in ten in 1994) believed the Bible to be the inerrant word of God, and that view correlated with perceptions about homosexuality as a choice and the view that deviation from heteronormative, patriarchal gender roles has the potential to upend families. These views, along with rhetoric from Evangelical ministers and conservative politicians, further constructed the faithful as millenarian warriors against subversive others and LGBT people as choosing to engage in immoral behavior and, therefore, forsaking God—even though, as I show later in this chapter, many LGBT and allied religious people refute this claim.

By the mid-1990s, negative public sentiment toward LGBT people, the political acumen of the Religious Right, and an unexpectedly successful chal-

TABLE 1.2 CROSS-TABULATION OF INERRANCY, GENDER ROLES, AND FAMILY

Feelings about the Bible	(Strongly) Agree	Neither Agree nor Disagree	(Strongly) Disagree	Can't Choose	Total
Word of God	96 (33.6%)[a]	52 (18.2%)	135 (47.3%)	2 (0.7%)	285 (100%)
Inspired Word	95 (19%)	110 (22%)	289 (57.8%)	6 (1.2%)	500 (100%)
Book of Fables	21 (14.6%)	23 (16%)	98 (68.5%)	1 (0.7%)	143 (100%)
Total	212 (22.8%)	185 (19.9%)	522 (57.2%)	9 (0.9%)	928 (100%)

Source: Data from the 1994 General Social Survey, row variable (*bible*), column variable (*mrmom*).
Notes: $\chi^2 = 39.0$, $p = .000$; Cramer's V = .145.
[a] Row percent.

lenge to Hawaiian relationship recognition law had opened new fronts in the culture war on LGBT people as well as new "policy windows" (see Cravens 2019). Local, state, and even federal bans on same-sex marriage were considered or enacted, and a slew of conservative "family values" policies were promoted through health care and tax regulations. Evangelicals staked out clear policy preferences on most of these positions and mobilized politically to help enact them (Fetner 2008; Stone 2012). Over time, however, the political power of the Religious Right (and affiliated groups such as the Moral Majority and Christian Coalition) has waxed and waned while public sentiment toward gays and lesbians has steadily improved among almost all demographic groups in the United States, including many religious groups (Public Religion Research Institute 2020). The fundamental principles of Evangelicalism that have guided both political mobilization and the construction of LGBT people, however, persist.

Notably, in the Pew Research Center's (2015) study of American religion, more than half (68%) of those who identify as Evangelical and believe "holy scripture" is the "word of God" that "should be taken literally" also said homosexuality should be "discouraged." Although the study did not ask about attribution, encouraging/discouraging homosexuality implies that sexuality, or at the very least sexual behavior, is not innate but a choice. Of those Evangelical respondents who believe scripture should not be taken literally, only about one-quarter (25%) believe homosexuality should be discouraged. Nearly half (45%) of those who believe scripture should not be interpreted literally also believe homosexuality should be accepted.

These trends have not gone unnoticed by the general population. In a 2010 Public Religion Research Institute (PRRI) study, Americans demonstrated cognition of negative messages about LGBT people among many religious institutions and attributed negative health outcomes among LGBT people to the perpetuation of those messages by religious leaders (Cox and Jones 2010). Figure 1.1 and Figure 1.2 are constructed using data from the study, highlighting responses from those who report an opinion ("don't know" responses suppressed for space). As Figure 1.2 shows, a plurality of the sample with an opinion (42%, $n = 362$) think "messages on the issue of homosexuality coming from America's places of worship" are generally negative. While fewer than one in ten (8%, $n = 77$) think the messages are positive, just over one-third (38%, $n = 420$) report that most places do not talk about the issue. The report highlights the finding that more than four in ten Americans gave religious organizations a D (18%, $n = 169$) or an F (24%, $n = 233$) when asked to "grade America's places of worship on how they are handling the issue of homosexuality" (Cox and Jones 2010). Yet it appears the negativity is perceived as systemic rather than congregation-specific, as fewer than one-quarter of respondents would grade their own place of worship a

D (6%, $n = 64$) or an F (11%, $n = 102$) on how they handle the issue of homosexuality.

As Figure 1.2 shows, about two in ten (22%, $n = 199$) respondents believe "messages about the issue of homosexuality coming from places of worship" do not contribute to "negative views of gay and lesbian people," while nearly three-quarters (76%, $n = 670$) say they do contribute either a little or a lot. Perhaps most astounding, when asked how much they believe messages about the issue of homosexuality coming from places of worship contribute to "higher rates of suicide among gay and lesbian youth," more than two-thirds of respondents say they contribute a lot (35%, $n = 295$) or a little (36%, $n = 303$), whereas about one-quarter (27%, $n = 224$) say not at all. Given the sample is almost evenly divided between respondents who believe "sexual relations between two adults of the same gender" is a sin (44%, $n = 435$) and those who do not (46%, $n = 465$), this data suggests even some of those who disbelieve attribution recognize that negative messages from religious institutions are harmful to LGBT people.

Differences in these attitudinal patterns, however, arise between respondents who report being "born again" and those who do not. Like biblical literalism, being "born again" is a doctrinal feature of fundamentalism, Evangelicalism, Pentecostalism, and other charismatic Protestant groups—although the moniker may be adopted by other religious groups (see Burge 2021). The phrase references a passage in the gospel of John in which the author attributes the words to Jesus when addressing Nicodemus, a religious leader who questioned Jesus's divinity. Among Evangelicals, the phrase refers to a personal conversion experience (sometimes called "being saved") that compels one to "leave" their "sinful" life and become a follower of Christ (see Oldfield 1996). This precept further reifies the notion that behaviors considered sinful by scripture *can* and should be changed. In this sample, respondents who identify as "born again" are more likely to give their own places of worship higher grades for how they "handle the issue of homosexuality" than respondents who do not identify as "born again." In addition, "born again" respondents are also more likely to report messages about homosexuality from American places of worship have little or nothing at all to do with the perpetuation of negative views about gays and lesbians. (See Online Statistical Appendix I. All appendixes are available via Harvard Dataverse at https://doi.org/10.7910/DVN/M87Q1V; for additional citation information see Cravens 2022b.)

These trends are consistent with other research that suggests religious heterosexuals negatively view "identities that result in the greatest violations of normativity." Namely, religious heterosexuals severely penalize religious LGBT (especially transgender) people for holding what the heterosexuals believe to be completely incongruent identities. For example, in their analysis,

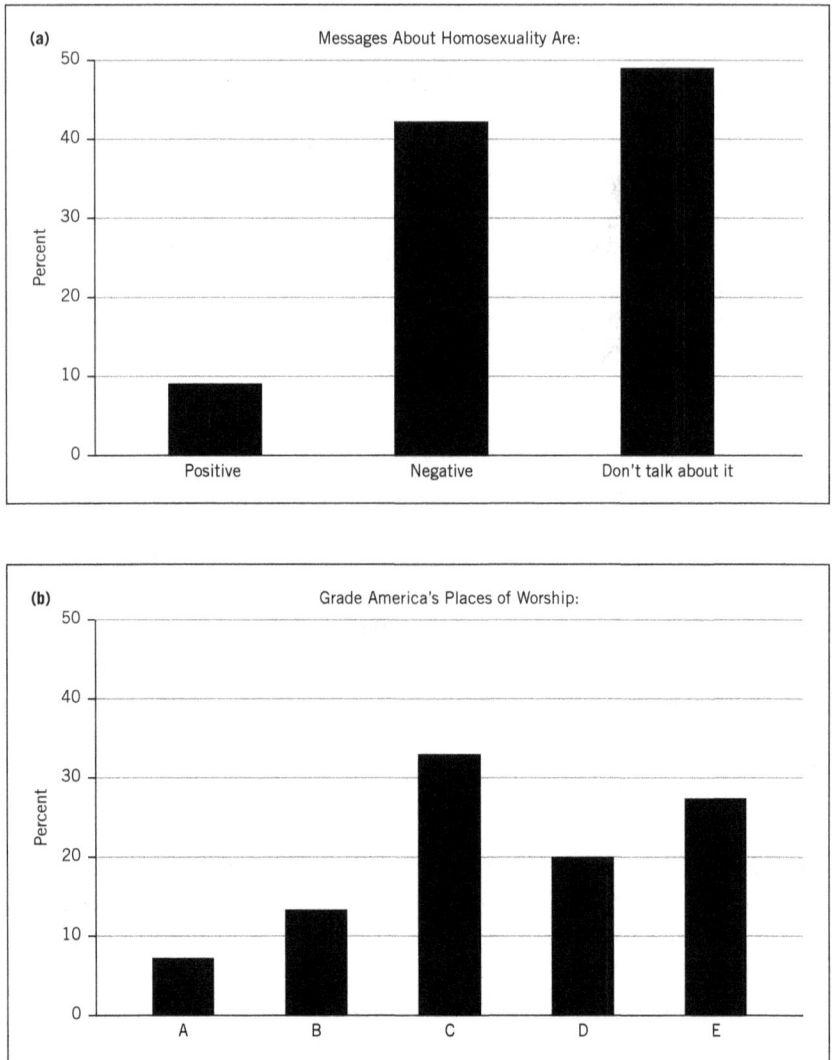

Figure 1.1 Perceived Homophobia in American Religious Institutions. *n* = 1,010. (*Data from Cox and Jones [2010]*)

Cragun and Sumerau (2017) find religious heterosexuals believe religious transgender people "taint religious identity," yet again confirming the oppositional construction of LGBT and religious identities (Cragun and Sumerau 2017, 8).

The close relationship between cisnormativity and the foundational unit of the family among Evangelicals has resulted in an attitudinal entrenchment and political mobilization to deny civil rights protections to transgen-

(a) Contributes to Negative Views:

[Bar chart: Percent on y-axis (0 to 50). "A lot" ≈ 42, "A little" ≈ 35, "Not at all" ≈ 23]

(b) Contributes to Self-Harm:

[Bar chart: Percent on y-axis (0 to 50). "A lot" ≈ 36, "A little" ≈ 37, "Not at all" ≈ 27]

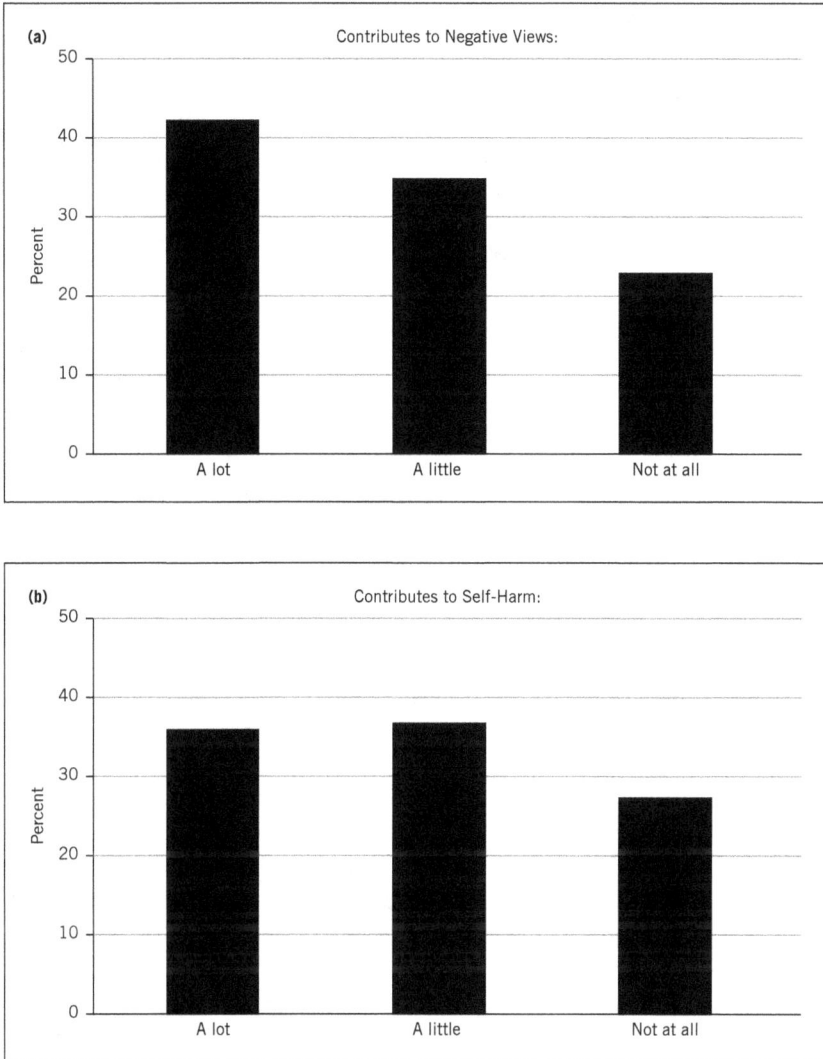

Figure 1.2 Perceived Consequences of Homophobia in American Religious Institutions. n = 1,010. (*Data from Cox and Jones [2010]*)

der people, especially at the local level (see Stone 2012). For example, a 2019 PRRI study found that across all religious groups surveyed, self-reported measures of change in support for transgender rights improved. However, white Evangelicals were the group least likely to support civil rights for transgender people, including openly serving in the military, teaching in schools, and using public facilities that match their gender identity rather than sex assigned at birth (Greenberg et al. 2019). In each case, the disbelief in attribution (i.e., gender identity is not innate) likely contributes to the negative attitudes.

Since the Supreme Court's decisions in three cases—*Obergefell v. Hodges* (2015), striking down state same-sex marriage bans; *Masterpiece Cakeshop v. Colorado Civil Rights Commission* (2018), upholding the right of a private business to refuse to serve same-sex couples based on a religious objection; and *Bostock v. Clayton County, Georgia* (2019), affirming that discrimination in employment on the basis of sexual orientation and gender identity amounts to illegal sex discrimination under Title VII of the Civil Rights Act of 1964—Evangelicals have, again, mobilized around a competition-based model of civil rights and liberties that further reinforces the message that LGBT people cannot be religious. As with the political response to HIV/AIDS, the competition is overtly political, with conservative religious groups promoting the belief that government action to protect LGBT civil rights comes at the expense of religious civil liberties.

Again, the messages of incompatibility (between religious and LGBT identities) and competition (between religious civil liberty and LGBT civil rights) are promoted by Evangelical religious leaders and resonate with lay members and conservative politicians alike. In a June 2018 statement "welcoming" the Supreme Court's *Masterpiece* decision, for example, Leith Anderson, president of the National Association of Evangelicals, an organization representing tens of thousands of local congregations across multiple denominations, said, "This decision is a win . . . for all Americans who care about freedom of conscience and religion." Continuing, "Government must not demonize the religion or religious beliefs of its citizens" (National Association of Evangelicals 2018). In response to the 2019 passage of the Equality Act in the U.S. House, a bill that would amend the Civil Rights Act of 1964 to include protections based on sexual orientation and gender identity (not just in employment), the seventy-eighth convention of the more fundamentalist American Council of Christian Churches adopted a resolution holding that "Bible believers, whose anthropology comes from the pages of Scripture, understand 'sexual orientation' and 'gender identity' to be false religious doctrines, which, when codified into law, would discriminate against them and violate their constitutional rights of religious liberty" (American Council of Christian Churches 2019).

Through the networks established by the Religious Right in the late twentieth century, these scriptural interpretations find their way into public policy position papers and amicus curiae briefs and onto the agenda of policymakers. The conservative Heritage Foundation, founded by Paul Weyrich in 1973 to focus the power of Christian Right political organizing into shaping Republican policy positions in government (Oldfield 1996), released a position statement on religious freedom in 2019 asking and answering the question, "Should florists, photographers and bakers be forced to provide their services for same-sex weddings and celebrations that violate their religious beliefs?" "The answer," they conclude, "should be no." Why? Because "forcing individuals and faith-based organizations to choose between living out their religious beliefs or serving their neighbors actually harms our communities" (Heritage Foundation 2020). In this case, the religiously informed positions of the National Association of Evangelicals and American Council of Christian Churches, which, at least in the case of the former, characterize LGBT identity as an unscriptural life choice incompatible with the Christian family, finds a subtler (more palatable?) but consistent voice in the Heritage brief. The Heritage Foundation appears to accept the premise that one must "choose between" serving one's faith and serving LGBT people, as if the two must be incompatible. To do so would cause irreparable harm to "our communities," likely built on the Evangelical heteronormative, patriarchal ideal.

Similar constructions also found voice in the very place where, five years earlier, same-sex marriage was legalized. In the fall of 2020, Justice Clarence Thomas, joined by Justice Samuel Alito, released an opinion dissenting from the six-member majority's decision to deny review of an appeal from Kim Davis, a Kentucky county clerk who refused to issue marriage licenses to same-sex couples. Davis, who had been held in contempt, went to jail, and was eventually sued by the couples whom she refused to serve, was represented by the group Liberty Counsel, an Evangelical legal organization that often litigates cases in which religious liberties and the civil rights of LGBT people are adjudicated. Justice Thomas's dissent in *Kim Davis v. David Ermold* (2020) argued, "Davis may have been one of the first victims of this court's cavalier treatment of religion in its *Obergefell* decision," which "enables courts and governments to brand religious adherents who believe that marriage is between one man and one woman as bigots, making their religious liberty concerns that much easier to dismiss." Until it is overturned, Thomas concludes, the Supreme Court's precedent in *Obergefell* "will continue to have ruinous consequences for religious liberty."

Whether related to inerrancy, fear of religious persecution, or animosity toward LGBT people, American public opinion is divided over the issue of religion-based service refusals. In 2018, PRRI found that almost half of Americans (46%) believe that private business owners should be allowed to refuse service to same-sex couples if providing service violates their religious beliefs. The report also found denominational cleavages. For example, "seven in ten (70%) white evangelical Protestants" believe that private business owners should be allowed to refuse service to same-sex couples. Comparatively, "white mainline Protestants (48% vs. 45%) are about as likely to support this policy as they are to oppose it." On the other hand, nearly six in ten "religiously unaffiliated Americans (58%) say these types of businesses should not be allowed to refuse services to gay and lesbian couples" (Vandermass-Peeler et al. 2018b). Given that the same report finds nearly three-quarters (71%) of Americans support laws that prohibit discrimination against LGBT people, framing of LGBT people and religiosity as incompatible and the rights of each as zero-sum appears to be a strong driver of negative opinions and political activism among many American Christians but especially white Evangelicals.

Research shows Evangelical identification is also associated with negative attitudes toward LGBT people among both Black and Latinx Americans (see Vegter and Haider-Markel 2020). Black Americans are no more or less homophobic than any other racial group (Battle, Pastrana, and Harris 2017). However, Black Americans are more religious and more likely to identify with a Protestant faith tradition than other racial groups, and religiosity among the group is associated with opposition to same-sex marriage, specifically (Sherkat, de Vries, and Creek 2010). While the institution of marriage may evoke specific religious connotations, the opinions of Black and white Evangelical Protestants diverge over their willingness to allow state-sponsored discrimination against LGBT people.

Specifically, a 2021 PRRI study finds Black Protestants are less likely than white Evangelical Protestants to support government and business discrimination against LGBT people in the provision of goods or services, even if the business owner claims doing so violates their religious beliefs (PRRI 2021). Distinctions between Black and white Evangelical Protestants are further nuanced by studies examining the effects of economic class within each group. In an analysis of data from the General Social Survey, for example, Irizarry and Perry (2017) suggest economic or class distinctions, more than denominationalism, explain the variation in attitudes since middle-class Black respondents show larger attitude gaps with nonreligious whites than economically disadvantaged Black respondents. Even with these nuances, Evangelical Protestantism remains a significant predictor of negative affect toward LGBT people among white, Black, and Latinx Americans (Ellison, Acevedo, and Ramos-Wada 2011).

Black and Latinx Evangelical theology as it relates to LGBT identity, same-sex sexual attraction, and gender diverse behavior, however, is likely a response to white perceptions of racial minorities as sexual deviants. The history of Black and Latinx religious development in the United States demonstrates both groups have experienced social and religious discrimination because white Christians believed them to be sexually deviant (see Griffin 2006). While Griffin (2006) argues this point among Black Protestants, Marti (2012) suggests a similar dynamic among Latinx Americans. In each case, Evangelical Protestantism functions as a bridging social structure that emphasizes religious similarities (rather than racial differences) between Latinx, Hispanic,

Black, and white communities. Any characteristic that could undermine racial parity (e.g., LGBT identity or behavior) is potentially a threat and should not be tolerated (Green 1998; Griffin 2006). In this way, white supremacy works to suppress sexual identity development and impose religious strictures to internally police heteronormativity.

Beyond negative affect toward LGBT people, this also affects social, religious, and political identity development *among* Black and Latinx LGBT people. Namely, while religious disassociation may be more prominent among white LGBT people, Black and Latinx LGBT people may find it more difficult than whites to sever ties with such an important cultural institution despite pervasive heterosexism. Instead, Black and Latinx LGBT people attempt to integrate their faith and LGBT identity or even maintain ties to nonaffirming and heterosexist religious communities. Other options, including seeking LGBT-affirming congregations, are often less appealing because these predominantly white denominations do not provide the same supportive environment for congregants' racial identity or may be overtly racist (see Chen and Jeung 2012; Griffin 2006).

The rise of the Religious Right and its anti-LGBT political activism was accompanied by a burgeoning struggle to recognize LGBT people as part of God's chosen (see Swartz 2012; Thumma and Gray 2005). As in the days of the New Deal, progressive Christians largely hold to the collectivist vision of the Social Gospel. Like conservative Evangelicals, progressive Evangelicals, mainline Protestants, and Catholics have also mobilized politically to press reform when government actions and public policies violate moral imperatives. This is especially true of younger religious cohorts.

Along with trends in survey research that suggest the American public notices anti-LGBT bias emanating from religious institutions, recent research shows American young people are willing to change their religious behavior because of it. A 2014 report from PRRI, for example, shows "seven in ten (70%) Millennials [born between 1981 and 1996] believe that religious groups are alienating young adults by being too judgmental about gay and lesbian issues." Continuing, "Among Millennials who no longer identify with their childhood religion, nearly one-third say negative teachings about, or treatment of, gay and lesbian people was either a somewhat important (17%) or very important (14%) factor in their disaffiliation from religion" (Cox, Navarro-Rivera, and Jones 2014).

Attitudes toward LGBT people continue to improve, assisted by the increasing number of "out" LGBT people in the United States and a shift in both elite support and media portrayals of the group (see Garretson 2018). Yet the lasting impact of conservative politico-religious activism has been a sharp divide in attitudes based on partisanship, racial identity, religiosity, and denominational affiliation. The ongoing public debate over LGBT rights is increasingly framed as a battle between religious liberty and LGBT civil rights, a tactic that both resonates with the American public and drives further conservative politico-religious engagement. The perpetuation of this framing by both LGBT and conservative religious groups contributes to the view that LGBT people have no place in American religion. Yet, a substantial proportion of LGBT people are religious. Theories of identity development among this group must account for the negative socioreligious environment attributable to Evangelical activism. The balance between political activism, LGBT identity, religiosity, and, in many cases, racial identity must also be negotiated, and these cross-pressures produce additional cleavages. In the remaining sections of this chapter, I undertake a macro-level review of the development of LGBT politico-religious structures and describe how LGBT people have navigated the American pluralist landscape. In the next chapter, I review data from large-scale surveys of LGBT people to expound several important patterns in individual-level LGBT religious belief and behavior.

Queer Approaches to Religious and Political Reform

Like other minority groups in American politics, over time the LGBT movement has vacillated between liberationist and assimilationist tendencies with corresponding inclusive and exclusive constructions of what it means to be "gay" and who is welcome in the community. Notably, religious belief has regularly been on the periphery of those constructions. Historical accounts of the emergent LGBT movement suggest urbanization after World War II, which brought together same-sex-attracted individuals in numbers never before possible, contributed to the development of a subcultural identity (see Bérubé 1990; D'Emilio 1998; Duberman, Vicinus, and Chauncey 1989; Katz 1983). Along with the shared characteristic of same-sex attraction or diverse gender expression, these early communities of LGBT people also shared experiences with heterosexism.

Dating to colonial statutes based in Christian legal theory that criminalized same-sex sexual behavior, heterosexuality has long been established as normative in American law and society. Those who transgressed this norm were often punished (see Katz 1983). The same heterosexist standard persisted through the twentieth century, when science, medicine, politics, and religion all contributed to the creation and pathologizing of a "homosexual identity" characterized by "deviant" sexual behavior (see Somerville 2000). The long history of religious-inspired bigotry toward LGBT people caused many early LGBT rights activists to consider religion the enemy of the movement (see Mecca 2009). However, the LGBT movement is not simply the foil of the Religious Right in the narrative of American pluralism. LGBT people, many inspired by religious conviction, have reimagined social, political, and religious spaces, both testing and ensuring American religious pluralism for themselves and future generations.

In the mid-twentieth century, LGBT activism was supported by the development of several organizations, including the Mattachine Society, the Daughters of Bilitis, and the Council on Religion and the Homosexual. Coley (2020) describes several strategies these and other groups employ to bring about social, political, and religious change, including direct action, education, and solidarity-building. The early LGBT movement organizations were generally formed to educate "homosexuals," building solidarity and facilitating assimilation into heterosexist society, although this often involved educating heterosexuals as well. However, each group had members who preferred social and political action that highlighted the uniqueness of LGBT experiences, especially when they were subjected to harassment by public officials. This "identity for critique" strategy often involved confrontational tactics that produced headlines that, even though they often inspired backlash, also increased the visibility of LGBT people in society (see Bernstein 1997). Fueled by the increased visibility of LGBT people and a solidifying sense of shared injustice among members of the group, both education and confrontation between gay rights activists and heteronormative social structures occurred during this period. Several important examples from LGBT history include the picketing of the White House in 1965 led by Frank Kameny, the Compton's Cafeteria Riot in 1966, and the more famous Stonewall Riot in June 1969. Borrowing the activist W. Dorr Legg's characterization, Faderman (2015, 91) describes the efforts of this earliest iteration of the LGBT movement as contentions against the "four horsemen" of society, science, the law, and, of course, religion.[4]

Because the gay rights movement was still in its infancy, the established religious views (i.e., homosexuality is sinful behavior and represents individual moral failure) dominated the narratives around LGBT lives, experiences, and rights (see Bull and Gallagher 2001; Fetner 2008). It was the heteronormative messages of these groups that laid the prejudicial foundation that the Religious Right used to construct LGBT identity as incompatible with religion. Despite this framing, religious LGBT people consistently asserted their sexual, gender, and religious identities and demanded both recognition and affirmation from religious communities. As Coley (2020, 51) suggests, the strategies and tactics pursued by religious LGBT activists may vary depending on the orientation (i.e., "friend or foe") and social situation (i.e., leadership or members of a religious group) of the audience. Friendly audiences, for example, may be inspired by sympathetic characterizations of religious LGBT people with relatively little effort; while unfriendly audiences (i.e., religious conservatives) may take more work to persuade, let alone mobilize (see Harrison and Michelson 2017). Similarly, religious LGBT people may appeal to religious leaders with messages of broad cultural resonance "rooted in authoritative cultural discourses" that situate LGBT people within the tradition's theological context, while religious membership may only require contact that generates resonance with the "lived experiences of [the] individual members" (Coley 2020, 51).

Building a Seat at the Table

The Council on Religion and the Homosexual (CRH) provides a case study in early LGBT religious activism consistent with Coley's (2020) classifications. According to Faderman (2015), in 1964, a meeting was held between LGBT activists (both religious and nonreligious) and heterosexual Methodist, Episcopal, Presbyterian, Lutheran, and Church of Christ ministers in Northern California. Among these supportive religious leaders, discrimination against LGBT people in American public and religious life resonated, and the three-day meeting produced a new organization, the CRH. CRH was an "outgrowth" of several San Francisco–area gay and lesbian organizations, including Mattachine, Daughters of Bilitis, and the Glide Memorial Center—a United Methodist congregation founded in 1930 but remade in the 1960s to serve marginalized communities in the Tenderloin neighborhood (see Holly 2013).

By 1965, the CRH had drafted a nine-point mission statement. Most points involved education of religious communities and fostering dialogue between homosexuals and religious groups. The CRH, however, was also committed to engaging American clergy to use their considerable moral authority on behalf of LGBT equality (see Council on Religion and the Homosexual, n.d.). To raise money for this venture 1,500 tickets were sold to a Mardi Gras–themed ball in San Francisco in 1966. While tame by contemporary standards perhaps, this provocative event occurred at a time when local laws forbade many businesses from serving "known homosexuals," state and federal law made same-sex sexual behavior a crime, and many law enforcement agencies routinely entrapped gay men for trumped-up charges of solicitation for the purpose of publicly humiliating them in the press (D'Emilio 1998).

When fifty local police officers wearing riot helmets and brandishing batons, and a phalanx of squad cards, cameras, and reporters, arrived outside the venue, heterosexual clergy experienced firsthand the kind of intimidation, suppression, and violence that was common to LGBT people. The event ended when uniformed officers invaded the venue and began arresting objectors for obstructing a fire code inspection. The publicity resulting from the arrest of heterosexual clergy forced the hand of the local political elite and led to the development of a community relations board "to demonstrate that the police were willing to listen to the clergy, and to the homosexuals who were under church protection" (Faderman 2015, 108). As Faderman (2015, 108) concludes, "No group of men wearing the collar—no moral authority of any kind—had ever before pleaded the homosexual's case so well to the general public."

The council continued to operate into the 1980s with chapters in the United States and Canada. While CRH promoted dialogue, the group's mission was predominately to educate religious heterosexuals (in the laity and clergy). Yet, the 1960s also witnessed religious activism that sought to democratize and queer religious participation. In many cases, this religious activism spilled into the political sphere as religious LGBT people contributed their talent and unabashed visibility to the political efforts of the burgeoning LGBT movement.

In the 1960s, some LGBT people, including clergy who came out as part of the gay liberation movement, were rejected by their families and excommunicated by their denominations. Yet, many still found emotional support and moral guidance in their faith. For these LGBT people, religion remained authoritative in their lives, but they recognized the potentiality of reconciling or integrating their faith and their LGBT identity. Having been rejected by their faith traditions, they faced two options: First, they could potentially advocate for inclusion within their unwelcoming tradition. Second, they could pursue a new faith tradition grounded in LGBT-inclusive theology. In the first instance, groups like Affirmation, mentioned at the beginning of this chapter, were founded to work within existing faith communities. In the supplemental online appendix, I show a table of similar organizations and the dates they were founded. From Pentecostal to Presbyterian, Orthodox Catholic to Orthodox Jewish, Baptist to Buddhist, there are numerous organizations (and innumerable contemporary online communities) dedicated to LGBT advocacy within most every religious tradition represented in the United States.

The advocacy work of religious LGBT people and allies within unsupportive faith traditions has led many of those traditions to reconsider their theological objections and welcome LGBT congregants, members, and leaders. Religious LGBT people and these denominational affinity groups are sources of spiritual resources for LGBT members and converts. In addition, LGBT affinity groups raise awareness of inequities among the broader denominational membership, giving the groups leverage in theological debates and placing pressure on recalcitrant denominations. Importantly, it is clear that many young people, even if they do not identify as LGBT, are willing to change or end their religious affiliation over the issue of LGBT inclusion (Cox, Navarro-Rivera, and Jones 2014). Religious LGBT people and affinity groups also advocate for secular policy changes, such as same-sex marriage and adoption rights for same-sex couples, and encourage their denominations to affirm these developments with changes in denominational theology or liturgy.

In the second table of the online supplemental appendix, I show the stance on LGBT inclusion of most major religious denominations in the United States. While some of the labels are overly broad and some denominations allow more local variation, the table classifies most of the major denominations along a continuum from the least (denounce) to the most (full inclusion) accepting. As the online appendix shows, there are generally inclusive and exclusive traditions within every denomination. Furthermore, many denominations, including most of the largest Christian denominations in the United States, are partially inclusive (i.e., welcome openly LGBT congregants but do not afford them membership, grant them leadership positions, or sanction same-sex relationships). While denominations like the UMC are still confronting heterosexism within their theology, the list of inclusive denominations is much longer now than at any previous time. This is largely due to the efforts of religious LGBT people who confronted heterosexism within their faith traditions.

The growing number of inclusive denominations and congregations means that many LGBT people may not feel the need to seek out more affirming denominations after coming out. Since the 1960s, several congregations and denominations have made reputations for their LGBT-inclusive theology largely because they were founded or led by religious LGBT people. Several studies have examined why LGBT people join these LGBT-led denominations and congregations, including the Metropolitan Community Church (MCC), Reform Judaism synagogues, or Unitarian Universalist congregations (see Griffin 2006; Shokeid 1995; Thumma and Gray 2005; Wilcox 2003). Some religious LGBT people, especially those who are learning to reconcile their LGBT and religious identities, find LGBT-led congregations helpful in alleviating psychological stress or conflict instigated by internalized homophobia (Primiano 2005; Shokeid 2005). Indeed, some newly out LGBT people may join an LGBT-led denomination or congregation, but once identity integration is achieved or at least conflict between one's religious and sexual identities has been sufficiently mitigated, they move on (see Thumma and Gray 2005). For others, LGBT identity is a central part of their sense of self, and social, religious, and political behaviors are extensions of their identity. For this group, it is important to make an overt (i.e., confrontational) political statement about the uniqueness of LGBT religious experiences.

In the middle of the twentieth century, few LGBT-led religious communities existed in the United States and no large denominations allowed LGBT people to hold leadership positions. For some religious LGBT people, then, it was necessary to create new congregations, and even denominations, grounded in LGBT-affirming theology and led by LGBT people. Three examples, the MCC, Faith Temple, and the Unity Fellowship Church movement highlight the importance of these religious pioneers and further nuance the strategy of pursuing LGBT and religious identity integration, especially among LGBT POC.

The MCC, also known as the Universal Fellowship of Metropolitan Community Churches, was founded by the Reverend Troy Perry in Los Angeles, California, in 1968 and has the distinction of being the first Christian denomination to allow full participation of openly LGBT people (although Perry did not characterize MCC as a "gay church"; see Perry 1974). Perry, a former ordained minister in the Church of God of Prophecy, a Pentecostal Holiness denomination headquartered in Cleveland, Tennessee, had been removed from ministry after coming out as gay in the early 1960s. After a tumultuous period of self-doubt, Perry recognized the dearth of spiritual and political representation among the Los Angeles LGBT community and began holding services (Perry and Lucas 1987). Given the intense heterosexism of the time and the underdevelopment of organized LGBT social groups, LGBT people of faith often struggled with questions of faith and legal discrimination independently. However, the rise of the homophile movement and the development of new social and political organizations designed to serve and educate LGBT people provided a framework for mass politico-religious mobilization (Faderman 2015).

From the beginning, Perry's religious vision included aspects of political mobilization. As Perry told the *Friends Radio* broadcast in Washington, DC, in 1974, the theology of MCC is "three-pronged," with equal attention given to the "gospels of salvation, community, and social action." Perry believed the "MCC should never take a back seat to any organization . . . when it came to . . . righting those wrongs . . . that have been committed against the gay community" (Perry 1974). Members of the MCC participated in early demonstrations against discrimination, including police entrapment of gay men and the firing of gay and lesbian employees. Perry and the MCC helped organize the first Christopher Street West parade, what would come to be known as the Los Angeles Pride March, in 1970, commemorating the one-year anniversary of the Stonewall Riots (Perry 1974). In addition, the MCC devoted significant resources to defeating the Briggs Initiative, the 1978 California ballot measure to ban gays and lesbians from working in public schools (see Stone 2012). Perry famously held a sixteen-day fast on the steps of the Federal Building in Los Angeles to raise money and awareness for the campaign against the initiative, which was defeated, despite the support of Anita Bryant (*Call Me Troy* 2007).

Since its founding, MCC has grown to over two hundred congregations in more than thirty countries. While its mission has always been inclusive of social justice, the denomination has developed a cosmology that explicitly socializes LGBT people into a shared affirmative understanding of LGBT identity within the Christian faith. Indeed, the quote at the beginning of this chapter is from a prayer suggested by the MCC for a special celebration of LGBT Pride month in June. It continues, "Red is for life, the root of spirit. Living and Self-Loving Christ, you are our Root. Free us from shame, and grant us the grace of healthy pride so we can follow our own inner light. With the red stripe in the rainbow, we give thanks that God created us just the way we are" (Cherry 2012). From these special Pride liturgies and worship services to rainbow vestments, flags, and decorations in church buildings, inclusive rituals, and affiliation with secular LGBT organizations, MCC demonstrates Fuist's (2016) titular observation about the ease with which LGBT and religious identities can be incorporated among some LGBT people: "It just always seemed like it wasn't a big deal."

For LGBT POC, however, being LGBT might not "be a big deal" in LGBT-led congregations, but being a person of color often *can* be in these predominantly white spaces. While some scholars have suggested differing religious worship styles explain the lack of racial diversity among the largest LGBT-led congregations, others suggest the importance of race-affirming religious traditions in predominantly white cultures combined with racism from within predominantly white LGBT-led religious spaces lead many LGBT POC to either remain in denominations and congregations that denounce LGBT identity or seek out LGBT POC-led denominations and congregations. Griffin's (2006) foundational work on the development of Black LGBT Christian identity notes this rationale among some Black religious LGBT people. Namely, some Black religious LGBT people may prefer to stay in unwelcoming Black Protestant denominations rather than join white LGBT-led Protestant congregations because they do not experience racism within Black-led congregations. Since the 1980s, however, some Black religious LGBT people have joined congregations that are led by LGBT POC.

In overcoming homophobic experiences within predominantly Black Protestant congregations and racist experiences within predominantly white LGBT-led Protestant congregations, two Black gay religious pioneers founded congregations that give expression to both Black and LGBT culture in their religious practice. First, Faith Temple in Washington, D.C., was founded by Dr. James Tinney in 1982 as the "first Black gay communion" (Griffin 2006, 189). Dr. Tinney was an ordained minister in the Church of God in Christ but had been excommunicated when he organized a "gay revival," focusing on outreach to Washington, D.C.'s, LGBT population. Dr. Tinney viewed Christianity as a liberation theology but recognized that liberation had been siloed within discrete Black and LGBT cosmologies. For both Black and LGBT Protestants, religion connects families and communities and empowers those who are oppressed by society, yet neither recognizes the intersectional position of Black Christian LGBT people. Instead, each demands conformity—

one through heterosexism, the other through racism—before experiencing full fellowship.

Similarly, Bishop Carl Bean sought to minister to the unique position of Black religious LGBT people after experiencing tension between heterosexism and his Protestant faith. Conflicted, according to Griffin (2006), Bean took an offer to record the song "I Was Born This Way," which celebrates being born gay. It became a hit on the Billboard music charts in the 1970s and became an auspice to minister to religious LGBT people. After years of ministry focusing on people with AIDS in Los Angeles, Unity Fellowship of Christ Church was chartered in 1982. Since 1992, the Unity Fellowship Church movement has expanded to include sixteen congregations in the United States. Founded on liberation theology, the church prioritizes social justice, antiracism, antihomophobia, and antitransphobia as well as inquisitiveness about the nature of faith and the teachings of all religions about sexuality and gender.

Bates (2005) explores religious practice in one of the Unity Fellowship congregations, Liberation in Truth (now UFC NewArk), in Newark, New Jersey. Like the MCC, Unity Fellowship weaves LGBT history and culture into its liturgy, worship, and community service. Following the Pentecostal tradition, for example, church attendees offer testimonies reflecting on their experiences negotiating life as Black religious LGBT people; and, taking its cue from Bishop Bean, the congregation operated an outreach center to educate the community on safe sex practices and HIV/AIDS. Unlike MCC, however, Unity Fellowship incorporates Black history and culture as well as religious pluralism into its service. For example, Bates (2005, 222) notes the Yoruba word *Ashe* or "sacred power" is often repeated, and references to African ancestors are peppered throughout the liturgy, while blessings invoke "the spirits, and various leaders in African American history ranging from Sojourner Truth to Malcom X."

Just as Black Americans are more religious (across measures of public and private devotion) than other populations, religion is more important to Black LGBT people in the United States than any other LGBT subpopulation (Battle, Pastrana, and Harris 2017). Studies of religiosity among communities of color demonstrate the importance of religion as a bonding institution (see Putnam 2000), (re)producing cultural and ethnic traditions and reinforcing attachments to ethnic communities and family, both nuclear and extended (Chen and Jeung 2012). In addition, predominantly POC-led religious organizations have a long history of service provision, including education, health care, and civic empowerment (see Eck 2001; Griffin 2006). For some POC it is difficult to contemplate leaving the religious communities they were raised in because it may also mean leaving behind familial, community, and ethnoracial attachments. Among religious LGBT POC, then, joining LGBT-inclusive denominations or congregations may not be as easy as it is among some white religious LGBT people. The Unity Fellowship Church movement and LGBT POC-led congregations like Dr. Tinney's Faith Temple help LGBT POC reduce psychic conflict between their religious, LGBT, and racial identities by affirming each equally.

Finally, in several studies, Wilcox (2009; 2012) notes women are less likely to participate in LGBT-led Christian congregations and denominations than men. Although both the MCC (Wilcox 2003) and the Unity Fellowship Church movement (Bates 2005) explicitly affirm the participation of women in leadership roles, Wilcox (2009; 2012) suggests religious LGBT women are more likely to hold individualist, rather than authoritative, perspectives on religion. Ecumenical or even multireligious viewpoints on sex(uality) and gender help many people reconcile their faith and LGBT identity. Learning to (re)interpret scriptures that were taught as homophobic cudgels is a central part of spiritual development among LGBT people, although not all religious LGBT people are interested or willing to undertake this individualized approach to religious studies. For some who maintain that conservative interpretations are authoritative, it is more important to attempt to change their sexual orientation or gender identity rather than alter their beliefs (Erzen 2006). Most in this group, however, learn that celibacy may be possible, but no religious therapy can reprogram human sexuality (Erzen 2006). Along with rejecting the authority of homophobic religious traditions, many religious LGBT women also reject sexist beliefs in the sacredness of male religious leadership. Among Wilcox's (2009; 2012) interviewees, the combination of these facets of individualistic religiosity primarily explained the patterns of religious belief among LGBT women.

In addition to Christian traditions, LGBT people from other faith traditions have pursued advocacy strategies that have resulted in strong LGBT faith communities. Griffin (2006), Shokeid (2005), and the edited volumes by Thumma and Gray (2005), Browne, Munt, and Yip (2010), Taylor and Snowdon (2014), and Hunt (2015), for example, explicate the ways LGBT people across faith traditions, LGBT POC, and LGBT immigrants and second-generation Americans have pushed their religious traditions toward acceptance and full participation of LGBT people and, subsequently, pushed the boundaries of American religious pluralism. Many LGBT-led meditation centers, synagogues, and affinity groups for LGBT Muslims and Hindus are established to educate LGBT people and heterosexual co-religionists, and even confront exclusive religious leadership. Expressions of queer religion also take form in queer Faerie and New Age, Wiccan, and Pagan spiritualities that have long challenged heteronormative and gendered social systems (see Hasbrouck 2005; Neitz 2005). With such a diverse array of religious denominations and traditions that either partially or fully accept LGBT people, it is not surprising that a majority of LGBT people in the United States hold a religious affiliation.

Despite the efforts of early and contemporary LGBT religious activists, it is worth noting distrust toward most religious institutions persisted among many LGBT people. While the gay liberation movement inspired efforts to democratize religious institutions, some LGBT people viewed religion as an existential threat to LGBT identity and culture. Sometimes based on personal experiences with religious bigotry, sometimes emerging out of concern for American pluralism, and sometimes emerging from a Marxist critique of Western culture popular among gay liberation activists, support for "organized religion" among some LGBT people was less than enthusiastic. Religious bigotry and subsequent political activity to limit the rights of LGBT people was a continuation of centuries of "queer-baiting and sex role reinforcement" that "oppressed the masses, helped capitalism," and maintained the patriarchy, opined the Philadelphia-based Gay Pagans and Atheists in the mid-1970s (Mecca 2009, 244). Similarly, the Gay Atheist League of America in New York (1978) asserted, "When organized religion uses its power to control government and forces its belief and social practices on unpopular minorities and lifestyles, it becomes dangerous and a serious threat to society."

The distrust toward major religious denominations continues among contemporary LGBT people. Using a probability sample of lesbian, gay, and bisexual people collected by the Pew Research Center to evaluate attitudes toward the major American religious traditions, Barringer (2019) finds relatively few respondents evaluate any denomination positively. Specifically, greater than three-quarters of respondents rated "Evangelical Protestant churches," the "Catholic church," the "Muslim religion," and the "Mormon church" as "unfriendly" toward LGBT people. Only the "Jewish religion" (11.6% evaluate as "friendly") and "non-Evangelical Protestant churches" (14.7% evaluate as "friendly") merit evaluations of "friendly" among more than one in ten respondents.

As Barringer (2019) shows, evaluations of the largest American religious denominations are contingent on a variety of factors, including political orientation, race and ethnicity, age and education, relationship status, and personal importance of religion. For example, respondents who report being in a committed relationship are less likely to report favorable views of any major religious tradition, perhaps a reaction to opposition to same-sex marriage among many of the groups. This is consistent with the low number of coupled religious LGBT people in the Williams Institute Study of LGBT religion (Conron, Goldberg, and O'Neill 2020). Notably, Barringer (2019) shows evaluations of the major American religious traditions are more positive among sexual minorities who describe religion as important in their lives. The trend even extends to evaluations of Evangelical Protestant churches, which have arguably been the most vocal opponents of LGBT rights.

This leads to another question: How religious are LGBT people? I answer this question in the next chapter by reviewing data from large-scale surveys of LGBT people. I start by visualizing LGBT religiosity from data gathered by the CCES, the Pew Research Center, and others, focusing on the major correlates of political participation—that is, measures of public and private devotion. In the remaining chapters of this text, I examine more closely the effect of religious socialization and the resources that accrue to religious participants as potential explanations for LGBT political behavior.

2

The LGBT Faithful in America

There's this mystical thread that is tied through my life and
my whole faith, and that is that everything hard that
happens to me, pushes me into music. And that's where
God lives inside of for me. . . . I knew I had to leave
organized religion and that I had to leave my template and
go into something scary, dark, and beautiful.

—Brandi Carlile

I never walked away from the church. I just quit going.

—Leslie Jordan, interviewed
by Shania Twain (2021)

The tension I articulate in the previous chapter between conservative
religion and LGBT identity is, more often than not, the dominant narrative that appears in popular media and even scientific literature about
LGBT people. To be sure, the tension is real and has defined the lives of many
LGBT people. However, the point I wish to reiterate is that the tension between LGBT identity and conservative religion is a construct—a mutable
component of society defined by shared social experiences—derived from
a conservative interpretation of religious traditions that has been reified
throughout our society. At the macro level, Fetner (2008) provides a good
example of the way LGBT politics has been constructed in reaction to conservative political mobilization. In the same way that LGBT social movement
organizations in the United States constantly respond to attacks from conservative politico-religious forces, the politico-religious attitudes and behavior of individual LGBT people are often developed in reaction to experiences
with conservative religious forces, a point to which I return in Chapter 4.

Both of the quotes at the beginning of this chapter highlight this idea. The
famed musician Brandi Carlile, self-described as a "Jesus freak mama with
a really complicated perspective on faith and the wreckage that it's left," discussed in an interview the necessity of leaving organized religion for a per-
sonalized spirituality grounded in self-discovery (Masters 2021). It is true
that LGBT people, on average, are less likely to identify with a faith tradition
than non-LGBT people and that LGBT people are overrepresented among

non-Christian faith communities in the United States (Murphy 2015; Sherkat 2016). Yet, despite the dominance of the conflict narrative, most LGBT people report little change in their religiosity after coming out (see Egan, Edelman, and Sherrill 2008). As Carlile discusses, changing affiliations and updating beliefs are important parts of *maintaining* ties to one's religious roots, not severing them.

In most of this chapter, I explore the religious beliefs and behavior of LGBT people using data from representative samples that were gathered by other researchers. It is helpful to begin with data from larger samples of LGBT people because it helps contextualize the patterns of behavior I identify later using data I collected from nonprobability samples and it offers a robust, generalizable picture of LGBT religiosity. Specifically, I use survey data from the Cooperative Congressional Election Study, a national annual survey of more than fifty thousand people that measures American political attitudes and behaviors. In the next chapter, I introduce the unique data sets that I have constructed to fully investigate the relationships between LGBT religiosity and politics in the remainder of the book.

The data I present in this chapter show that, similar to the late actor and comedian Leslie Jordan's quote at the beginning of this chapter, religion is a nuanced subject for many LGBT people. In Jordan's case, the actor (and gospel singer) implies that one's religious affiliation may change after coming out, but spirituality remains important despite distance from religious institutions. Rather than turning away from religion or being unreligious, as the conservative Evangelical narrative suggests, many LGBT people see themselves as either religious or spiritual. In short, LGBT identity, religiosity, and spirituality are not destined to be zero-sum identities. Despite popular misconceptions, LGBT people are and will continue to be a religious and spiritual population. Furthermore, when LGBT people experience displeasure with religion, it is almost certainly viewed as a fault of "organized religion" or the Christian Right, usually not individual religious actors, and especially not religious people within the LGBT community. Yet, experiences vary significantly across gender and racial identities. As I explain in the concluding section of this chapter, my contention is that religious variation (stemming from both pre–coming out and post–coming out socialization) is responsible for differences in LGBT politico-religious experiences.

LGBT Identity in the United States

The total population of LGBT people in the United States is unknown. However, recent estimates suggest that about one person in twenty (5.6%) of the American adult population identify as LGBT (J. Jones 2021). The trend is especially pronounced among younger generations, with about one in six

(15.9%) born between 1997 and 2002 (Generation Z) and nearly one in ten (9.1%) born between 1981 and 1996 (millennials) identifying as LGBT. The data suggests the growing rejection of gender and sexual binarism may be driving the trend among younger Americans since more Americans identify as bisexual than gay or lesbian.

In 2020, the Williams Institute estimated there are about 5.3 million LGBT adults in the United States who identify as religious (Conron, Goldberg, and O'Neill 2020). There are similarities in demographic patterns between these LGBT people and religious heterosexuals in the United States. Namely, older LGBT people are more likely to report religious affiliation than younger LGBT people. Nearly two-thirds (64.9%) of LGBT respondents age sixty-five and older in the Williams Institute study are religious, whereas about four in ten (40%) LGBT respondents age eighteen to thirty-four are religious (Conron, Goldberg, and O'Neill 2020). In addition, many religious LGBT adults are parents (45.8% to 57.7%, depending on the measure of religiosity) or live in the South (54.1%), while fewer than two in ten (14.8%) are married or cohabitating with a same-sex partner (Conron, Goldberg, and O'Neill 2020).

Social scientific research also shows distinctive patterns of religiosity among this growing proportion of the population. First, LGBT people are less likely to report a religious affiliation than non-LGBT people. As Coley (2020) suggests, this is likely because some LGBT people attempt to alleviate perceived conflict between their religious and LGBT identities by disassociating with religion after coming out (see also Cravens 2018). Indeed, in an analysis of a representative sample of lesbians, gays, and bisexuals in the United States, Egan, Edelman, and Sherrill (2008, 22) find more than one-quarter (27%) of the sample report becoming "less religious" after coming out, while just over one in ten (15%) report becoming "more religious" after coming out. This is also consistent with other research that suggests LGBT people are less likely to identify as Christian than heterosexuals (see Murphy 2015). Taken together, such evidence is generally marshaled to confirm stereotypes that LGBT people, as a whole, are unreligious. However, in Egan, Edelman, and Sherrill's (2008) study, more than half of the respondents (53%) reported no change in their religious affiliation after coming out, while recent studies confirm a majority of LGBT people identify with some faith tradition (Cravens 2018; Sherkat 2016).

Sherkat (2016) identifies a second distinctive pattern in LGBT religious affiliation. Namely, LGBT people are overrepresented among non-Christian religious traditions, including Buddhism, Judaism, and Unitarianism. Vegter and Haider-Markel (2020) suggest these traditions are more egalitarian and have fewer (if any) formal restrictions on same-sex attraction, behavior, and gender diverse expression. Indeed, the Reform and Conservative Judaism movements (the latter after about 2006) have long pursued an inclusive theology that informs a progressive politics with room for LGBT people and LGBT rights. The Orthodox movement, guided by its strict adherence to Jewish law, which is generally interpreted as antiattribution, is somewhat less progressive in both its acceptance of LGBT identity and LGBT civil rights (see Schnoor 2006). However, on average, Jewish Americans represent the second-most supportive religious group on LGBT civil rights (slightly behind Unitarian Universalists), with a PRRI study finding as many as 80% of Jewish Americans supporting civil rights laws protecting LGBT people against discrimination, while more than two-thirds (68%) oppose laws allowing business owners who express religiously based objections to refuse service to LGBT people (PRRI 2020). LGBT people have responded positively as Judaism is evaluated as the friendliest religious tradition by LGBT people in Barringer's (2019) study. Similarly, Buddhism has generally been perceived as friendly to LGBT people, and LGBT people are more likely than heterosexuals to be Buddhist in the United States (Vegter and Haider-Markel 2020).

Trends in LGBT Religious Affiliation

Data from the CCES help demonstrate the patterns of religious affiliation among sexual minorities. The CCES began asking the sexual orientation of respondents in 2016, with the question "Which of the following best describes your sexuality?" The choices given are "heterosexual/straight," "lesbian/gay woman," "gay man," "bisexual," "other," and "prefer not to say." In the same year, the CCES began asking respondents the question "Have you ever undergone any part of a process (including any thought or action) to change your gender / perceived gender from the one you were assigned at birth? This may include steps such as changing the type of clothes you wear, name you are known by or undergoing surgery." The response options are "yes," "no," or "prefer not to say." The sample sizes fluctuate between election years, with larger samples collected during 2016 and 2018 in both pre- and postelection waves. Respondents are largely recruited from YouGov panels and are supplemented through online recruitment. Although not a random sample, researchers use a "pruning" process to ensure the sample is representative of the American population (see Ansolabehere and Schaffner 2017), and the survey offers one of the largest samples of LGBT people with measures of religious behavior in the United States.

Table 2.1 shows the distribution of religious affiliation among respondents who identify as lesbian, gay, bisexual, or as a sexual orientation other than heterosexual across four years of the CCES, 2016–2019. As the table shows, fewer than one-quarter of lesbian, gay, and bisexual respondents consistently identify as atheist or agnostic, while a plurality of each sample, about one-quarter in each, consistently identify as "nothing in particular." Religious

TABLE 2.1 DISTRIBUTION OF RELIGIOUS ID AMONG LGB AND "OTHER" RESPONDENTS, CCES 2016–2019								
	2016 CCES		2017 CCES		2018 CCES		2019 CCES	
Religion	Freq.	%	Freq.	%	Freq.	%	Freq.	%
Protestant	993	20.9	316	17.4	1047	18.4	321	17.8
Roman Catholic	645	13.6	217	11.9	637	11.2	217	12.0
Mormon	23	.49	17	.94	39	.69	13	.72
Eastern or Greek Orthodox	17	.36	15	.83	25	.44	8	.44
Jewish	126	2.6	56	3.0	167	2.9	70	3.8
Muslim	34	.72	16	.88	33	.58	14	.78
Buddhist	93	1.9	33	1.82	103	1.8	28	1.5
Hindu	14	.30	8	.44	17	.30	7	.39
Atheist	720	15.2	274	15.1	911	16.0	322	17.8
Agnostic	580	12.6	229	12.6	777	13.7	225	12.4
Nothing in Particular	1,046	22.1	470	25.9	1,419	25.0	448	24.8
Something Else	441	9.3	163	8.9	495	8.7	128	7.1
Total[a]	4732		1,814		5,670		1,801	

Sources: Data from Ansolabehere and Schaffner (2017); Schaffner and Ansolabehere (2019); Schaffner, Ansolabehere, and Luks (2019); and Ansolabehere, Schaffner, and Luks (2020); in response to the question "What is your present religion, if any?"
[a] Column percentage does not sum to 100% due to rounding.

participation may be a better measure of religious devotion, but it is important to note that given the opportunity to identify as atheist, these respondents chose "nothing in particular" instead. This lends support to the literature that suggests religiosity remains an important component of sexual minority identity even after coming out.

Across each year of the survey, a majority of sexual minorities identify with a particular faith tradition. Between 17% and 20% of respondents identify as Protestant, while 11% to 14% identify as Roman Catholic. Between 2% and 4% identify as Jewish, and fewer than 1% identify as Mormon, Christian Orthodox, or Hindu. Consistent with Sherkat (2016), Buddhists are well represented among the samples, while a large proportion of each sample, between 7% and 9%, identify as "something else," eluding to the myriad ways LGBT people practice religion beyond the scope of traditional categorial measures (see Taylor and Snowdon 2014; Thumma and Gray 2005).

Table 2.2 shows the distribution of religious identification among respondents who identify as transgender across four years of the CCES, 2016–2019. While there is some overlap[1] between the two tables (i.e., some transgender people in the samples also identify as a sexual minority), the trends in affiliation are similar. Yet, larger proportions of transgender respondents than sexual minorities in each sample report a religious affiliation. Notably, be-

TABLE 2.2 DISTRIBUTION OF RELIGIOUS ID AMONG TRANSGENDER RESPONDENTS, CCES 2016–2019

Religion	2016 CCES		2017 CCES		2018 CCES		2019 CCES	
	Freq.	%	Freq.	%	Freq.	%	Freq.	%
Protestant	228	21.9	88	19.1	221	19.7	127	19.5
Roman Catholic	295	28.3	114	24.8	230	20.5	206	31.6
Mormon	21	2.0	8	1.7	11	.98	23	3.5
Eastern or Greek Orthodox	19	1.8	13	2.8	11	.98	16	2.4
Jewish	32	3.0	17	3.7	41	3.6	24	3.6
Muslim	38	3.6	22	4.7	21	1.8	14	2.1
Buddhist	20	1.9	10	2.1	23	2.0	10	1.5
Hindu	9	.86	4	.87	16	1.4	7	1.0
Atheist	83	7.9	46	10.0	118	10.5	57	8.7
Agnostic	65	6.2	26	5.6	96	8.5	33	5.0
Nothing in Particular	149	14.3	75	16.3	236	21.0	101	15.5
Something Else	81	7.7	35	7.6	97	8.6	33	5.0
Total[a]	1,041		459		1,121		651	

Sources: Data from Ansolabehere and Schaffner (2017); Schaffner and Ansolabehere (2019); Schaffner, Ansolabehere, and Luks (2019); and Ansolabehere, Schaffner, and Luks (2020); in response to the question "What is your present religion, if any?"
[a] Column percentage does not sum to 100% due to rounding.

tween 19% and 22% of transgender respondents identify as Protestant and 20% to 30% identify as Roman Catholic. Non-Christian faith traditions are also better represented among transgender respondents, but smaller proportions of transgender people than sexual minorities identify as atheist (between 7% and 10%) or agnostic (between 5% and 9%). Although transgender people are less likely to affiliate with a faith tradition than cisgender people, sociological and psychological research suggests religion may act as a source of resiliency among transgender people, either through its bridging function (i.e., building supportive relationships) or by constructing a cosmology that affirms transgender people, helping to alleviating psychic conflict (see Sumerau and Mathers 2019).

To better understand how religious affiliation is distributed across racial identities, Table 2.3 and Table 2.4 disaggregate the data from the 2016 and 2018 CCES (with the largest samples). As the tables show, smaller proportions of Black and Hispanic sexual minorities identify as atheist than others in the samples. This is consistent with both the Williams Institute study (Conron, Goldberg, and O'Neill 2020) and data from a 2010 study conducted by the Social Justice Sexuality Project using a large oversample of LGBT POC (Battle, Pastrana, and Harris 2017). In both CCES samples, about one-third of Black sexual minorities identify as Protestant, while about one-third of

TABLE 2.3 DISTRIBUTION OF RELIGIOUS ID AMONG LGB AND "OTHER" RESPONDENTS BY RACE, CCES 2016

Religion	White Freq.	White %	Black Freq.	Black %	Hispanic Freq.	Hispanic %	Asian Freq.	Asian %	Another Freq.	Another %
Protestant	726	20.9	154	39.5	47	11.9	16	11.4	50	14.5
Roman Catholic	441	12.7	19	4.8	143	36.2	13	9.2	29	8.4
Mormon	15	.43	3	.77	2	.51	0	0	3	.87
Eastern or Greek Orthodox	12	.35	1	.26	3	.76	0	0	1	.29
Jewish	109	3.1	4	1.0	0	0	3	2.1	10	2.9
Muslim	13	.37	8	2.0	3	.76	3	2.1	7	2.0
Buddhist	53	1.5	6	1.5	7	1.7	19	13.5	8	2.3
Hindu	0	0	1	.26	1	.25	11	7.8	1	.29
Atheist	593	17.0	22	5.6	41	10.3	19	13.5	46	13.4
Agnostic	466	13.4	18	4.6	35	8.8	16	11.4	45	13.1
Nothing in Particular	724	20.8	122	31.3	86	21.7	36	25.7	80	23.3
Something Else	317	9.1	30	7.7	27	6.8	4	2.8	63	18.3
Total[a]	3,469		388		395		140		343	

Source: Data from Ansolabehere and Schaffner (2017).
[a] Column percentage does not sum to 100% due to rounding.

TABLE 2.4 DISTRIBUTION OF RELIGIOUS ID AMONG LGB AND "OTHER" RESPONDENTS BY RACE, CCES 2018

Religion	White Freq.	White %	Black Freq.	Black %	Hispanic Freq.	Hispanic %	Asian Freq.	Asian %	Another Freq.	Another %
Protestant	807	19.4	140	31.6	47	8.6	16	8.4	64	15.3
Roman Catholic	394	9.4	20	4.5	178	32.9	28	14.8	35	8.3
Mormon	34	.82	2	.45	3	.55	0	0	1	.23
Eastern or Greek Orthodox	15	.36	6	1.35	2	.37	0	0	3	.71
Jewish	142	3.4	4	.90	7	1.29	3	1.5	11	2.6
Muslim	10	.24	6	1.3	1	.18	7	3.7	10	2.3
Buddhist	69	1.6	7	1.5	2	.37	19	10.0	7	1.6
Hindu	2	.05	0	0	1	.18	8	4.2	6	1.4
Atheist	741	17.8	25	5.6	63	11.6	34	17.9	50	11.9
Agnostic	607	14.6	23	5.1	66	12.2	31	16.4	54	12.9
Nothing in Particular	977	23.5	177	39.9	137	25.3	39	20.6	101	24.1
Something Else	354	8.5	33	7.4	34	6.2	4	2.1	76	18.1
Total[a]	4,152		443		541		189		418	

Source: Data from Schaffner, Ansolabehere, and Luks (2019).
[a] Column percentage does not sum to 100% due to rounding.

Hispanic sexual minorities identify as Catholic. Similar proportions of white and Asian sexual minorities identify with no particular religious tradition, but greater proportions of Asians in both samples identify as Buddhist or Hindu than any other racial identity group. Similar proportions of Black (in 2016), Asian, and those sexual minorities with another racial identity identify as Muslim. This is not surprising given the history of Islamic faith among Black Americans and in Asian and Middle Eastern cultures, the latter of whom are represented among the "another" category.

The "another" category collapses responses including Native American, mixed-race, Middle Eastern, and "other" racial identities. In both samples, nearly two in ten respondents in this group identify with a different religious tradition than those provided to the respondents by researchers. This is especially true of Native American and mixed-race sexual minorities, who likely practice Indigenous faith traditions or incorporate multiple facets of spirituality from the different cultures that influence their lives, respectively. Similarly, the largest proportion of Jewish respondents identify as white or in the "another" category. Among this group, about one in ten Middle Eastern sexual minorities also identify as Jewish in both samples.

Table 2.5 and Table 2.6, again, disaggregate 2016 and 2018 CCES response data to better describe the distribution of religious affiliation by racial identity among transgender respondents in each study. The number of respon-

TABLE 2.5 DISTRIBUTION OF RELIGIOUS ID AMONG TRANSGENDER RESPONDENTS BY RACE, CCES 2016

Religion	White Freq.	%	Black Freq.	%	Hispanic Freq.	%	Asian Freq.	%	Another Freq.	%
Protestant	140	20.7	37	38.5	36	22.7	6	14.2	9	12.6
Roman Catholic	193	28.6	18	18.7	77	48.7	6	14.2	1	1.4
Mormon	14	2.0	3	3.1	2	1.2	1	2.3	1	1.4
Eastern or Greek Orthodox	14	2.0	0	0	5	3.1	0	0	0	0
Jewish	24	3.5	3	3.1	2	1.2	1	2.3	2	2.8
Muslim	22	3.2	2	2.0	4	2.5	4	9.5	6	8.4
Buddhist	10	1.4	1	1.0	0	0	6	14.2	3	4.2
Hindu	2	.3	0	0	1	.63	6	14.2	0	0
Atheist	65	9.6	2	2.0	4	2.5	2	4.7	10	14.0
Agnostic	50	7.4	3	3.1	3	1.9	2	4.7	7	9.8
Nothing in Particular	92	13.6	20	20.8	15	9.4	6	14.2	16	22.5
Something Else	48	7.1	7	7.2	8	5.0	2	4.7	16	22.5
Total[a]	674		96		157		42		71	

Source: Data from Ansolabehere and Schaffner (2017).
[a] Column percentage does not sum to 100% due to rounding.

TABLE 2.6 DISTRIBUTION OF RELIGIOUS ID AMONG TRANSGENDER
RESPONDENTS BY RACE, CCES 2018

Religion	White		Black		Hispanic		Asian		Another	
	Freq.	%	Freq.	%	Freq.	%	Freq.	%	Freq.	%
Protestant	133	19.5	44	35.2	26	14.8	3	5.3	13	15.6
Roman Catholic	118	17.3	15	12.0	73	41.7	12	21.4	12	14.4
Mormon	7	1.0	0	0	2	1.4	1	1.79	1	1.2
Eastern or Greek Orthodox	6	.88	4	3.2	0	0	0	0	1	1.2
Jewish	28	4.1	5	4.0	3	1.7	2	3.5	3	3.6
Muslim	10	1.4	4	3.2	1	.57	3	5.3	3	3.6
Buddhist	9	1.3	4	3.2	2	1.1	7	12.5	1	1.2
Hindu	1	.15	2	1.6	2	1.1	8	14.2	3	3.6
Atheist	86	12.6	5	4.0	13	7.4	3	5.3	11	13.2
Agnostic	76	11.1	5	4.0	7	4.0	5	8.9	3	3.6
Nothing in Particular	143	20.9	31	24.8	40	22.8	11	19.6	11	13.2
Something Else	65	9.5	6	4.8	6	3.4	1	1.7	19	22.8
Total[a]	682		125		175		56		83	

Source: Data from Schaffner, Ansolabehere, and Luks (2019).
[a] Column percentage does not sum to 100% due to rounding.

dents in each of the columns is noticeably smaller than in the previous tables, especially among Asian and "another" subsamples. While this limits the generalizability of statistical inferences, the data are still useful for understanding the basic distribution of religious affiliations among these relatively large samples of transgender respondents.

As the tables show, fewer Black, Hispanic, and Asian transgender people than white and transgender people of another racial identity in the samples identify as atheist. Even among white respondents, religious affiliation appears more common for transgender people compared to sexual minorities. Notably, between 14 % and 17% of white sexual minorities identify as atheist; however, between 9% and 12% of white transgender respondents identify as atheist in the two samples. Similar to sexual minorities, a plurality of Black transgender respondents in both samples identify as Protestant, while a plurality of Hispanic transgender respondents identifies as Catholic. In both samples more than three in ten Black transgender respondents identify as Protestant, whereas more than four in ten Hispanic transgender respondents identify as Catholic. Between 3% and 4% of white transgender respondents identify as Jewish across the samples, while the Muslim religion is most common among Asian transgender people in the samples, as is Buddhism and Hinduism, reported by between 12% and 14% of the group.

White, Black, Hispanic, and Asian transgender respondents report no particular religious affiliation at higher rates than transgender respondents of another racial identity. Specifically, nearly two in ten white, Black, Hispanic (except in 2016), and Asian respondents identify with no particular religious tradition. However, in both samples, about two in ten transgender respondents of another racial identity report their religious affiliation as something different from the denominations provided by the researchers. Again, this is likely reflective of the Indigenous spiritualities and spiritual adaptations that take place among transgender respondents from multiracial or multiethnic backgrounds.

In the end, most LGBT people in these samples affiliate with some faith tradition. POC, especially Black and Hispanic LGBT people in these samples, are more likely than white LGBT people to identify with a faith tradition. In addition, fewer transgender people in the samples identify as atheist, but higher percentages of transgender people report affiliating with a faith tradition compared to sexual minorities. Denominational affiliation, however, is not the same as personal devotion or public expression of religion or faith. Both are important components of religiosity, but each may have unique effects on identity and political development. Before unpacking the effect of religiosity on LGBT politics, it is important to have a basic understanding of how LGBT people participate in religion. In the next section, I use data from the CCES to examine patterns of LGBT religious participation.

Trends in LGBT Religious Participation

Research suggests that LGBT people are less religious than heterosexuals across several measures of religiosity, including church attendance and personal devotion (Vegter and Haider-Markel 2020). There are nuances, however, as religiosity also varies across race, ethnicity, gender, education, as well as denomination and other demographic indicators. Religious participation among LGBT people is also more nuanced than among heterosexuals because survey measures of religious participation generally assume religious participation is open to heterosexual and LGBT respondents equally. However, as the table of religious denominations in the supplemental online appendix makes clear, not every tradition allows LGBT people to become members, let alone fully participate in religious activities. Furthermore, while heterosexuals may hold ideological or political opinions that differ from the theological stance of their faith traditions, or even engage in behavior that their faith tradition deems immoral or sinful, very few heterosexuals have experienced condemnation and consequent psychic conflict related to their religious beliefs in the way LGBT people report.

Given these conditions, what are the patterns of religious participation among LGBT people? The CCES asks three standard religiosity questions. The first, a measure of personal or private devotion, asks respondents, "How important is religion in your life?" The second, a measure of public devotion, asks respondents, "Aside from weddings and funerals, how often do you attend religious services?" The third, also a measure of personal or private devotion, asks respondents, "People practice their religion in different ways. Outside of attending religious services, how often do you pray?"

Table 2.7 shows the distribution of responses to each question among respondents who identify as lesbian, gay, bisexual, or with another sexual identity across four years of the CCES, 2016–2019. In each year, a plurality of re-

TABLE 2.7 RELIGIOSITY AMONG LGB AND "OTHER" RESPONDENTS, CCES 2016–2019								
	CCES 2016		CCES 2017		CCES 2018		CCES 2019	
Religiosity	Freq.	%	Freq.	%	Freq.	%	Freq.	%
Importance								
Very	949	20.0	333	18.3	926	16.2	295	16.3
Somewhat	985	20.7	360	19.7	1,175	20.6	362	20.0
Not too	870	18.3	350	19.2	1,044	18.3	304	16.8
Not at all	1,930	40.7	777	42.3	2,539	44.6	846	46.8
Total[a]	4,737		1,813		5,684		1,807	
Prayer								
Several times/day	760	16.0	243	13.3	744	13.1	266	14.7
Once/day	457	9.6	164	9.0	497	8.7	131	7.2
Few times/day	477	10.0	188	10.3	571	10.0	161	8.9
Once/week	113	2.3	62	3.4	125	2.2	37	2.0
Few times/month	329	6.9	141	7.7	372	6.5	97	5.3
Seldom	844	17.8	306	16.8	1,068	18.8	309	17.1
Never	1,651	34.8	660	36.2	2,149	37.8	741	41.0
Don't Know	105	2.2	51	.27	155	2.7	64	3.5
Total[a]	4,736		1,815		5,681		1,806	
Attendance								
More than once/week	174	3.6	63	3.4	152	2.6	58	3.2
Once/week	413	8.7	168	9.2	433	7.6	137	7.5
Once or twice/month	283	5.9	130	7.1	340	5.9	114	6.3
A few time/year	572	12.0	197	10.8	650	11.4	185	10.2
Seldom	1,068	22.5	362	19.8	1271	22.3	364	20.1
Never	2,182	46.0	865	47.5	2,761	48.6	920	50.9
Don't know	44	.02	29	.33	73	1.2	29	1.6
Total[a]	4,736		1,814		5,680		1,807	

Sources: Data from Ansolabehere and Schaffner (2017); Schaffner and Ansolabehere (2019); Schaffner, Ansolabehere, and Luks (2019); and Ansolabehere, Schaffner, and Luks (2020).
[a] Column percentage does not sum to 100% due to rounding.

spondents, between 40% and 47%, indicate religion is "not at all" important in their lives. Between 36% and 40% indicate religion is very or somewhat important. The table also shows a majority of sexual minorities engage in prayer, another private measure of devotion, at least sometimes. Specifically, a plurality of the respondents, between 35% and 41%, report never praying; however, more than one in ten respondents, between 13% and 16%, report praying several times per day. A majority of respondents indicate never engaging in only one measure of public devotion—church attendance. Specifically, among the 2019 sample, a small majority of respondents (50.9%) report never attending church outside of weddings and funerals. Like Leslie Jordan's statement quoted at the beginning of this chapter, many sexual minorities in the CCES studies may not attend religious services, but this does not appear to diminish the importance of faith in their lives.

Table 2.8 shows the distribution of responses to the same questions among respondents who identify as transgender across the four years of the CCES, 2016–2019. In each year, a plurality of respondents, between 37% and 45% indicate religion is "very" important in their lives while between 18% and 28% indicate religion is "not at all" important. Similarly, a plurality of respondents, between 17% and 24%, indicate they pray "several times per day," while between 18% and 24% indicate "never" praying. This relationship is reversed in the 2018 data, which suggests more transgender respondents indicate "never" praying than praying "several times per day"; however, most transgender respondents in every year of the CCES indicate praying at least once per day. Finally, a plurality of transgender respondents, between 28% and 44%, indicate attending religious services at least once per week, although a similar proportion, between 33% and 46%, indicate seldom or never attending; again, however, the relationship is reversed in the 2018 data.

As with the general population, religious affiliation is more common among sexual minorities in the United States than religiosity. That is, fewer people actually attend religious services or pray than identify with a faith tradition. This is, of course, nuanced by racial and gender effects. For example, a more detailed analysis of data from the 2018 CCES, with the largest sample of sexual minority and transgender respondents (see online Statistical Appendix II. All appendixes are available via Harvard Dataverse at https://doi .org/10.7910/DVN/M87Q1V; for additional citation information see Cravens 2022b), demonstrates LGB and "other" respondents are more likely to report religion is "not too" or "not at all" important in their lives than heterosexuals. However, transgender respondents are more likely than cisgender respondents to report religion is "very" important in their lives and attend religious services more frequently than cisgender respondents.

In addition, patterns of religiosity differ between white and LGB and "other" sexual minority POC. Specifically, data from the 2018 CCES suggest

TABLE 2.8 RELIGIOSITY AMONG TRANSGENDER RESPONDENTS, CCES 2016–2019

Religiosity	CCES 2016 Freq.	%	CCES 2017 Freq.	%	CCES 2018 Freq.	%	CCES 2019 Freq.	%
Importance								
Very	467	44.8	199	43.3	346	30.8	243	37.3
Somewhat	269	25.8	103	22.4	293	26.0	186	28.5
Not too	107	10.2	61	13.2	168	14.9	85	13.0
Not at all	196	18.8	95	20.7	316	28.1	137	21.0
Total[a]	1041		459		1123		651	
Prayer								
Several times/day	226	21.7	109	23.7	198	17.6	158	24.2
Once/day	222	21.3	67	14.6	155	13.8	114	17.5
Few times/day	143	13.7	66	14.3	150	13.3	88	13.5
Once/week	72	6.9	39	8.5	66	5.8	48	7.3
Few times/month	69	6.3	28	6.1	76	6.7	38	5.8
Seldom	96	9.2	46	10.0	158	14.1	63	9.6
Never	191	18.3	89	19.3	276	24.6	121	18.5
Don't Know	20	1.2	15	3.2	41	3.6	21	3.2
Total[a]	1041		459		1120		651	
Attendance								
More than once/week	165	15.8	66	14.3	132	11.7	102	15.6
Once/week	294	28.2	110	23.9	185	16.5	189	29.0
Once or twice/month	105	10.0	67	14.6	119	10.6	65	9.9
A few time/year	106	10.1	34	7.4	138	12.3	53	8.1
Seldom	125	12.0	55	11.9	156	13.9	74	11.3
Never	228	21.9	119	25.9	367	32.7	143	21.9
Don't know	16	.19	8	1.7	23	2.0	25	3.8
Total[a]	1041		459		1120		651	

Sources: Data from Ansolabehere and Schaffner (2017); Schaffner and Ansolabehere (2019); Schaffner, Ansolabehere, and Luks (2019); and Ansolabehere, Schaffner, and Luks (2020).
[a] Column percentage does not sum to 100% due to rounding.

Black, Hispanic, Asian, Native American, and mixed-race LGB and "other" sexual minorities indicate religion is more important in their lives than their white peers. Furthermore, while heterosexual Asian respondents are less religious than white heterosexuals, LGB and "other" sexual minority Asians are more religious than white LGB and "other" sexual minorities. Conversely, while heterosexual Middle Eastern respondents are more religious than white heterosexuals, LGB and "other" Middle Eastern respondents pray and attend religious services less frequently than LGB and "other" sexual minority whites (see Online Statistical Appendix II). Relatedly, these descriptive statistics must also be understood in the context of Christian religiocentrism, since several faith traditions in which LGBT people are overrepresented may not regard regular service attendance or frequent prayer as important faith practices.

Religious affiliations among LGBT people provide important context, as do the basic religious practices of LGBT people. However, data in even the largest sample surveys of LGBT people rarely capture information about how LGBT people negotiate their religious and sexual identities. Specifically, the notion of psychic conflict stemming from one's religious upbringing or current belief system has been a centerpiece of LGBT religious research, perhaps because of the underlying assumption among scholars and the general population that LGBT identity and religion are incompatible (Cravens 2018). To this point, I have shown a majority of LGBT people do affiliate with a faith tradition. Although many do not engage frequently in devotional activities, a substantial proportion of LGBT people do believe faith to be an important part of their identity. Among this group, some do experience conflict between their religious beliefs and their LGBT identity, and this conflict does have repercussions for their political activism (Cravens 2018). Just as identity conflict affects political behavior, it is my contention in later chapters that religious affirmation also has an effect on political behavior. For now, I review data from a different survey of LGBT people, conducted by the Pew Research Center, to explore the patterns in identity conflict.

Trends in Identity Conflict

Research shows that for some LGBT people religiosity is nuanced by psychic conflict between one's religious and LGBT identities. In 2013, the Pew Research Center gathered data from a probability sample of LGBT respondents in the United States (see Pew 2013a). Figure 2.1 shows the distribution of responses when respondents were asked if they feel there is conflict between their religious beliefs and their sexual orientation or gender identity. In a previous analysis, I found that nearly one-quarter of sexual minorities report experiencing conflict (Cravens 2018). As the figure shows, among the group who report conflict, nearly two-thirds describe experiencing "a lot" rather than "a little" conflict. Importantly, conflict is common among LGBT people who also identify as atheist or agnostic (the Pew public data release does not disaggregate the categories). This suggests psychic conflict can persist among LGBT people even after they come out *and* after they disassociate from any faith tradition (see Cravens 2018).

While religious and LGBT identity conflict affects political participation among LGBT people, it also affects religious participation. An extension of my original analysis reveals respondents in the Pew (2013a) study who report conflict between their religious beliefs and sexual orientation or gender identity are more likely to report religion is "very" important to them and

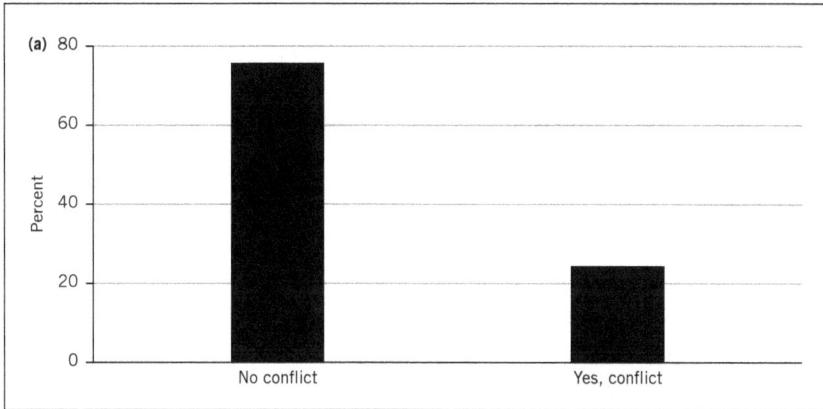

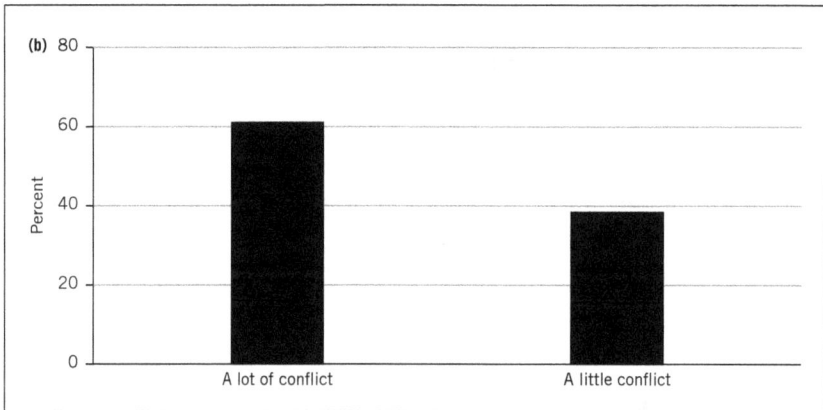

Figure 2.1 Distribution of Religious and SOGI Conflict among LGBT People. A. "Do you personally feel that there is a conflict between your religious beliefs and your sexual orientation/gender identity?"; n = 1,187. B. "How much conflict do you feel there is?"; n = 1,187. (*Data from Pew [2013a]*)

report attending religious services at least once per week than respondents who report no conflict (see Online Statistical Appendix III). In this case, it may be that conflict evokes an "identity threat" response whereby LGBT people who experience conflict will often attempt to resolve it by avoiding stressful situations—that is, contexts that foreground the conflict (Sevelius 2013). Politically, LGBT people who experience conflict are less likely to engage in political activism on behalf of LGBT people, such as attending Pride events (Cravens 2018). Spiritually, however, experiencing conflict may be a proxy for a conservative-authoritative perspective on religion and sexuality (see Coley 2020). That is, religion is more important to LGBT people who experience conflict; therefore, they may be more likely to accept the conservative views of their faith tradition about sexual and gender identity. To alleviate the conflict, then, it may be that these LGBT people more frequently participate in religious activity. It is not clear at this point, however, if the religious behavior is intended to help them embrace or change their LGBT identity. I return to this point in later chapters.

As the supplemental online appendix shows, since the 1970s, dozens of religious groups have emerged that explicitly affirm LGBT identity. Not only are they theologically welcoming, but many of these groups also allow LGBT people to fully participate in the religious community by becoming members and holding leadership roles. This dramatic change in religious acceptance is consequential because it produces opportunities for LGBT people to practice their faith in ways denied to previous generations. This can potentially reduce psychic conflict while allowing LGBT people to maintain ties with their preferred faith tradition. Yet, we do not have longitudinal (over time) data to demonstrate trends in either conflict or participation in affirming religious traditions. Perhaps more important, we have not had panel data (data from the same respondents at different periods in their lives) to understand how religious behavior changes over time and in relation to important life events like coming out. The data I draw on in the remainder of the book was collected so that we can begin to fill this gap in our knowledge.

The Faith Factor in LGBT Politics

As the data in this chapter show, faith, spirituality, and religion are major components of the LGBT experience. Yet, there is significant variation in how LGBT people practice their faith and the importance of faith to their lives. On the whole, most seem to understand that faith can be just as important to one's identity as sexuality, gender, and race (although there is variation here too). LGBT people are, however, somewhat distrustful of "organized religion," which, coupled with the conservative political movement since the 1970s, has been weaponized against LGBT identity and rights.

Despite conflictual social constructions of LGBT identity, LGBT people are not antagonistic toward religious people. Yet, here again, variation in cultural context and social location seem to indicate faith and LGBT identity are not monolithic experiences. For example, as I will show in Chapter 4, LGBT POC—who are more religious overall and whose faith is generally a source of racial identity maintenance and support—experience more religious discrimination from predominantly white LGBT people. It is my contention that these differences in religious experiences and participation are the sources of variation in LGBT political attitudes and activism.

Defining the contours of LGBT religious experiences is a crucial but underdeveloped task in LGBT political studies. Like LGBT religious activists pushing to expand the pluralist landscape, LGBT political studies push the discipline to better understand how minority groups shape political outcomes in majoritarian societies (Mucciaroni 2011). Looking back, many of the case studies in the text to this point have demonstrated aspects of several important theories that attempt to explain religious effects on politics, including socialization, political resource, and identity theories. Moving forward, I situate the present study within current theory and literature about religious effects on politics and expand these traditional theories to include the unique perspectives of LGBT people.

Using data from surveys I describe in the next chapter, I begin, as it were, at the beginning and examine the early religious socializing experiences of LGBT people. After describing religious socialization, I turn to its effect on politics. Then, using the paradigms of religious resource and identity theories, I explore how contemporary religious participation affects political attitudes and behaviors of LGBT people. As I explain later, having the opportunity to participate in religious organizations is a major step toward increasing political activism. But, political activism is only one side of the coin. In addition to a set of beliefs, personal actions, and/or a set of institutions, religion is also an identity that shapes how we view the world and politics. So, it is also important to understand how LGBT and religious identities interact to affect political attitudes.

As I will show, faith and its practice are major factors in the politics of LGBT people. They often define the contours of LGBT identity even before LGBT people come out. While some change their faith after coming out, many do not. Many also follow similar paths to those described at the beginning of this chapter by Leslie Jordan and Brandi Carlile. Faith and its practice set boundaries, but faith also expands opportunities to participate in politics. This appears to be even more true of LGBT-affirming religious traditions than traditions that do not explicitly affirm the identity and participation of LGBT people. Time will tell if the patterns in affiliation and practice I identify among LGBT people hold. From the data presented thus far, it is likely that as long as faith is a major factor in American society, it will remain a major factor in LGBT politics. In the remainder of the text, I focus on the task of understanding how faith shapes LGBT identity and politics.

3

Faith and Early LGBT Identity Development

Train up a child in the way [they] should go,
and when [they] are old [they] will not depart from it.

—Proverbs 22:6 (NKJV)

In a study of LGBT people living in heavily religious rural American communities, Bernadette Barton (2012) describes numerous interviewees whose lives have been influenced by their experiences growing up as a "Bible Belt gay." In one particularly salient passage, Barton (2012, 24) tells of a middle-age lesbian woman from Oklahoma who said "she no longer had to hear homophobic statements to evaluate my appearance as too dykey or change my pronouns." Instead, "all it takes now is to see a hand with a cross ring on it, or a fish key chain." Barton (2012, 24) continues, "Simply seeing a Christian symbol on another prompts her to be careful about how she does or does not reveal that she is a lesbian." In a nod to theorists Jeremy Bentham and Michel Foucault, Barton (2012) describes the experiences of these interviewees as having taken place within the "Bible Belt panopticon" in which "tight social networks of family, neighbors, church, and community members, and a plethora of Christian signs and symbols sprinkled throughout the region" exert power on LGBT people to conform to the values of the hegemonic Christian religious institutions (Barton 2012, 24).

I allude to a similar situation when describing the practices of the MCC in Chapter 1. Specifically, the Rainbow Christ Prayer, developed by Kittridge Cherry, priest of the MCC, and the gay theologian Patrick Cheng, uses the symbology of the rainbow Pride flag and Christian iconography in supplication but also to convey to congregants the values of the denomination as they relate to LGBT identity. Red, for example, reminds congregants to give thanks that God created LGBT people "just the way we are." The prayer continues with orange "for sexuality, the fire of spirit," invoking "Erotic Christ" to "free us from exploitation, and grant us the grace of mutual relationships," then yellow "for self-esteem" and a petition to "free us from closets of secrecy, and give us the guts and grace to come out." With green for love, violet for vision, and blue for self-expression, congregants invoke the "Liberator Christ," whose voice "speak[s] out against all forms of oppression," beseeching "free us from apathy, and grant us the grace of activism" (Cherry 2012).

In both situations, social interactions define and reinforce different religious understandings of LGBT identity. For Barton's (2012) interview subject, religion forecloses LGBT identity and interactions with nongay Bible Belters require Bible Belt gays to police their own actions and behaviors to avoid detection, while everywhere religious iconography reinforces the dominant view of society that one cannot be LGBT and Christian. For MCC parishioners, religion embraces LGBT identity and interactions with other believers encourage identity expression that reflects the sexual and gender diversity inherent to God's creation, while everywhere religious iconography reinforces the dominant views of the community that LGBT people can be Christians too.

Each situation, although only viewed cross-sectionally here, is part of a broader process known as socialization. As these two examples illustrate, socialization can be defined as the process by which groups and individuals construct meaning from social interactions (Berger and Luckman 1966; Goffman 1959). From the symbolic jewelry of strangers to the rainbow flag and communal invocation of Rainbow Christ, social interactions help construct our understanding of ourselves and our place in society. Throughout one's lifetime, interactions with various "agents" of socialization, including family, friends, teachers, religious leaders, and so on, teach us about our group memberships, including how society accepts or rejects them (Erikson and Tedin 2015). Studies of socialization typically focus on the transmission of social, cultural, and political values from one generation to the next (i.e., the relationship between parents and children); however, the process can correspond with major life changes at any age.

Socialization is one potential explanation for how we acquire both religious and political identities. Research shows both of these attributes can be conveyed from parents to children; however, both are also malleable in early adulthood and generally stabilize later in life (Margolis 2018a; 2018b). Political socialization theory attempts to explain this process of solidifying political orientations, including identities, values, and behaviors, that occurs through social interaction (Neundorf and Smets 2017). Consistent with the quote from the Book of Proverbs at the beginning of this chapter, political socialization theory holds that early and consistent experiences with partisan or political subjects can predict political attitudes and behavior later in life (Erikson and Tedin 2015). The political socialization canon is split, however, in its determinations about the permanency of socialization. On the one hand, research suggests political experiences early in life produce relatively stable political orientations that endure throughout adulthood. On the other hand, some research suggests political orientations are malleable throughout the lifespan as people "update their preferences and behavior" when they "experience important life events" (Neundorf and Smets 2017, 2).

The socialization literature generally characterizes religious upbringing as an important factor that determines later political behavior (see Perry and Longest 2019). The relationship between Evangelical Protestantism and political activism to oppose LGBT rights described in Chapter 1 clearly illustrates this notion. Namely, it is thought that children raised in conservative religious traditions are more likely to identify as a religious conservative, hold conservative political opinions, or identify with the Republican Party later in life. However, recent research suggests partisanship likely drives religious behavior.

As Margolis (2018a; 2018b) notes, while both religious and partisan affiliations are malleable in early adulthood, partisanship generally solidifies earlier than religious identity. Many adolescents disassociate with religion but as young adults may return. Those who do return generally do so after major life events such as getting married and having children alter the relative importance of religious institutions in their personal social calculus. During this same period, however, Margolis (2018a) finds, partisanship and associated political values have solidified and any decision to return to a faith tradition is influenced by the political beliefs of the young adults—especially if they are politically knowledgeable. In short, Margolis (2018a) finds Republicans return to religion more frequently than Democrats; however, the relationship between Democratic partisanship and religiosity among Black Protestants is more similar to white Republicans than white Democrats. The resultant political asymmetry within many religious communities results in more homogeneous Republican-leaning white congregations that fuel conservative political mobilizations (Djupe and Gilbert 2009; Margolis 2018a).

The underlying life-cycle theory is very similar to findings about the religious and political behavior of LGBT people. While early life experiences can influence the decision to openly identify as LGBT (i.e., "come out of the closet"; see Egan 2012), the coming out process is recognized as a formative event (an agent of socialization) that can take place at various times throughout one's life course (Guittar and Rayburn 2016). Since the first decade of the twenty-first century, research shows, LGBT people began coming out earlier in life than LGBT people in previous decades (Savin-Williams 2006). Political socialization theory suggests coming out results in lived experiences that may require LGBT people to "update" their political identities, preferences, and behavior, generally resulting in ideological liberalism (see Alwin and Krosnick 1991; Egan, Edelman, and Sherrill 2008). An application of Margolis's (2018a; 2018b) life-cycle theory suggests coming out, and its association with Democratic partisanship and ideological liberalism, will drive many LGBT people to make decisions about their religiosity based on their experiences as openly LGBT people. This likely leads some to reject religious identity and others to seek out religious communities that affirm their LGBT identities (see Coley 2020).

Coming out, then, should be associated with distinctive political and religious orientations among LGBT people, especially those who are partisan identifiers and are politically knowledgeable. These relationships, however, have never been fully interrogated. Furthermore, the extent to which negative religious socializing experiences factor into later political and religious decisions for LGBT people is unspecified in existing theory. As described in Chapter 2, although LGBT people are less likely than heterosexuals to identify as Christian, a majority of LGBT people retain ties to religious traditions, sometimes even when those traditions are overtly hostile to their LGBT identity. In addition, more than one-third believe religion is important in their lives and at least occasionally engage in public and private religious devotion. Given LGBT people exist in both conservative and progressive congregations, how does coming out affect religious and political behavior? In the following, I use survey data that I collected with both quantitative and qualitative responses to analyze the religious socialization of LGBT people. In this chapter, I focus on pre–coming out socializing experiences. In the next chapter, I focus on post–coming out religious and LGBT identity development. Afterward, I turn to the question of motivation for religious and political activity (Chapter 5) and then examine how religiosity affects political behavior (Chapter 6) and political attitudes (Chapter 7) among group members.

Constructing Religious and Political Identities

There is no singular definition of identity, yet social identities have been used to organize society throughout history (Gleason 1983). Social science generally understands identity as a social category in which one claims membership, the cognitive or affective meaning one attaches to it, and behaviors one engages in to maintain it (Tajfel 1978; see also Greene 2002). Identities are socially constructed and products of power dynamics in society. Like identity, religiosity is somewhat nebulously defined in the social science literature (Greeley 1972; Greene 2002). Religion, for example, is generally regarded as a set of beliefs about the divine, but it can mean different things. To some, religiosity itself constitutes a social identity. In the United States, this often takes the form of a denominational affiliation (Greeley 1972). Religious practices and interaction with religious institutions reify the identity. In addition, the identity may be shared by members of one's familial and social networks, further reinforcing identity salience. To others, religiosity may not implicate formal institutions or practices, or be tied to a particular denominational affiliation, but still represents an important component to one's sense of self.

Partisanship is also a social identity, generally referring to affiliation with a particular political party. Greene (2002) and others note that partisanship, as well as other social identities, can have cognitive, affective, and behavioral components. Party affiliation, but also vote choice, (e.g., selecting a member of one's party in an election), beliefs about one's party or other partisans, and values reflected in policy positions all encompass one's political identity. In previous decades, partisanship was weakly correlated with policy positions; however, contemporary partisans are increasingly polarizing, and ideological sorting and homophily affects myriad social behaviors (see Levendusky 2010; McPherson, Smith-Lovin, and Cook 2001).

Identities such as these are characterized as socially constructed because their meaning is derived from a common understanding of what constitutes an identity in a given place and at a given time (e.g., romantic or sexual attraction, religious belief, political affiliation). Identities are characterized as the product of power dynamics because the categorical labels we give identities are the "primary organizing principles of society," locating and positioning groups "within that society's opportunity structures" (Baca Zinn and Dill 1996, 322). Identities provide structure to our interactions with society because they act as mental heuristics both conveying (externally) and filtering (internally) information about how one *should* believe and act, or where one *should* belong in the social system (see Pierce et al. 2014). Like Barton's (2012) "Bible Belt panopticon," identities are policed and maintained by society through interactions with social and political institutions as well as by those within the identity group.

Identities can be transmitted from one generation to the next through socialization. For example, children whose parents frequently engage in partisan activity are more likely to identify as partisans in adulthood (Erikson and Tedin 2015). Similarly, religious identities often persist into adulthood when children have experienced strong religious enculturation (Neundorf and Smets 2017). Social identities can also develop throughout the course of one's life. Typically, social interactions with nonfamilial agents of socialization expand over time; for some, social networks diversify (Erikson and Tedin 2015). New experiences introduce new information that often causes individuals to update their sense of self (Alwin and Krosnick 1991). Identity, then, is not static. While some identities, like partisanship and religiosity, can and do stabilize, this does not mean they will never be updated to reflect changing life circumstances.

How do interactions with religious and political communities convey social identities and values? An important mechanism that contributes to the effectiveness of socialization is framing. Goffman (1974, 21) refers to frames as "the schemas of interpretations that enable individuals to locate, perceive, identify, and label occurrences within their life space and the world at large." Importantly for political mobilization, McAdam, McCarthy, and Zald (1996, 6) characterize framing as "conscious strategic efforts by groups of people to fashion shared understandings of the world and of themselves that legitimate and motivate collective action."

Framing is a process of creating heuristics, or mental shortcuts, that allow us to more easily process information we observe and relate it to our understanding of the world (Goffman 1974). Social and political networks help people form a cohesive understanding of social and political problems as well as how best to respond to various social and political stimuli (Gamson 1992). Frames are not the same thing as political ideologies, although political ideologies can, and do, function as frames that help political actors situate themselves within struggles to promote or resist social changes (Oliver and Johnson 2000).

Framing is an especially important mechanism for politics because the average American is relatively uninformed about political issues (Converse 1964; Delli Carpini and Keeter 1996). The social interactions that convey frames and develop religious, racial, sexual, gender, political, and other identities provide members of society with low-cost information that helps them make decisions about complex topics. For example, religious communities, which Wald, Owen, and Hill (1988, 532) describe as "well suited to the transmission and maintenance of group norms," often bring people together across economic and social classes, emphasizing solidarity under a faith tradition. At the same time, social interactions bond communities together by emphasizing differences between the in-group and the out-group, usually the broader society (Tajfel 1978). According to political socialization theory and social capital theory, interactions with religious communities allow for the development and maintenance of a religious identity, but also other social identities, such as race or ethnicity, gender, or LGBT identity (Liu, Austin, and Orey 2009; Putnam 2000; Putnam and Campbell 2010). Furthermore, bonding facilitates frame transference among religious communities, which helps create cohesive understandings of social and political problems, like homosexuality, same-sex marriage, and so on, among group members (Margolis 2018a; 2018b; Slothuus and de Vreese 2010).

Political parties serve similar bridging and bonding functions that facilitate frame transference among group members. First, because American voters are relatively uninformed about candidate issue positions and voters must expend resources in order to acquire information, partisan labels help

lower informational barriers to participation by giving voters an approxima-
tion of a politician's position on a variety of issues (Popkin 1991). Consistent
with framing theory, party leaders also frame specific issues of public policy, often in simplistic terms consistent with an underlying political ideology
or social norm, that are conveyed to group members through group communications, group activities, or media outlets. Group members then align
their views with those of the organization's elites and other members of the
group (Slothuus and de Vreese 2010).

Among religious groups, the relatively consistent messages the laity receives from religious leaders help socialize believers into a shared understanding of the world they occupy. Through ritualized practices, religious authorities provide adherents with a consistent set of values and directions that guide
other social interactions (O'Brien 2014). O'Brien (2014, xv) refers to this common understanding as a "script" offering "deeply meaningful cosmologies
that weave together spirit, intellect, body, and community." By participating
in these communities, congregants learn how the world should be arranged,
socially and politically, and their place in it. Public opinion surveys of religious Americans, for example, note the relative cohesion of believers' attitudes toward social and political issues such as abortion, same-sex marriage,
gender roles, environmentalism, foreign policy, and what it means to be
"American" (Glazier 2013; Hoffmann and Johnson 2005; Jelen 1994; Olson,
Cadge, and Harrison 2006; Read 2003; Taylor, Gershon, and Pantoja 2014).
Overall, social interaction and "the extent to which the individual relies on
the religious group for instruction, worship, and understanding" contribute
to cohesive voting and attitudinal patterns among religious adherents (Jelen
and Chandler 1996; Wald and Shye 1995, 496). Importantly, this bridging
effect also potentially reduces barriers to other forms of social engagement,
like political participation, a point I return to later.

Religious interactions are also important for establishing and maintaining ethnic, racial, and cultural identities (Putnam and Campbell 2010). As
I elaborated in Chapter 1, LGBT people have adapted religious practices to
the purpose of cultivating LGBT identity. Similarly, predominantly Black,
Hispanic, Latinx, Asian, immigrant, and white religious communities adapt
religious practices to strengthen racial, ethnic, and cultural identities. For
example, Wilcox and Gomez's (1990) examination of data from the National Survey of Black Americans demonstrates that attendance and involvement
in predominantly Black Protestant church activities are associated with a
positive view of respondents' racial identity. Other research demonstrates
religious interactions help forge a shared, destigmatized, racial consciousness among Black congregants (Brega and Coleman 1999; Calhoun-Brown
1996; 1999; Griffin 2006; Nelsen and Nelson 1975). Similarly, Calvillo and

Bailey (2015, 57) suggest Catholicism among Latinx immigrants, as compared to Evangelical Protestantism, is associated with stronger Latinx cultural identity and "reinforces ethnic salience." Davenport's (2016, 76) study of college students also finds "cultural overlap between certain religious identities and racial/ethnic backgrounds—[specifically] Baptist for blacks; Catholic for Latinos; and Hindu, Buddhist, and Muslim for Asians—reinforces identification with that minority group."

As this research suggests, one may hold many identities throughout the course of one's life, and even the most seemingly fundamental social identities, including religiosity, sexuality, and gender, are not static. Identities may conflict or a particular identity and associated behaviors may take precedence in a given context (e.g., at a LGBT Pride rally) while others are more muted. Once formed, identities and their associated political orientations are reinforced through the interconnected social-psychological mechanisms of socialization and framing. Because identity is also a product of power dynamics, it is important to note that these mechanisms do not act in isolation and that their effect on behavior is often dependent on the social location of the individual.

For LGBT people, the power relations that constructed LGBT identity as deviant described in Chapter 1 also constructed a social system in which LGBT politics was based on the requirement that LGBT people "come out of the closet," or publicly affirm their LGBT identity. By balancing the tensions between liberation and assimilation, the visibility of LGBT people has contributed to public policy successes and positive shifts in public opinion toward LGBT identity (Garrettson 2018). The requirement that LGBT people come out, identifying themselves as "different" from the heterosexual prototype, also privileges those who can afford the repercussions or can otherwise "pass" in hetero- and cisnormative societies.

While sexuality and gender identity may be innate and the ascriptive traits of same-sex sexual attraction or gender variance randomly distributed across society, as Egan (2012) notes, the distribution of LGBT identity is not random but occurs among a subset of the population of people who experience these traits yet also choose to self-identify as LGBT. Studies comparing political behavior of people who report experiencing same-sex attraction and self-identified LGBT people, for example, demonstrate that LGBT identity is a powerful predictor of political behavior as people who experience same-sex sexual attraction but do not identify as LGBT exhibit political behavior more similar to heterosexuals (Cravens 2020). Coming out, then, is a key component of LGBT identity and related politico-religious behavior. In the following, I analyze the relationship between religious and political socializing experiences and the coming out process.

Faith and the Coming Out Process

For LGBT people, coming out, or openly identifying as LGBT, represents a major developmental milestone with implications for religious and political identity development. Coming out is a process, a series of interactions that is perhaps never fully complete (Guittar and Rayburn 2016). Like other socializing experiences, coming out creates a situation that often compels LGBT people to "update" their religious and political preferences to match their lived reality as an openly LGBT person (Egan 2012). Studies of LGBT politics recognize the powerful effect of coming out on LGBT sociopolitical behavior and suggest it is the cause of most distinctive features of LGBT sociopolitical life (Cravens 2020).

Namely, LGBT social and political theory suggests coming out represents a "conversion" experience after which attitudes and behavior measurably change among self-identified LGBT people (see Egan 2012). Regardless of one's views on sexual orientation or gender identity as innate characteristics, identifying as LGBT is a different social process than experiencing and even acting on same-sex desire and/or gender nonconformity (Schanabel 2018). Namely, recent estimates suggest about 7.1% of the U.S. population identify as LGBT (Gates 2017; J. Jones 2022; Newport 2018); however, survey data also suggest between 8.2% and 8.7% of U.S. adults experience same-sex sexual attraction but do not identify as lesbian, gay, or bisexual (see Twenge, Sherman, and Wells 2016).

Important for political socialization theory, research shows self-identified LGBT people are more likely to report a liberal shift in political ideology after coming out (Egan, Edelman, and Sherrill 2008). Similarly, self-identified LGBT people are less likely to identify as religious after coming out. Accordingly, the conversion theory of LGBT liberalism suggests the socialization that newly "out" LGBT people undergo explains this variation. That is, after coming out, LGBT people embed within LGBT communities, join LGBT interest groups, and develop or maintain social networks with other LGBT people. Like familial or religious networks, LGBT communities and organizations transmit information about the marginalized status of the group that cultivates a common group identity through shared history, culture, rhetoric, and internal policing.

Social interactions within networks centered on one's sexual or gender identity foster and/or reinforce group consciousness and "linked fate," or the notion that one's fate is tied to the fate of others who share one's identity (see Miller et al. 1981). In addition, among LGBT people, liberation ideology, outness, and cognitions that foster identity integration are other psychological resources that accrue through social interaction within LGBT networks and especially LGBT religious communities (see McQueeney 2009; Minwalla et al. 2005; Rodriguez and Ouellette 2000). Notably, each of these are characterized by social science as cognitive political resources that affect political attitudes and augment political activism among LGBT people (see Duncan, Mincer, and Dunn 2017). While I examine these resources in later chapters, for now, I focus on the religious socialization of LGBT people.

In the remainder of the text, I analyze data from two surveys. Specifically, I surveyed two samples of LGBT people and asked them to reflect on their religious and political experiences before and after coming out as LGBT. The surveys were conducted online during the spring and winter of 2021–2022.[1] Each consists of about sixty questions. Both surveys are self-administered questionnaires that ask respondents about their religious and political experiences.

One survey, piloted with a smaller sample ($n = 261$), includes open-ended questions that allowed respondents to express more detailed thoughts about the role of religion in LGBT cultural and identity development. When I offer quotes from survey respondents, the responses are derived from this data set. Quantitative analyses in the remainder of the book are derived from the larger representative sample of LGBT adults in the United States conducted during the winter of 2021–2022 ($n = 1,100$).[2] Respondents for both surveys were recruited using nonprobability sampling techniques,[3] although the recruitment methods differed significantly. A full description of the survey methodologies and text of the survey questions and response sets are in the supplemental online Methodological Appendix (all appendixes are available via Harvard Dataverse at https://doi.org/10.7910/DVN/M87Q1V; for additional citation information see Cravens 2022b).

Keeping the Faith and/or Coming Out?
It's about Finding the Right Recipe

When asked to describe the relationship between LGBT culture and religion, a white lesbian woman raised in the western United States who identified as Protestant before coming out expressed a view shared by about 20% of the respondents in my exploratory survey. The woman said LGBT people are often tasked with emotionally supporting one another as they come to terms with their religious upbringing. "For me," the woman said, "the way religion comes into LGBT spaces is the frequently shared trauma." She continued, "It's helpful to share that terrible experience with others and learn to grow out of that mindset that being gay is a sin or deviant." As I show in Chapter 1, the ideas that homosexuality and gender diverse expression are sinful or moral failures are a tenet of the conservative Christian construction of LGBT identity. It is not surprising, then, that this idea permeated the upbringing of a significant proportion of the LGBT people I surveyed. But how does this belief affect the coming out process and, ultimately, the political behavior of LGBT people?

In this section, I explore how religious beliefs and behaviors prior to coming out influence identity and religious development of LGBT people. I begin by analyzing responses to several question about when the people I surveyed came out, the extent to which they are out, and their religious experiences before they came out. For most of the survey participants, responses represent their experience during preadolescence and adolescence. For some, the timeline extends further into adulthood. This underscores the fact that coming out is a dynamic process that is, for some people, never truly complete (Guittar and Rayburn 2016). It also underscores the fact that the experiences of LGBT people are not monolithic. The factors that shape coming out are myriad (Egan 2012), and the intersecting social locations that potentially influence LGBT identity development are many. In the following pages, I am particularly focused on the influence of religion on the process.

I first asked the survey participants to share details about their coming out experiences, including the degree to which they are currently out about their LGBT identity on a scale from 1 to 5, where 1 means not at all and 5 means completely. The average score was about a 4 on the scale (3.97). More than two-thirds of the sample (69%) report a score of 4 or 5, meaning they are completely or almost completely out about their LGBT identity. Fewer than one in five (15%) report a score of 1 or 2, meaning they are not out at all or only out to a limited number of people. Outness, however, is significantly influenced by the race of the survey participant. Namely, white survey participants report being out to more people than any other group, while Latinx and survey participants who identify as another racial identity than white, Black, or Latinx are out to fewer people.

A majority of the respondents are out to most or all of their immediate family (66%), extended family (50%), people they socialize with (66%), and people they work with (54%). Of the LGBT people who answered the question about their religious community (about half the sample), about two in five (42%) are out to most or all of their religious community; however, more than one-third (35%) are not out to anyone in their religious community. From these measures I constructed an "outness index" by averaging scores across the five groups. Figure 3.1 graphically depicts the average score on the index across categories of religious affiliation among the people I surveyed. The important thing to note is that the affiliations represent the survey participants' religion prior to coming out as LGBT. Affiliations are collapsed into the most common categories.

As the figure shows, the average score on the index appears highest among survey participants who identified with Christian traditions other than Prot-

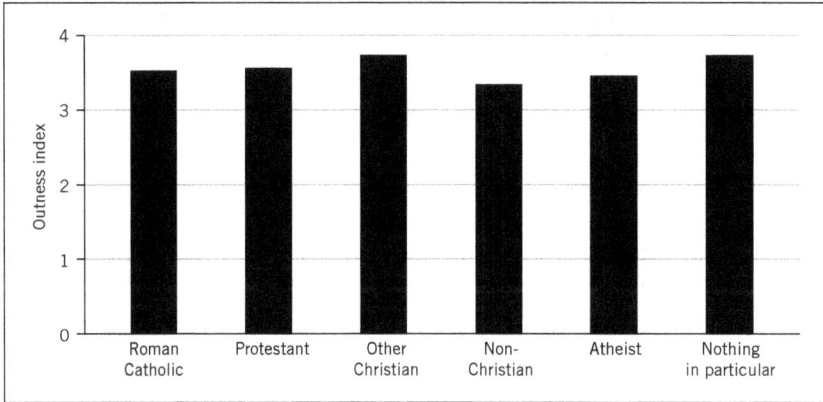

Figure 3.1 Outness in Relation to Past Religious Affiliation. $n = 1,058$. (*Author data available from Cravens [2022]*)

estant or Catholic and those with no particular religion prior to coming out as LGBT. The lowest average scores on the index appear among traditions including Jewish, Hindu, Buddhist, and Muslim.

Statistical tests mostly confirm what appears in the visual representation of the data. First, there is no discernible difference in outness between LGBT people who identified as Catholic, Protestant, or another Christian tradition before coming out and the rest of the sample. Compared to the rest of the sample, however, LGBT people who identified with a faith tradition other than Christianity are out to fewer people in their lives. On the other hand, LGBT people who identified with no particular faith tradition prior to coming out are contemporaneously out to more people than others in the sample. Notably, there is no statistical difference in outness between LGBT people who identified as atheist before coming out and the rest of the sample, although this is most likely due to low statistical power since I classify atheists separately from agnostics, resulting in a relatively smaller subsample. Finally, although not graphically represented, I also asked the survey participants if they identified as "born again" prior to coming out. Analysis of these data also show there is no difference in outness between survey participants who identified as "born again" before coming out and those who did not. In this case, however, there is no concern over statistical power. (See Online Statistical Appendix IV. All appendixes are available via Harvard Dataverse at https://doi.org/10.7910/DVN/M87Q1V; for additional citation information see Cravens 2022b.)

In addition to contemporary measures of outness, I also asked when the respondents first thought they might be LGBT, when they decided for sure they were LGBT, and when they first told someone they were LGBT. The findings underscore the importance of studying coming out as a process that is ongoing. On average, the LGBT people in the sample were about ten years old when they first thought they might be LGBT but about fifteen years old when they decided for sure. It was an additional two years for most to actually tell someone they are LGBT. Again, the results vary significantly by race of the survey participant. Specifically, white survey participants reach coming out milestones significantly later than POC. On average, the white people I surveyed were about ten years old (nine for POC) when they first thought they might be LGBT, about fifteen years old (thirteen for POC) when they first decided they were LGBT, and eighteen years old (sixteen for POC) when they first told someone they were LGBT.

For most, there was nearly eight years of social, political, and religious development between the time they suspected they might be LGBT and the time they publicly disclosed their sexual orientation or gender identity. As I show later in this chapter, this intervening time can critically shape the religious and political behavior of LGBT people. Figure 3.2 shows the average age of each coming out milestone across religious traditions. Again, the religious traditions represent affiliations before the respondent came out as LGBT.

As the figure shows, the average age at which the LGBT people I surveyed achieved each coming out milestone is fairly consistent across religious traditions. Statistical tests show there is no difference between religious groups in the average age survey respondents thought they might be LGBT. I find the same pattern in nearly every other case except the following. First, LGBT people who identified as Protestant prior to coming out decide at a later age they are LGBT than people from every other religious group. Whereas non-Protestants decided their sexual orientation and gender identity around age

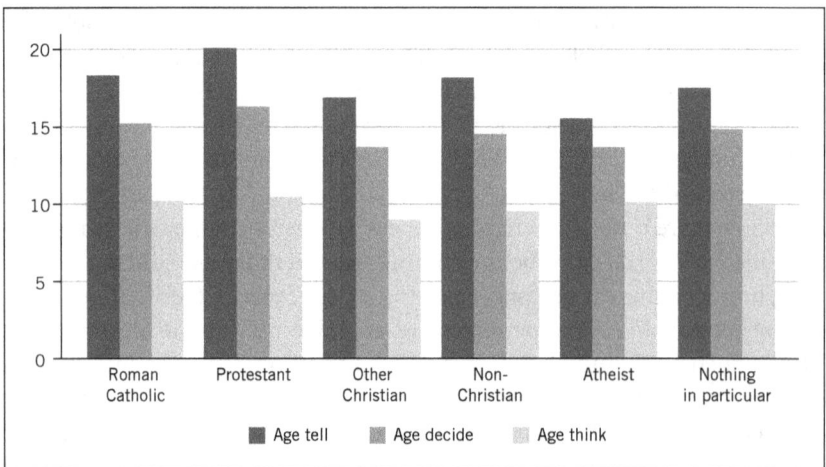

Figure 3.2 Average Age of Coming Out Milestones across Pre–Coming Out Religious Traditions. *n* = 1,072. (*Author data available from Cravens [2022]*)

fourteen, on average, LGBT people raised Protestant were age sixteen when they decided they were LGBT. Second, and relatedly, LGBT people who identified as Protestant before coming out disclosed their sexual orientation and gender identity at a later age than non-Protestants. Non-Protestants were about seventeen years old when they first told someone they are LGBT, whereas Protestants were about twenty years old. Third, LGBT people who identified as "born again" prior to coming out also decided and disclosed their sexual orientation and gender identity at a later age. On average, LGBT people who identified as "born again" prior to coming out decided they were LGBT at age sixteen and first told someone they were LGBT at nineteen, about two years later than the other survey participants. Finally, LGBT people who identified as atheist prior to coming out disclosed their sexual orientation and gender identity at a significantly younger age than LGBT people who identified as religious. Members of the former group were, on average, about fifteen years old when they first disclosed their LGBT identity, whereas members of the latter group were about eighteen years old (see Online Statistical Appendix IV).

In summary, race and religion are significantly related to the coming out experiences of the LGBT people I surveyed. White LGBT people are out to more groups of people than LGBT POC; however, LGBT POC reach each coming out milestone at a younger age. Similarly, religious LGBT people who identified with no particular faith tradition prior to coming out are contemporaneously out to more people than people from any other faith tradition in the sample. Yet, this group is no more likely to reach a coming out milestone earlier than LGBT people from any other religious group.

There is also no difference in the average age at which the people I surveyed first thought they might be LGBT when compared across religious traditions. However, LGBT people who identified as either Protestant or "born again" before coming out both decide and disclose their LGBT identity later than LGBT people from other faith traditions. For both groups, the average age is almost two years higher than for other groups. For Protestants, broadly speaking, this is around age twenty; for those who identified as "born again," this is around age nineteen. On the other hand, LGBT people who identified as atheist prior to coming out disclosed their LGBT identity almost two years earlier than religious people. On average this was around age fifteen.

The Devil You Know: Specific Socializing Experiences and LGBT Identity Development

Knowing that coming out milestones are related to religious upbringing is different from knowing the effect of religious socialization on coming out or, ultimately, how it affects political behavior. To start to piece together this puzzle, it is important to consider the agents of socialization that LGBT people encounter and the messages they receive from these people or groups. It is also important to analyze a specific psychological concept that is shown to affect political behavior—that is, whether or not one experiences conflict between one's religious beliefs and LGBT identity.

Whether or not one learns that LGBT people are normatively "good" or "bad" from social, familial, and religious networks can affect how LGBT people see themselves and their place in society (Trammell 2015). Similarly, research suggests the messages about LGBT people that the survey participants received during their formative years will be important predictors of future social and political behavior (Yip 1997). In addition, these experiences are expected to either generate or mitigate psychological conflict between LGBT and religious identities. While I rely on associational findings, after examining the dynamics and logical progression of events, I am able to make a case for the path to politico-religious activism I specify in this text.

To measure socializing experiences, I suggested a series of groups that represent potential sources of information about LGBT people or culture that the survey participants may have encountered prior to coming out. They were also given the option to identify additional sources of information. After identifying the sources, they were asked to describe the tone of the messages they received, whether positive, negative, or neutral. Not all of the people I surveyed got messages about LGBT identity from each of these sources. While every survey participant indicated receiving messages about LGBT identity from at least one source in the survey, on average, the people I surveyed received messages from two of the sources. Interestingly, LGBT people who identified with a non-Christian religious tradition before coming out report receiving information from the highest number of sources I suggested (see Statistical Online Appendix IV). Table 3.1 shows the breakdown of these experiences.

As the table shows, the messages were generally positive or neutral, although there are notable exceptions. On the one hand, university classes, friends and acquaintances, websites or chatrooms, and social media appear to provide the most neutral-to-positive messages about LGBT identity among the people I surveyed. On the other hand, primary and secondary school classes and religious leaders appear to provide the most neutral-to-negative messages. However, because only a limited number of people reported *any* messages from these latter sources, it is difficult to say with certainty that each represents generalizable experiences. That is, even though the negative messages from schools and religious leaders reported by these respondents likely represent significant formative events in their lives, these experiences are

TABLE 3.1 SOURCES AND PERCEPTIONS OF INFORMATION ABOUT LGBT PEOPLE

Source	Positive (%)	Neutral (%)	Negative (%)	Total Responses
Family	41.0	30.1	28.8	229
Friends and Acquaintances	59.7	32.5	7.6	572
Strangers	33.6	46.6	19.7	208
Primary/Secondary School Classes	26.6	41.1	32.2	90
Print Media	35.6	51.1	13.2	348
Entertainment TV or Movies	40.1	49.1	10.6	431
TV News	31.3	44.5	24.1	182
College/University Classes	61.8	34.0	4.1	97
Religious Leaders	13.7	10.9	75.3	73
Internet Websites/Chatrooms	54.8	39.3	5.7	348
Social Media	49.1	43.0	7.7	362
Other	24.5	61.4	14.0	57

Source: Author data available from Cravens (2022).
Note: Row percentages may not sum to 100 due to rounding.

not shared by enough members of the sample to analyze, statistically, their impact on attitudes or behaviors of the group.

But how do these experiences differ across religious traditions? In short, there is no statistically significant variation across religious traditions in the tone of messages about LGBT identity received by the people I surveyed. Neither an analysis of variance nor means comparisons support the claim that identifying with any one faith tradition before coming out is associated with either more positive or more negative messages about LGBT identity than any other faith tradition.

Although the people I surveyed largely did not identify religious leaders as a source of information about LGBT people in their formative years, this does not mean they had no religious socializing experiences. In addition to the majority of survey participants who identified with a faith tradition prior to coming out, several participated in religious programs to change their LGBT identity. I also found that more than two-thirds (68%) of the people I surveyed participated in a religious rite of passage as a child, such as a baptism, communion, or bar or bat mitzvah. Moreover, one in five people I surveyed (20%) attended a private religious school for K–12 education.

There is also some evidence to suggest Protestantism, but especially Evangelicalism, can be a source of conflict over LGBT identity for young people and that this information can lead LGBT people to delay coming out and potentially attempt to change their LGBT identity later in life (see Ratcliff and Haltom 2021). First, cross-tabulation shows the people I surveyed who identified as "born again" before coming out are significantly more likely to undergo a religious rite as a child ($\chi^2 = 37.7$, p = .000). Second, I asked the survey participants if they ever participated in a religious program to change their sexual orientation or gender identity, and, while the vast majority had not (96%), of those who did report participating in a conversion therapy program, significantly more identified as "born again" prior to coming out as LGBT ($\chi^2 = 23.2$, p = .000). These programs are generally designed around essentialist constructions of sexuality and gender that encourage LGBT people to adopt behaviors consistent with stereotypical heterosexual and cisgender men and women (Ezren 2006).

Without knowing the diversity of the pre–coming out social networks of the people I surveyed, it is impossible to say that Evangelicalism itself delays coming out milestones. However, such a scenario is consistent with research about the network of Protestant ministries dedicated to changing one's sexual orientation and/or gender identity (Ezren 2006). That is, Evangelical denominations have established religious networks that touch almost every aspect of congregants' lives beyond the church. From private Christian schools and Christian homeschool networks, to television, entertainment, and radio networks, to publishing houses and recording labels, to websites and Internet hosting and monitoring services, Evangelicals have created the infrastructure to provide Protestant Christians with alternative social and political institutions free from secular influences (Barton 2012; Ezren 2006; White 2015).

As I have described previously, one major focus of this work is sustaining the heteronormative family as the central unit of American life. Key to that work is the maintenance of heterosexuality and cis-sexist gender roles. It is common for all of these conservative Evangelical networks to amplify such messages and to attempt to convince questioning Christians to abandon their LGBT identity (Ezren 2006; Goldberg 2006; Stewart 2020). Given that the Protestant and "born again" LGBT people I surveyed thought they might be LGBT at roughly the same time as LGBT people from every other religious group, that they took longer to accept it and came out later suggests they encountered substantial pressure not to affirm their LGBT identity.

Past Religious Belief and Current Identity Conflict

As I detail in previous chapters, LGBT people whose lives were influenced by religion before coming out may adopt several strategies to ensure religious and LGBT identity congruence after coming out. The strategies are largely predicated on the existence or nonexistence of psychological conflict between one's religious and LGBT identities. Some LGBT people may not feel psychic conflict. So they have no need to update their religious beliefs to align with their LGBT identity. Others may feel conflict between their religious beliefs and LGBT identity. Among this group, many update their religious prefer-ences (i.e., seek out congregations or denominations that welcome LGBT people) or disassociate with religion (Coley 2020). Others, primarily those who adopt a conservative-authoritarian approach (see Coley 2020), will not attempt to update their religious beliefs. Instead, LGBT people in this group may live celibate or closeted lives or seek to change their sexual orientation or gender identity through religious aversion programs (Ezren 2006). Reli-gious and identity conflict is associated with negative health outcomes among LGBT people (Lease, Horne, and Noffsinger-Frazier 2005). For this reason, many states have banned what activists call "conversion therapy" programs, especially for young people (see Movement Advancement Project 2022).

LGBT and religious identity conflict has also been shown to reduce soli-dary political participation among the group. In Chapter 2, I showed that conflict is associated with religious importance and attendance. This likely reflects the salience of religion to the lives of some LGBT people after com-ing out. In previous work, using survey data from both random and nonprob-ability samples of LGBT people, I showed that LGBT people who experience conflict with their religious beliefs are less likely to participate in political activism that directly implicates their LGBT identity (Cravens 2018). I theo-rized that the relationship exists because LGBT people who experience con-flict, like anyone who experiences psychological stress due to cognitive dis-sonance, will attempt to reduce the stress by avoiding situations that highlight the conflict. In the case of LGBT people, they are less likely to attend Pride rallies, work for political campaigns, or volunteer with LGBT organizations, but more likely to attend religious services if they experience conflict between their LGBT identity and religious beliefs.

But what role does religious socialization play in fostering religious and LGBT identity conflict? To better understand this dynamic, I analyze respons-es to several survey questions. First, I asked survey participants if they felt there is conflict between their religious beliefs and their LGBT identity. Re-spondents either answered "yes" or "no." If they answered yes, they were then asked how much conflict they experienced, either "a lot" or "a little." Among the group, about six in ten (65%) said they did not experience conflict, while about one-third (34%) said they did experience conflict. Of that group, two-thirds (66%) said they experienced a lot of conflict.

How does the type of message about LGBT people as well as specific re-ligious experiences before coming out affect identity conflict later in life? To answer this question, I conduct a statistical test using the measure of conflict (yes/no) as a dependent variable. In addition to the tone of socializing mes-sages about LGBT people, described previously, I also control for the region of the country where the respondent was raised, the size of the community in which the respondent grew up, the religious tradition the respondent affiliated with prior to coming out, whether or not the respondent identified as "born again" before coming out, whether or not the respondent underwent a religious rite as a child, and whether or not the respondent attended a private religious school as a child.[4] I also controlled for several demographic measures, including age, race, sexual orientation and gender identity, and the age of the respondent when they first disclosed their LGBT identity. Because I am interested in the effect of pre–coming out socializing experiences, I limit the variables in the model to those indicators that measure such experiences. I describe several models with contemporary indicators in the next chapter.

The results (shown in Online Statistical Appendix V) suggest religious socialization is an important predictor of religious and LGBT identity conflict later in life. That is, regardless of where a person was raised, their race and ethnicity, their sexual orientation, their gender identity, or when they came out as LGBT, having participated in a religious rite as a child and attending a private religious school both increase the likelihood that a survey participant experiences conflict between their religious beliefs and LGBT identity. Specifically, attending a religious school increases the likelihood of identity conflict by about 71%, and having participated in a religious rite of passage as a child increases the likelihood of identity conflict by about 91%.

In addition, LGBT people who identified with a non-Protestant or Catholic Christian tradition, including Latter-Day Saints, Jehovah's Witness, and Orthodox traditions, are, on average, as much as 135% more likely to experience identity conflict than Protestants. On the other hand, LGBT people who affiliated with a non-Christian faith tradition like Judaism, Hinduism, and Buddhism before coming out, LGBT people who identified with no particular faith tradition, and LGBT people who identified as atheists are significantly less likely to report conflict between their religious and LGBT identities than Protestants. Specifically, LGBT people who identified with no particular religion before coming out are about 39% less likely than Protestants to report conflict. LGBT people in non-Christian faith traditions prior to coming out are about 54% less likely than Protestants to report conflict; and LGBT people raised as atheists are about 82% less likely than LGBT people raised as Protestants to report conflict.

The importance of a positive social environment is apparent when examining how faith traditions and specific religious experiences before coming out are used to construct that positive social environment. Specifically, I included several interaction terms to model the relationship between positive messages about LGBT identity and religious affiliation, attending a religious school, and undergoing a religious rite before coming out. The results suggest that the effect of positive socialization on reducing identity conflict extends across faith traditions and religious socializing experiences. That is, positive socializing experiences before coming out reduce the variation in identity conflict between religious traditions to the point of statistical insignificance. In other words, increasing exposure to positive messages about LGBT people before coming out is associated with a decreased likelihood of experiencing religious and LGBT identity conflict among almost all the faith traditions in the sample—including Evangelicals. The results support similar claims about specific religious experiences like attending a religious school or undergoing a religious rite. Namely, even though these experiences predict identity conflict, when they happen in a social environment supportive of LGBT people, the likelihood of experiencing conflict is reduced to the point of statistical indistinguishability from those who did not attend a religious school or undergo a religious rite as a child.

Taken together, what do these findings mean? First, socialization significantly affects LGBT identity development by generating, but also mitigating, religious and LGBT identity conflict. In terms of generating conflict, LGBT people raised in Christian traditions other than Protestantism or Catholicism (traditions classified as such in this study, such as Latter-Day Saints, Orthodox, and Seventh-Day Adventist, are generally conservative) are as much as 135% more likely to experience conflict than LGBT people raised Protestant or Catholic. In addition, young LGBT people who participate in religious rites of passage and public affirmations of faith are more likely to experience identity conflict later in life, and so are young LGBT people who attend private religious schools for K–12 education. In terms of mitigating conflict, LGBT people I surveyed who identified as atheist prior to coming out or who affiliated with no particular religion and non-Christian traditions are less likely to experience identity conflict than LGBT people raised as Protestant or Catholic. Furthermore, among all groups and experiences, when the social environment is accepting of LGBT people, or at least survey participants receive positive messages about LGBT people from a variety of sources, identity conflict can be reduced.

The positive association with identity conflict is not a normative comment on any of the religious experiences I model. Instead, the results provide evidence to suggest participation in religious experiences should not be compulsory. One person I surveyed, a Latino man from the Northeast who was raised in no particular religious tradition, said the following when asked to describe the relationship between LGBT culture and religion: "If a person is LGBT and religious that is their choice and should be respected as a valid part of their identity. Religion, however, should not be forced on a person either." In another instance that speaks directly to the way private religious education can induce both conflict and anger, a white lesbian woman I surveyed said, "While I've been an atheist my entire life, I was incarcerated in Catholic boarding school as a teenager, and still hate organized religion violently because of that experience."

In these instances, organized religious institutions are seemingly used as weapons to shape or train young LGBT people without their consent. It is intuitive, then, that LGBT people who experienced religious socialization in these ways would carry a sense of anger, resentment, or distrust toward religious institutions into their adulthood. Conflict, especially when left unresolved and/or internalized, can have serious effects on an LGBT person's mental and physical health (Lease, Horne, and Noffsinger-Frazier 2005). The absolutist and essentialist ideologies about gender and sexuality that accompany many conservative Christian traditions also seem to be especially strong predictors of conflict, and this conflict is reinforced through socializing institutions like religious schools.

Second, LGBT identity development is significantly different for Protestants and "born again" Christians. Compared to LGBT people raised in other faith traditions and LGBT people raised nonreligious prior to coming out, the LGBT people I surveyed who were raised Protestant or identified as "born again" both decided and disclosed their LGBT identity later in life, sometimes as much as five years later. Although coming out later does not appear to affect whether or not one experiences conflict between one's religious beliefs and LGBT identity, the Evangelical milieu seems to incentivize young religious LGBT people to wait until they are old enough to survive away from their religious community to come out publicly.

Third, positive socialization offers a way to mitigate religious and LGBT identity conflict. This is consistent with psychological research that shows LGBT young people who are affirmed by their families are less likely to experience negative mental and physical health outcomes than LGBT young people who are rejected by their families (see Family Acceptance Project n.d.). Combined with findings about religious socialization and coming out, it appears that building supportive social networks is important for younger religious LGBT people, especially if they are raised in conservative religious communities. This is a function that uniquely implicates LGBT-affirming religious denominations and congregations. I will return to affirming religious experiences in the next chapter. In the next sections, I will address how the early religious experiences of the LGBT people I surveyed affected their LGBT identity later in life.

How Early Faith Shapes LGBT Identity and Social Behavior in Later Life

In order to understand the effects of religious socialization on LGBT identity development, in this section I compare the effects of many of the data points I have already described on perceptions of LGBT identity among the people I surveyed. Since I am mostly concerned with how religion affects LGBT identity, I focus my analyses on affective (or how the survey participants think about their LGBT identity) and behavioral (or what the survey participants do related to their LGBT identity) components of LGBT identity. This understanding of identity is consistent with Greene (2002) and others who similarly conceptualize identity as encompassing more than just self-categorization.

The specific measures of interest relate to the importance of LGBT identity to the people I surveyed and specific religious behaviors that LGBT people engage in to support their identity. The first set of measures are derived from Sellers et al.'s (1998) Multidimensional Model of Racial Identity, which measures how strongly one identifies with a group—or more specifically, how central a particular identity is to one's sense of self. Table 3.2 shows the statements and distribution of responses to each. Again, strongly agree and agree and strongly disagree and disagree categories are collapsed for space.

Among the people I surveyed, the majority feel that being LGBT is important to who they are and defines their social relationships. A plurality of the people I surveyed report a strong sense of belonging to the broader LGBT community, but they are split when it comes to how closely they feel their destiny is tied to the fate of other LGBT people, and most view their LGBT identity as having little do to with how they feel about themselves. How, then, does religion shape LGBT identity? I start to answer this question by first examining how socialization and religious experiences before coming out affect contemporary religious behavior and LGBT identity.

TABLE 3.2 STRENGTH OF LGBT IDENTITY			
	(Strongly) Agree (%)	Neither Agree nor Disagree (%)	(Strongly) Disagree (%)
Being LGBT has very little to do with how I feel about myself	45	17	36
Being LGBT is an important part of my self-image	53	25	20
My destiny is tied to other LGBT people	28	34	36
I have a strong sense of belonging to the LGBT community	47	30	20
Being LGBT is an important reflection of who I am	51	25	21
Being LGBT is not a major factor in my social relationships	51	22	25
Source: Author data available from Cravens (2022). **Note:** Row percentages do not sum to 100 due to rounding. $N = 1,100$.			

Religious Socialization and LGBT Identity

In order to understand how religious socialization shapes contemporary LGBT identity, I model two regression equations. (The full models are shown in Online Statistical Appendix VI.) In each model, the dependent variable is based on responses to the statements in Table 3.2, and the independent variables of concern are those that represent religious and socializing experiences prior to coming out. The results demonstrate that religious socialization can have persistent effects throughout the lifespan of the LGBT people I surveyed.

First, LGBT identity is more important to survey participants who received positive social messages about LGBT people before coming out compared to those who did not. I have already shown that receiving positive social messages about LGBT identity prior to coming out is negatively associated with religious and LGBT identity conflict. Taken together, the results make a strong case for the assertion that a social environment welcoming to LGBT identity prior to coming out helps LGBT people see their LGBT identity as important to who they are but also reduces the likelihood that they will view their identity as in conflict with any preexisting religious notions of LGBT people later in life.

Interestingly, the benefits of positive socialization appear to be concentrated among those who identified as "born again" prior to coming out. Namely, LGBT people who identified as "born again" before coming out, on average, report values on the index of LGBT identity I constructed about 20% lower than those who did not identify as "born again." Moreover, among those who did not identify as "born again" prior to coming out, the effects of a positive social environment on the importance of LGBT identity later in life are relatively flat. For each additional positive source of information they encountered, there appears to be no change in the importance of LGBT identity later in life. However, among those who identified as "born again," each additional positive source of information about LGBT people they encountered before coming out is associated with about an 8% increase in the importance of LGBT identity later in life. For those raised in other religious traditions before coming out, positive social environments have a near uniform positive effect on LGBT identity—meaning positive social messages are associated with LGBT identity importance later in life.

This leads to the question of how likely a person raised in an environment hostile to LGBT identity is to encounter positive messages about LGBT people. With the rise of digital communication, social media, and so on, the likelihood is high that LGBT people raised in hostile environments can encounter positive information (see Gray 2009, for example). In addition, the proliferation of LGBT-affirming religious organizations provides options for questioning LGBT young people raised in hostile environments to form positive religious communities. The findings, here, underscore the importance of these organizations and digital communities for LGBT identity development.

Second, even after controlling for age of the survey participant, the results show that LGBT identity is less important to those who come out later in life. While I investigate changes in religious affiliation in the next chapter, in short, coming out later appears to increase the importance of maintaining one's faith tradition but decrease the importance of LGBT identity. Given that LGBT people who identified as Protestant and "born again" come out later than those raised in other faith traditions, it may be that denominational effects on LGBT identity development are moderated (or transmitted through their effect on) coming out milestones. In these cases, the cross-pressure of one's faith tradition and LGBT identity, on average, are resolved by maintaining the survey participant's Protestant or "born again" religious affiliation.

Conclusion

Religion can influence LGBT identity development in multiple ways. Socialization theory suggests that religious and other social messages about LGBT identity received in one's youth shape perceptions about LGBT people. These messages as well as participating in religious organizations can also shape when and how (or if) LGBT people come out. In addition, religious communities, including faith leaders and co-religionists, but also religious schools and other social institutions, help LGBT people understand how their LGBT identity comports with their faith tradition.

Religious communities also help shape what LGBT people know about their identities. Participation in some faith communities may induce conflict for LGBT people in their formative years. The data in this chapter show, for example, conflict is more likely among LGBT people who were raised or affiliated with the Latter-Day Saints, Orthodox Christianity, or Jehovah's Witness, among others. On the other hand, LGBT people who were raised Jewish, Hindu, Buddhist, with no particular affiliation, or as atheist are less likely to experience conflict. In every case, however, receiving positive social messages about LGBT people from a variety of sources during the years before one comes out lessens the likelihood of conflict.

LGBT-affirming religious organizations and communities are implicated in this dynamic, and I explore their role further in the next chapter. Namely, religious communities can either affirm or deny the lives of LGBT people. The messages that LGBT people receive, including the theology, affirmation through membership, leadership, and full inclusion in denominational and congregational life, are what lead some LGBT people to change their religious affiliation after coming out. Even then, because LGBT people have largely been constructed as nonreligious by opponents of LGBT rights, a significant portion of the LGBT community harbors distrust toward religion—especially organized religion—and contest the place of religion in the LGBT community.

As the data in this chapter show, distrust may be the product of compulsory religious education, as LGBT people who attended private religious schools and participated in a religious rite prior to coming out are more likely to experience identity conflict. The data also show that religious experiences are influenced by intersecting social identities, including race and ethnicity, gender, and social class. Whether or not it is safe to come out and the community and resources that one has available for support after coming out are important factors that LGBT people, and especially religious LGBT people, must consider.

In the next chapter, I continue to examine the role of socialization by focusing on the post–coming out religious experiences of LGBT people. To this point, most LGBT scholarship presumes that after coming out, religion becomes less important to LGBT people; however, as I show, faith remains a major part of the LGBT experience. This can be linked to pre–coming out religious experiences but also to the development of LGBT-affirming religious spaces. After showing the effect of religious affirmation on LGBT identity, I then explore its effect on LGBT politics.

4

Faith and LGBT Identity Development after Coming Out

In 2008, Hunter College commissioned a survey of LGBT people. Using a national probability sample, the researchers found that more than one in five LGBT people become "less religious" after coming out (Egan, Edelman, and Sherrill 2008).[1] Being "less religious," however, can have a variety of meanings. For some it could mean leaving religion or a specific tradition altogether. For others, it could mean attending fewer religious services, spending less time studying scripture or praying, and so on. It is important, then, to distinguish the ways the religious experiences of LGBT people change after coming out. Coley (2020) offers an archetype for how and why these changes occur.

Heteronormative and cisnormative interpretations of the sacred texts of the major monotheistic religions have generally been a source of negative attitudes toward LGBT people (Vegter and Haider-Markel 2020). Although *LGBT* is a culturally relative term, and many theologians have argued over the meaning and context of passages in the Talmud, Qur'an, and Bible that have been interpreted as "anti-LGBT," the harmful interpretations and negative attitudes persist. As described in previous chapters, one important consequence of this dynamic is the construction of LGBT people as antireligious by heteronormative society. Following the *Will & Grace* paradigm (see Preface), LGBT people are not only frequently depicted as non-normative, but a central component of their non-normativity is their disassociation from religion. In order to be religious, one cannot also be LGBT. In addition, LGBT cultural development suggests LGBT culture has internalized this notion and constructed an identity largely viewed as nonreligious. That is, in order to be LGBT, one cannot also be religious. Yet, as I have shown, rather than creating an unreligious category of people, the conflict over the construction of LGBT identity means religiosity and spirituality take many forms among LGBT people.

Coley's (2020) insightful study of LGBT approaches to religion and sexuality provides four archetypes for how LGBT people perceive and understand their LGBT and religious identities (see also Moon 2014). Importantly, research suggests each appears to be associated with religious behaviors that may also influence political mobilization among the group. Across one axis, Coley (2020) suggests LGBT people may hold "conservative" or "liberal" perceptions about the compatibility of their LGBT (or same-sex attraction or gender identity) and religious identities. As Coley (2020, 48) describes, LGBT people who adopt conservative perceptions "take seriously" the "condemnations" of LGBT identity, same-sex attraction, behavior, and/or gender diverse expressions. Among this group, some likely experience psychological stress or psychic conflict between their LGBT and religious identities and attempt to resolve the conflict by "attempting to rid themselves of homosexual desire" or remaining celibate (see Erzen 2006). Others may seek out supportive peer groups or join religious congregations that affirm their LGBT and religious identities (see Wolkmir 2006). Many in this group also attempt to resolve conflict by "reinterpreting church teachings," reimaging religious cosmologies inclusive of LGBT people (see Hunt 2015; Taylor and Snowdon 2014; Thumma and Gray 2005). Still others attempt to resolve the conflict by disassociating or abandoning their religious identities.

On the other hand, LGBT people who adopt liberal perceptions "reject the premise that any kind of conflict or tension exists" between their religious and LGBT identities (Coley 2020, 48). Because this viewpoint challenges religious condemnations, not surprisingly, studies have shown LGBT people who adopt the liberal understanding are likely to participate in politico-religious activities that further LGBT equality, even within religious denominations that are traditionally hostile to LGBT congregants (see Moon and Tobin 2018).

Coley (2020, 48) also identifies a second axis of understanding, "authoritative versus individualistic strategies," that informs LGBT politico-religious development. On one hand, LGBT people who hold an authoritative perspective view the teachings of their faith tradition on LGBT identity, same-sex sexual attraction, behavior, and gender diverse expression as authoritative and attempt to fully understand the implications for their lives. Such LGBT people can be found in both conservative and liberal religious traditions, and they generally "remain committed to religious institutions and submit" to the views of their faith tradition. On the other hand, LGBT people who hold an individualistic perspective are "much less committed to the formal teachings of religious authorities" as they relate to LGBT identity (Coley 2020, 49). Among this group, LGBT people are likely to "build a spirituality that personally suits them" by adopting perspectives and values from multiple faith traditions (Coley 2020, 49). As with the authoritative perspective, the individualistic viewpoint can be found among LGBT people who hold both conservative and liberal perspectives on the compatibility of LGBT and religious identities. Keeping these distinctions in mind, in the following I examine trends in religious behavior among LGBT people.

To determine whether these archetypes fit the experiences of LGBT people, I asked the survey participants several questions about how religious beliefs and experiences changed, but also what motivates their religious participation and, specifically, how their congregations and denominations recognize, accept, and affirm their LGBT identities. In short, I want to better understand how LGBT identities motivate and find expression in their religious behavior after they come out. I begin the analysis by examining how religious affiliation changes after coming out. Figure 4.1 shows the distribution of religious affiliations among the LGBT people I surveyed before and after coming out as LGBT.

Overall, about one-quarter of the people I surveyed reported changing their religious affiliation after coming out, and about three-quarters did not.[2] Consistent with Coley (2020) and other studies of LGBT religion, not all of the people I surveyed disaffiliated altogether; many simply changed their affiliation. As Figure 4.1 shows, the three categories of Christianity were most frequently abandoned. Specifically, the proportion of LGBT people who identified as Catholic, Protestant, or with another Christian tradition including Orthodox, Latter-Day Saints, Jehovah's Witness, and Seventh-Day Adventist, decline from one chart to the next in Figure 4.1. On the other hand, traditions including Judaism, Hinduism, Buddhism, and Islam, as well as atheists and those who identify as nothing in particular, represent larger proportions of the survey participants after they came out as LGBT.

Several of the people in the exploratory analysis volunteered why they left their religious tradition after coming out, and their reasoning warrants consideration here. For some, the decision was motivated by hetero- or cis-sexism, as with one biracial pansexual and nonbinary person from the western United States who told me, "My religion of my youth was homophobic. I'm into more earth-based spiritual practices. I'm not part of any [religious] organization now [after coming out]." While implied in this example, for some the desire to find a more welcoming religious experience is an important part of leaving their faith tradition. A clearer example of this theme comes from a white lesbian woman, also from the western United States, who offered the following about her decision to leave Catholicism: "Admittedly, my religious

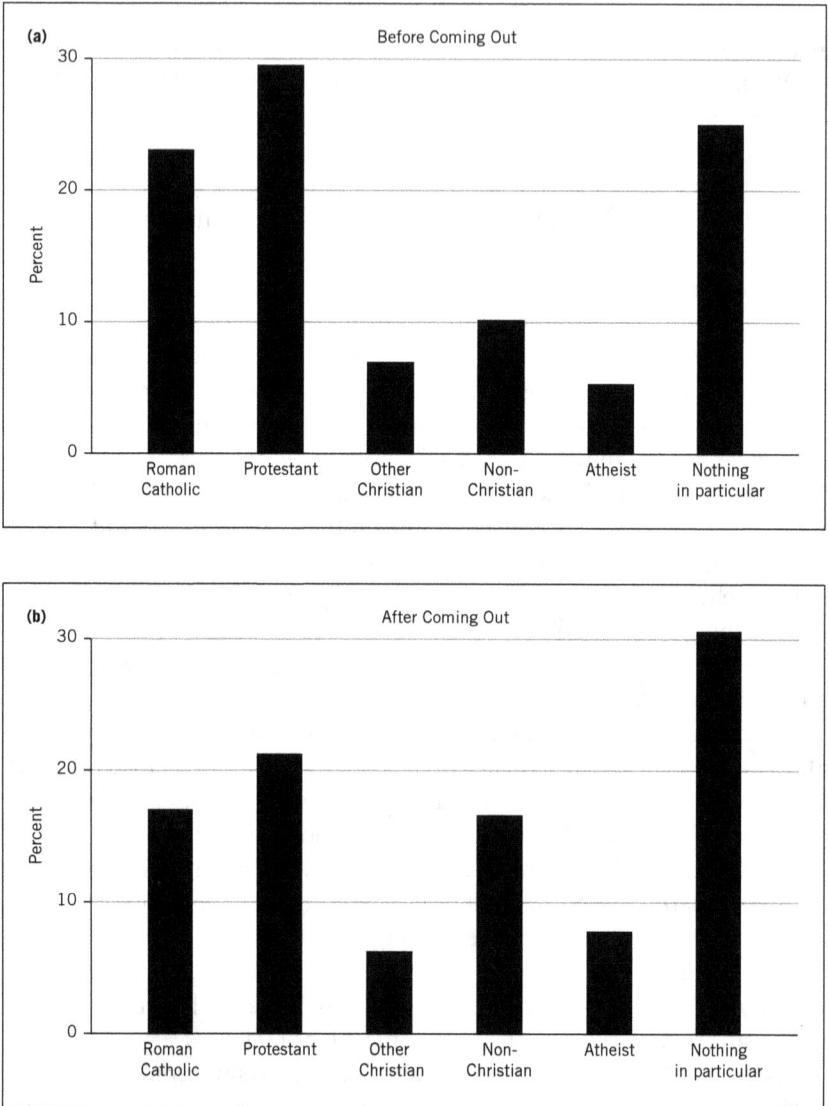

Figure 4.1 Religious Affiliation Before and After Coming Out as LGBT.
A. *n* = 1,072 (before); B. *n* = 1,100 (after). (*Author data available from Cravens [2022]*)

beliefs were skeptical from the beginning, having been baptized in my teens. I felt a condescending attitude toward females and those who questioned tenets of the faith. Once I came out to myself and learned what Catholicism embraced about my lifestyle, I left the church seeking a more accepting faith."

For others, experiencing prejudice made it easier to leave religion altogether. An example of this theme comes from a white queer woman from the

Midwest who responded to a question about the place of religion in LGBT culture by saying, "I left religion by choice very young. Even before I had thoughts of my sexuality, I rarely agreed with the teachings of my church, especially if they brought up social issues, which was quite often." As these examples suggest, coming out may coincide with one's decision to leave or change religious traditions, but underlying experiences with hetero- or cis-sexism, as well as philosophical or even political disagreements with religious teaching, are also factors the LGBT people I surveyed consider when deciding to leave or change their religious affiliation.

It is also possible to quantitatively model why LGBT people may change their religious affiliation after coming out. Using data from the representative survey and subtracting the measure of religious affiliation before coming out from the measure after coming out, I created a scale that ranges from −5 to 5. A score of 0 means the respondent did not change their religious affiliation after coming out. By transforming the scale into a binary variable that takes on the value of 0 if the survey participant did not change their religious affiliation and a value of 1 if they did, I can then model a logistic regression equation that predicts the likelihood of an outcome (change/no change) occurring based on a set of independent variables. For independent variables, I rely on measures previously described that capture the survey participants' past social and religious experiences as well as basic demographic controls. (The full model can be found in Online Statistical Appendix VII. All appendixes are available via Harvard Dataverse at https://doi.org/10.7910/DVN/M87Q1V; for additional citation information see Cravens 2022b.)

The results reveal several important findings that nuance our understanding of when and why LGBT people change their faith tradition after coming out. First, survey participants who received positive social messages about LGBT people before coming out are about 38% less likely to change their religious affiliation after coming out. Second, non-Christians (including those who identified as Jewish, Buddhist, Hindu, and so on before coming out), those who identified with no particular faith tradition, and those who identified as atheist are less likely than Protestants to change their faith tradition after coming out. Finally, for each additional year a survey participant did not come out, the likelihood of changing their faith tradition decreases by about 4%.

The results also demonstrate how religious and LGBT identity conflict can shape religious change after coming out. First, conflict is associated with change among certain traditions. Specifically, while non-Christians, those who identified as nothing in particular, and atheists are less likely to change their religious affiliation overall, experiencing conflict increases the probability of change to the point that it is statistically indistinguishable from Protestants. In other words, even in the faith traditions with the least change, conflict increases the likelihood of changing one's faith tradition after coming out. Second, the older an LGBT person is when they come out, the less likely they are to change their religious affiliation, even if they experience identity conflict. It is probable that the older an LGBT person is when they come out, the more likely their faith has solidified as a component of their identity and the harder it is for them to change or update their faith after coming out, no matter how much psychic conflict they feel between their religious and LGBT identities.

The results also show how the mechanisms of LGBT and religious identity formation may work differently for white and LGBT POC. Specifically, in models disaggregating the full sample into racial identity subsamples, it is apparent that denominational effects on affiliation change persist only among white LGBT people I surveyed. That is, among LGBT POC, no one denominational affiliation is more or less likely to change after coming out. However, white LGBT people who were raised or affiliated with non-Protestant or Catholic denominations, including Orthodox, Latter-Day Saints, or Jehovah's Witness, are more likely to change their religious affiliation after coming out than Protestants. Furthermore, there is no relationship between positive social messages about LGBT people and affiliation change among LGBT POC. Yet, LGBT POC who participated in a religious rite before coming out are less likely to change their religious affiliation after coming out. Positive social messages about LGBT people appear to have the strongest effect on retaining one's pre–coming out faith tradition, but only among white LGBT people.

Finally, it should be noted that the measure of affiliation change does not necessarily capture those religious LGBT people who went to a different congregation within the same denomination or otherwise changed their religious environment while maintaining the same overarching affiliation.

Expressions of LGBT-Affirming Faith after Coming Out

Having examined some of the major formative experiences that lead LGBT people to change their faith tradition after coming out, it is also important to know the extent to which LGBT people engage in affirming religious practices after coming out. As I describe in Chapter 1, the number of faith traditions that affirm LGBT people is growing (also see the supplemental online appendix). After coming out, LGBT people have a variety of religious options to choose from. As Coley (2020) suggests, they may change or remain in their faith tradition, but they may also seek out a new faith that affirms their LGBT identity, as the former Catholic woman quoted earlier in the chapter did. Among the people I surveyed, after coming out, two in five (46%) report religion is either very or somewhat important in their lives, while about half (52%)

report religion is not too or not at all important. One in ten (10%) participants report attending religious services at least once per week, while more than three in five (69%) report rarely or never attending religious services.

Again, there are significant differences in religious behavior after coming out across racial identities. Specifically, Black and Latinx LGBT people I surveyed are more likely than others to pray, attend a Bible study meeting, read scripture, attend religious services, and say religion is important in their lives. Black LGBT people are also more likely to share their faith with others. In short (as shown in Online Statistical Appendix IV), white LGBT people in the sample are significantly less religious than LGBT POC after coming out.

But most surveys of LGBT people do not explicitly ask about religious practices or distinguish between affirming and nonaffirming traditions when they do. We are, therefore, left with an incomplete picture of LGBT religion. To better understand the types of denominations and congregations that LGBT people attend, I asked survey participants a series of questions about how their religious institutions and places of worship include LGBT people. As Table 4.1 shows, the LGBT faithful I surveyed are generally split in terms of how their faith traditions accept and include LGBT people. While most affiliate with a denomination or broad tradition that blesses same-sex weddings and allows LGBT people to be members, a majority do not allow LGBT people to be clergy or affirm LGBT identity in their theology.

A larger proportion of the LGBT people I surveyed attend congregations that allow LGBT people to be members and bless same-sex weddings, but similar patterns hold for the other indicators. That is, most attend congregations that do not explicitly affirm LGBT people in their theology or ordain

TABLE 4.1 EXPERIENCE WITH AFFIRMING RELIGIOUS DENOMINATIONS			
Does your current religious tradition:	Yes (%)	No (%)	Total Responses
Affirm LGBT identity in its theology	43	56	584
Allow openly LGBT people to be congregation members	69	30	632
Allow openly LGBT people to hold leadership positions	55	44	581
Ordain openly LGBT ministers or clergy	45	55	571
Bless same-sex weddings	52	47	641
Does the congregation you attend:			
Affirm LGBT people in its theology	46	53	411
Allow openly LGBT people to be congregation members	72	27	458
Allow openly LGBT people to hold leadership positions	52	47	407
Ordain openly LGBT ministers or clergy	45	54	411
Bless same-sex weddings	51	48	428
Source: Author data available from Cravens (2022). Note: Row percentages do not sum to 100% due to rounding.			

LGBT ministers. LGBT people who identified as Catholic or with another Christian tradition (such as Orthodox, Latter-Day Saints, or Jehovah's Witness) before coming out report attending less-affirming congregations and denominations than those raised in other traditions. However, LGBT people who identified as Protestant or as non-Christian (such as Jewish, Hindu, or Buddhist) report attending more-affirming congregations and denominations than those raised in other traditions. Interestingly, patterns of affirmation are not significantly different among white, Black, and Latinx LGBT people; however, LGBT people who identify as another racial identity report attending significantly less-affirming congregations than others in the sample (see Online Statistical Appendix VIII.)

Although, at both the denominational and congregational levels, the LGBT people I surveyed affiliate with a religious tradition that affords them the opportunity to hold leadership positions, it is important for future analyses to recognize these patterns since structural hetero- and cis-sexism means that some people are fundamentally barred from fully participating within their places of worship, especially since religious participation is a socializing experience and can generate opportunities to engage politically (see Cravens 2018; Djupe, Sokhey, and Gilbert 2007; Friesen and Djupe 2017).

In addition to questions about the affirming characteristics of their denominations and congregations, I asked the survey participants a series of questions built on Coley's (2020) archetypes of LGBT religious and political participation. Specifically, I constructed several questions designed to engage with Coley's (2020) two axes of understanding that guide LGBT people as they try to navigate religious and political activism. As I describe earlier in this chapter, those axes are conservative-liberal understanding of LGBT identity and authoritarian-individualistic understanding of religion. The following survey results present the first quantitative evaluation of the prevalence of each of these attitudes, orientations, and experiences among a representative sample of LGBT people in the United States.

Since the conservative-liberal understanding of LGBT identity is constructed in the same way that conservative religious activists constructed LGBT identity (i.e., as sinful and as a moral failure), the questions I asked the survey participants follow suit. I asked the survey participants to rate their agreement with a series of statements about LGBT identity that implicates a religious understanding of LGBT people, same-sex sexual attraction, and gender diverse behavior and expression. Table 4.2 shows the distribution of responses to the nine items. Again, strongly agree and agree and strongly disagree and disagree responses are collapsed to conserve space. Also note that respondents are asked to think about some items in the context of "God or the divine." This was done intentionally to mitigate as much Christian religiocentrism as possible.

TABLE 4.2 RELIGIOUS UNDERSTANDING OF LGBT IDENTITY			
	(Strongly) Agree (%)	Neither Agree nor Disagree	(Strongly) Disagree
Same-sex attraction is not a choice	79	9	11
I would rather be celibate than have a sexual relationship with someone of the same sex	5	7	86
God or the divine accepts people if they are not heterosexual	78	15	4
Having a gender identity that does not match the sex you were assigned at birth is a choice	19	23	55
God or the divine accepts people if they are not cisgender (explained)	66	26	6
What it means to be a man or woman is determined by God or the divine	27	32	39
Same-sex sexual behavior is natural	93	11	4
Same-sex sexual behavior is not sinful	80	12	5
It is not a sin to be transgender	75	17	6

Source: Author data available from Cravens (2022).
Notes: n = 1,100. Row percentages do not sum to 100%, due to rounding.

On the whole, the people I surveyed largely reject the ideas that same-sex attraction, gender diverse expression, and LGBT identity are sinful or otherwise not accepted by God or the divine. In most cases, greater than seven in ten survey participants agree or strongly agree with this perspective. Perspectives on gender essentialism (or the notion that there is a fixed, biologically determined male and female gender), however, are not as clearly delineated as perspectives on sexuality. For example, while about one in ten survey participants either agree or strongly agree that same-sex attraction is a choice, twice as many or nearly two in ten say having a gender identity that does not match the sex you were assigned at birth is a choice. Similarly, while more than seven in ten either agree or strongly agree that God or the divine accepts people if they are not heterosexual, about six in ten say the same about not being cisgender. Similar proportions agree that same-sex sexual behavior and being transgender are not sinful; however, when it comes to gender essentialism, the sample is nearly evenly split. Specifically, almost two in five either agree or strongly agree with the idea that what it means to be a man or woman is determined by God or the divine. Fewer than one in five neither agree nor disagree, with slightly more either disagreeing or strongly disagreeing with the sentiment.

Because a relatively small proportion of the people I surveyed are transgender, nonbinary, or gender nonconforming, the responses shed light on the way sexual minorities view religion and gender more than anything. And, importantly, there appear to be significant differences in the way religious and nonreligious people respond to these questions. Table 4.3 shows the results of tests of association or means comparison tests. These tests compare the mean response to the statement "What it means to be a man or woman is determined by God or the divine" between two categories, the religious group in the leftmost column with everyone else in the sample. A positive *t*-value indicates the group is more likely to agree or strongly agree with the statement.

As the table shows, Catholics, Protestants, those from other Christian traditions, and those who identify as "born again" are all significantly more likely than other religious groups I surveyed to agree or strongly agree that gender is determined by God. On the other hand, non-Christians, atheists, and those who identify with no particular religion are all significantly more likely than other religious groups I surveyed to disagree or strongly disagree that gender is determined by God. Similar patterns hold with other statements. Protestants are more likely to say being transgender is a sin but are also more likely to agree that God accepts people who are not cisgender; however, people who are "born again" are more likely to say both being transgender is a sin and that being transgender is a choice. Both non-Christians and atheists are more likely to say being transgender is not a sin. Atheists are also more likely to say that being transgender is not a choice; however, they are less likely to say God accepts people who are not cisgender. Because the converse relationship exists among Protestants, this is likely a reflection of atheists' views of religion as unaccepting, in general, rather than a statement about their own acceptance of transgender people. While this analysis provides some insight, I return to this discussion in the final section of the chapter.

Coley's (2020) second axis of religious understanding, authoritarian-individualistic, is constructed around beliefs about the authority of religion to determine beliefs about LGBT people and identity. In short, LGBT people who hold an authoritarian view of religion will likely submit to their faith's

TABLE 4.3 LGBT CHRISTIANS VIEW GENDER AS DETERMINED BY GOD		
	Mean (n)	t (Degrees of Freedom)
Catholic	2.86 (248)	1.07** (1,070)
Protestant	3.01 (315)	4.45*** (1,070)
Another Christian	3.04 (75)	2.01** (1,070)
Non-Christian	2.34 (109)	−3.11*** (1,070)
Atheist	1.64 (56)	−6.23*** (1,070)
Nothing in Particular	2.57 (269)	−2.18** (1,070)
Born Again	3.26 (212)	6.50*** (1,044)
*** p ≤ .01; ** p ≤ .05		

teachings about LGBT people and identity, regardless of what they mean for LGBT equality. On the other hand, LGBT people who hold an individualistic view of religious authority will likely seek out their own understanding of LGBT people and identity and be more willing to hold views that contradict their faith tradition. I asked the survey participants a series of questions to measure these perspectives. Table 4.4 shows the distribution of responses.

As the table shows, LGBT people appear ecumenical in their views about how religion influences perceptions of LGBT identity. Namely, the people I surveyed are mostly resolute against the notion that any one religious leader should be the sole source of truth about LGBT identity. A plurality say they build their own understanding of LGBT identity and that their personal values about LGBT identities do not come from religious leaders. A similarly high percentage say they do not trust information about LGBT identity from religious leaders. It is likely, though, that there are differences in macro- as compared to micro-level perspectives. That is, if I had asked about the survey participant's own religious leader, I may have gotten a different, potentially more amenable perspective, much the way voters may evaluate their own members of Congress more favorably than the body as a whole (Cook 1979).

Again, there are denominational differences in perspectives. First, LGBT people who currently identify as Protestant hold significantly different views on all but one of the statements. They are more likely than other faith traditions to agree that it is important to understand what religion teaches about LGBT identity, to say their personal values about LGBT identity come from religious leaders and to trust that information, but also to say they seek out information from multiple faith traditions. However, they are more likely than other faith traditions to disagree with the statement that no single re-

TABLE 4.4 VIEWS ON RELIGIOUS AUTHORITY ABOUT LGBT IDENTITY			
	(Strongly) Agree (%)	Neither Agree nor Disagree (%)	(Strongly) Disagree (%)
It is important to understand what religion teaches us about LGBT identity	31	33	34
I trust the information religious leaders provide about LGBT identity	11	26	62
My personal values about LGBT identity come from religious leaders	6	14	78
I build my own understanding of LGBT identity by seeking information from multiple faith traditions	31	24	42
No single religious institution can define the truth about LGBT identity	76	17	5
Source: Author data available from Cravens (2022). Notes: Row percentages do not sum to 100% due to rounding. $N = 1,100$.			

ligious institution can define the truth about LGBT identity. Survey participants who are "born again" have the same profile. Like Protestants, LGBT Catholics I surveyed are more likely to say their information about LGBT identity comes from religious leaders and also to trust that information but that they seek out information from multiple faith traditions and believe that no single religious institution can define the truth about LGBT identity.

On the other hand, LGBT atheists I surveyed are less likely to say it is important to understand what religion teaches about LGBT identity. They are also less likely to say their personal values about LGBT identity come from religious leaders or trust information from religious leaders and to say they seek out information from multiple faith traditions. LGBT people from traditions other than Christianity are less likely to say that it is important to understand what religion teaches about LGBT identity but more likely to say that no single religious institution can define the truth about LGBT identity. Finally, LGBT people with no particular affiliation are less likely to say it is important to understand what religion teaches about LGBT identity and less likely to say they receive information about LGBT identity from religious leaders. They are also less likely to say they seek out information from multiple faith traditions. Furthermore, consistent with previous results showing LGBT POC are more religious than white LGBT people in the sample, statistical analyses show that LGBT POC also perceive their faith as more authoritative than white LGBT people (see Online Statistical Appendix VIII). Again, I return to this conversation in the final section of the chapter.

LGBT people can and do express their LGBT identity through their religious participation and behavior. Most religious LGBT people are part of a faith tradition that at least welcomes LGBT people as members if not complete equals in ministry and responsibility. For some of the people I surveyed, finding an affirming religious community was part of the reason they changed their faith tradition after coming out. Indeed, receiving positive messages about LGBT identity before coming out makes the religious LGBT people I surveyed less likely to change their religious tradition after coming out, at least the white LGBT people.

The religious LGBT people I surveyed generally reject heterosexist theology and believe sexual minorities should be welcomed in religious spaces. Their rejection of gender essentialism, however, is less clear. While the religious LGBT people I surveyed are supportive of transgender people, their views about religious acceptance of transgender people are demonstrably more negative than their views about religious acceptance of sexual minorities. Protestants, for example, are more likely to believe being transgender is a sin and that being transgender is a choice.

Even though the religious people I surveyed are, on average, likely to look to multiple faith traditions rather than relying on a single interpretation of faith as a guidepost for what to believe about LGBT identity, Protestants, Catholics, and people who identify as "born again" are more likely to look to religious leaders for information about LGBT identity and to trust that information, and LGBT POC are more likely than white LGBT people I surveyed to view their faith as a source of authority on topics of LGBT identity. What effect do these attitudes, beliefs, and experiences have on LGBT identity and other measures of religiosity after coming out? In the final sections of this chapter, I examine these relationships and show that affirming religious belief and participation significantly affect how LGBT people view their own identity.

How Contemporary Religious Affirmation Shapes LGBT Identity

In the last chapter, I showed positive socializing messages about LGBT identity help establish a foundation for LGBT identity development. Consistent with socialization theory, positive messages about LGBT identity, including from religious leaders, help LGBT people locate themselves in the social, religious, and political milieu but also help them understand that they are not inherently damaged, as many conservative faith traditions would have them believe. Knowing that early social experiences can have persistent effects on LGBT identity, I now turn to the effects of identity-affirming religious beliefs and practices in the context of post–coming out religious experiences. In another application of socialization theory, some scholars have hypothesized religious affirmation and especially participation in affirming religious communities can be an agent of socialization that influences LGBT identity development. Specifically, among those who experience religious and LGBT identity conflict, religious affirmation can offer a path to understanding, as those who experience positive socializing experiences before coming out do, that they are not inherently damaged.

To better understand these relationships, I model regression equations using the same LGBT identity measure and measure of religious and LGBT identity conflict I describe previously as the dependent variables. (The full models are shown in Online Statistical Appendix IX.) How does faith after coming out shape LGBT identity? Like positive social messages before coming out, affirming religiosity is associated with a decrease in the likelihood of identity conflict and an increase in the importance of LGBT identity. In addition, specific religious beliefs about LGBT identity and views on religion as an authoritative source of information about LGBT identity are important predictors of both religious and LGBT identity conflict and the importance of LGBT identity after coming out.

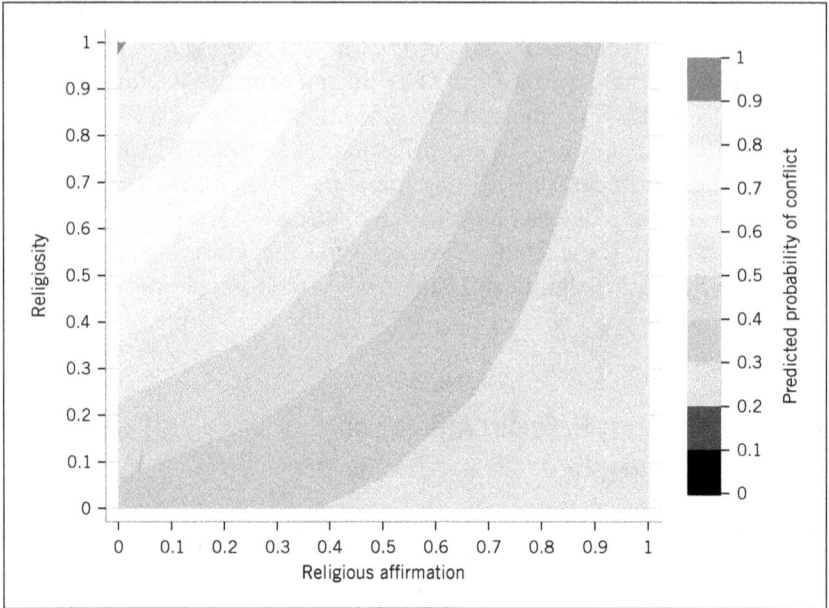

Figure 4.2 Effect of Affirming Religiosity on Identity Conflict. $n = 694$. (*Underlying model is estimated in Statistical Appendix X.*)

Concerning the relationship between affirming religiosity and identity conflict, Figure 4.2 graphically represents the effect of affirming religiosity on the probability that a religious LGBT person in the sample experiences conflict between their religious beliefs and LGBT identity. The y-axis represents values on a religiosity index I constructed from responses to questions measuring the importance of religion to the survey participant, how frequently the survey participant attends religious services, prays, reads scripture, attends scripture study meetings, meditates, and shares their faith. The x-axis represents values on a religious affirmation index I constructed from responses to statements in Table 4.1 (see also Online Statistical Appendix IX). The key on the right-hand side of the figure shows the grayscale arrangement of the colors in the figure correspond to probabilities from 0 to 1 of an event occurring. In this case, the event is that a survey participant reports experiencing religious and LGBT identity conflict.

As the figure shows, after controlling for religious tradition, changing faith traditions after coming out, religious-based beliefs about LGBT identity, outness, and other potential confounding variables, increasing values on the religiosity index, alone, are associated with an increased probability that a survey participant experiences identity conflict. In fact, a survey participant who reports the highest possible value on the religiosity index (top of y-axis) is nearly certain to experience identity conflict (p(conflict) = .9 – 1). However, as values on the religious affirmation index (x-axis) increase, the probability that a survey participant experiences identity conflict decreases by nearly 80% (p(conflict) = .2). Because all of the measures represent contemporary (post–coming out) experiences, the results suggest that after coming out, LGBT people who experience identity conflict can potentially mitigate it by engaging in affirming religious practices.

A similar relationship emerges between affirming religiosity and the importance of LGBT identity among the survey participants. Figure 4.3 graphically depicts the relationship across categories of religious and LGBT identity conflict. In the figure, the x-axis represents values of an interaction term between the religiosity and religious affirmation indexes. The y-axis represents predicted values of the LGBT identity index (how important being LGBT is to the survey participant). As the figure shows, affirming religiosity is positively related to the importance of LGBT identity, and the positive effect is the same among both those who experience and those who do not experience identity conflict. That is, affirming religiosity appears to have the same positive relationship with LGBT identity for those who experience conflict and for those who do not. The results suggest that, after coming out, LGBT people who engage in affirming religious practices view their LGBT identity as more important to who they are, even if they viewed the two identities as

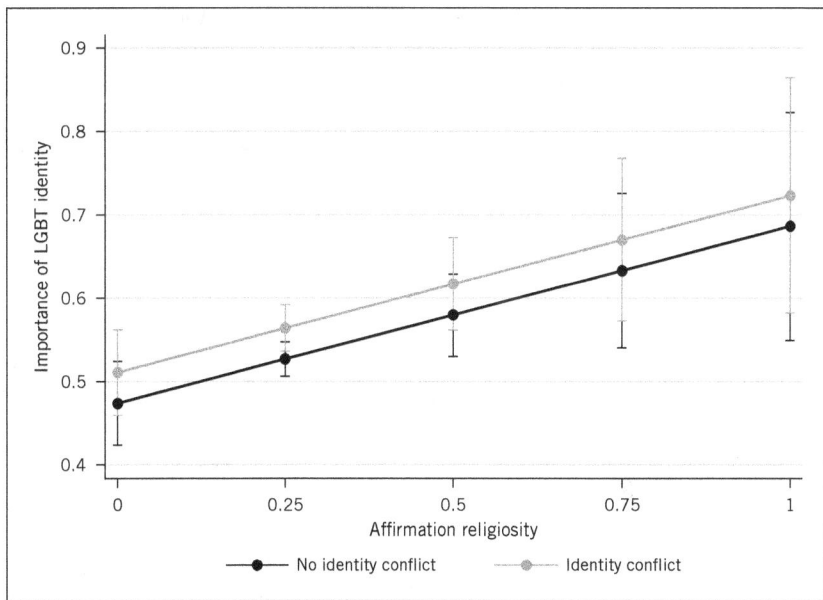

Figure 4.3 Effect of Affirming Religiosity on Importance of LGBT Identity. $n = 694$.
(*Underlying model is estimated in Statistical Appendix X.*)

in conflict. Not only does affirming religiosity reduce the likelihood of conflict; it also potentially increases the value of LGBT identity—an important precursor to political activism.

For comparison, in previous models, positive social messages received before coming out are related to about a 25% decrease in the likelihood of religious and LGBT identity conflict later in life and an increase in the importance of LGBT identity of about 2%. The results from these models suggest affirming religiosity is related to a 96% decrease in the likelihood of religious and LGBT identity conflict later in life and an increase in the importance of LGBT identity by about 21%, on average. The results seem to indicate that religious affirmation can be a powerful socializing experience for LGBT people that shapes their beliefs and identities even more strongly than early socializing messages.

Additional evidence from the analysis supports this assertion. Namely, the belief that being LGBT is not a sin is associated with both a decrease in conflict and an increase in the importance of LGBT identity. A similar relationship exists for religious authoritarianism—suggesting that religious leaders who share affirming messages have a powerful influence over the religious and LGBT identity development of their congregants. Yet the religious milieu also presents complicating factors. For example, the results suggest LGBT people who believe in attribution, or the view that homosexuality and gender diversity are innate characteristics, view their LGBT identity as more important; yet, the view is also associated with religious and LGBT identity conflict. It may be that those who experience conflict have already been enculturated to believe homosexuality and gender diversity are choices, so the belief in attribution represents a message that challenges preconceived notions and induces conflict. This has implications for affirming religious organizations because the way LGBT identity is framed to those who come from conservative religious backgrounds should be carefully tailored to avoid creating more conflict than it potentially resolves.

Importantly, these experiences are nuanced by the positionality of the individual. For example, even after controlling for religious affirmation, Black LGBT people are still more likely than others in the sample to report identity conflict. Given Black LGBT people in the sample are the most religious, this may not be surprising. In the next chapter, I show Black LGBT people in the sample are also more likely to avoid LGBT spaces because of religious discrimination. This suggests that the benefits of LGBT affirmation do not fall, disproportionately, to the most religious group. Instead, other factors, such as the influence of familial networks and strong religious enculturation early in life that are specific to Black LGBT people in the sample, are important in the identity calculus of Black LGBT people.

Conclusion: Toward a Model of LGBT Politico-religious Behavior

What do the findings from this and the previous chapter tell us about LGBT religious socialization, contemporary religious behavior, and how the two affect LGBT identity development? It is clear that religious and secular socialization about LGBT people prior to coming out explains both religious and identity development among LGBT people. It is also clear that coming out represents an ongoing socializing event that further affects religious patterns among out LGBT people. The results in these chapters support both claims. Positive social environments prior to coming out, religious affiliation prior to coming out, as well as specific religious socializing experiences like participating in a religious rite as a child or attending a religious school are significant predictors of religious changes after coming out, the likelihood of experiencing religious and LGBT identity conflict, and the importance of LGBT identity among the people I surveyed.

Furthermore, after coming out, most LGBT people do not abandon their faith. Some change their religious affiliation—most, but not all, of them in search of religious affirmation. The more affirming a religious congregation or denomination that LGBT people engage with, the less likely they are to experience identity conflict and the more likely they are to value their LGBT identity. LGBT people who engage with affirming traditions apparently learn to value their LGBT identity and integrate their faith with earlier (mis)conceptions about their sexuality and gender. Although not a perfect mechanism for identity integration, affirming religiosity is a major factor in identity development. It is reasonable to expect that most of these variables also explain variation in political attitudes and behaviors of LGBT people.

In this concluding section, I synthesize the information from this chapter and distill a model of these effects with predictions for political behavior that will be tested in the remaining chapters. Other scholars have more succinctly explored and explained the various ways that religious LGBT people attempt to integrate their religious and LGBT identities, as well as the successes and pitfalls they encounter (see Coley 2020; Erzen 2006; Griffin 2006; Shokeid 2005; Wilcox 2009; 2012; etc.). With the model I explain in this section, I am not attempting to account for every potential outcome; I am only attempting to demonstrate the most common and likely scenarios based on the data I have collected. Without longitudinal data or more robust samples of transgender and LGBT POC, it is not possible to fully account for the religious socialization effects on LGBT identity and political behavior; however, the relationships I have described to this point give some indications that help specify a theoretical framework.

Namely, the results in this chapter suggest two paths for religious LGBT people that lead to politico-religious activism. For clarity, I depict these observed and predicted relationships in Figure 4.4, where the dashed outlines and circles with italicized text are hypothesized relationships. In the first path, religious LGBT people who come out as LGBT and were raised in supportive social environments stay in their faith traditions, or may only switch congregations. This group is likely to work within their faith traditions to make them more affirming and through that process grow to better understand and value their identity. In the second path, religious people who come out as LGBT but are raised in hostile social environments experience conflict and some change their faith tradition, seeking out affirming religious experiences that help them better understand and come to terms with their identity. Those experiences increase the importance of LGBT identity in their lives. In one case, LGBT identity was cultivated earlier. In both cases, religious affirmation (the combination of religiosity and participation in affirming religious organizations) increases the salience of LGBT identity and contributes to politico-religious activism. In the former case, however, because LGBT identity is already salient, and their religious and LGBT identities are congruent, the likelihood of politico-religious activism is already high. In the latter case, affirming religiosity takes the place of early socialization but produces a similar behavioral result.

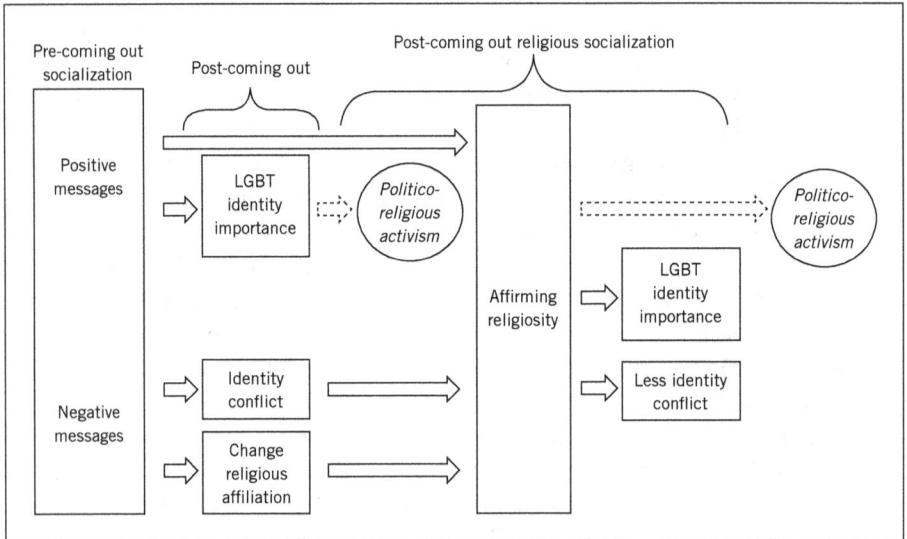

Figure 4.4 The Path to Politico-religious Activism for Religious LGBT People: Observed and Predicted Relationships

This framework does not foreclose other religious outcomes. Some LGBT people will stay in nonaffirming faith traditions and may eventually seek to change their LGBT identity (this is a small but not insignificant proportion of the sample I studied), while other LGBT people will disaffiliate from religion altogether. Others (fewer than half, but again, not an insignificant proportion) may have never viewed religion as important; for them these processes are moot.

Some observations help summarize the chapter and justify the construction of this framework. First, the LGBT people I surveyed were able to identify a faith tradition prior to coming out (even if this was nothing in particular). Although not a perfect indicator, this and the existence of conflict among many of the people I surveyed implies religiosity precedes LGBT identity and that many survey participants have a pre–coming out religious position on the subject of LGBT identity. Would, for example, conflict exist if there was no underlying religious belief that inspired the conflict? Second, religiosity is associated with conflict. It is likely because it is difficult for the most religious LGBT people to abandon their faith when a new experience that can be perceived as a challenge to their faith (e.g., coming out in conservative religious traditions) becomes a factor in their lives. Again, this implies a preexisting religious orientation that is confronted by the new experience of coming out as LGBT. Third, affirmation is associated with religiosity among both those who experience and those who do not experience conflict. While some LGBT people may seek out affirming religious spaces, even those who do not experience identity conflict but are part of affirming religious communities are more religious. This suggests that those who come to affirming religious spaces because they see their LGBT identity as important (rather than as a source of conflict with religion) still increase their religiosity.

How, then, does religious affirmation "work" to support LGBT identity development? Religious affirmation appears to serve several purposes simultaneously; however, the effect depends on both the social location of the individual (e.g., race or gender identity) and their socializing experiences prior to coming out. Affirmation can increase the importance of LGBT identity. This scenario is most likely among those to whom religion is important prior to coming out but who experience religious and identity conflict and then change their faith tradition after coming out. Among this group, the change in faith tradition likely represents a switch from a nonaffirming to an affirming faith, which, in turn, is associated with increased LGBT identity importance.

Affirmation may also help "normalize" LGBT identity so that it is no longer in conflict with one's religious beliefs. This scenario is also most likely among those who experience negative socialization prior to coming out and then change their faith after coming out. Among this group, for example non-Christians I surveyed, religious affirmation is associated with a decrease in the importance of LGBT identity. This is likely the result of identity integration processes whereby one's LGBT identity becomes one in the constellation of identities that make up a person's sense of self. In this case, a reduction in LGBT identity importance reflects a balanced perspective that allows both LGBT and religious identities to coexist.

The LGBT people I surveyed who changed their faith tradition after coming out do not appear to do so because they experience identity conflict, at least not directly. Instead, a change in faith tradition is associated with negative social messages prior to coming out. Because there is no association between social messages and religiosity, it is likely that the change in religious affiliation represents previously affiliated LGBT people disaffiliating with religion after coming out.

In describing their perspective on religion in LGBT culture, one survey participant, a lesbian woman raised Protestant in the northeast, shared a prescient metaphor that summarizes the findings and implications of the previous two chapters:

> [LGBT culture] is a seasoning mix of various concepts, faiths, adherences, beliefs, and values. Each has their unique quality that should not be dismissed because of its origin and can add to the overall flavor. But, it should be up to the individual on what seasonings they want, the amount that they want it, and how it is applied and what they want out of it . . . if not, you can destroy the dish.

Faith is a major component of the lives and identities of the LGBT people I surveyed. But, to reiterate, the model I describe in the previous section does not fit the experience of every LGBT person. The combination of "spices" that produce LGBT culture and identity are multitudinous. They cannot be contained in a simple flow chart. As this quote illustrates, however, LGBT people have incorporated faith into what it means to be LGBT often in spite of hetero- and cis-sexist institutions that would otherwise deny their spirituality. It is their resilience and commitment to perfecting their own recipe for identity that has spurred the development of numerous religious groups and organizations through which LGBT people can find spiritual community, contribute their gifts and talents, and receive healing if they need it. That affirmation also comes with the benefit of political mobilization.

Regardless of when or why LGBT people come to experience religious affirmation, it is my contention that religious affirmation is important for political participation because it acts as a form of socialization that helps convey the importance of both religion and LGBT identity to LGBT people. To better understand this relationship, in the next chapter, I examine the *why* of LGBT social, religious, and political behavior. I will not only establish the reasons LGBT people seek out faith communities and opportunities to express their religiosity after coming out but also distinguish these from the reasons LGBT people engage in other voluntary social activities. In the following chapter, I situate these perspectives within the context of political resource theory and explore the relationship between LGBT religiosity and political activism, paying special attention to the fact that religious affirmation, although cognizant of LGBT marginalization, is fundamentally religious socialization, and its effects on specific political views may not be the same as secular socialization that LGBT people may also undergo after coming out.

5

"I Cannot Separate Myself from Either My Religious Beliefs or My Sexual Identity"

Faith in LGBT Culture and Politics

The quote in this chapter's title comes from a white bisexual woman who was raised Protestant in the Midwest but now identifies as agnostic. The comment represents one way the LGBT people I surveyed view the relationship between their faith and LGBT identity (i.e., intrinsically). For some, faith defines their sexual identity—for good or ill. Others I surveyed see their faith and LGBT identity as wholly separate concepts. Similar patterns emerge when it comes to LGBT people's understanding of their faith and politics. The purpose of this book is to explore how faith shapes both LGBT identity and political development. To this point, I have focused on the former. The next three chapters will focus on the latter (i.e., faith and LGBT political development). Specifically, I will explore how religious identity, belief, and practice affect political participation and political attitudes of LGBT people. But, before testing the participatory model I outlined at the end of the previous chapter, it is important to understand how LGBT people view faith, religion, and spirituality as components of LGBT politics and why LGBT people engage in collective religious behavior.

So far, I have discussed several ways that faith shapes LGBT identity. For example, I have shown that positive pre–coming out socialization about LGBT people helps shape future cognitive and affective understandings of both faith and LGBT identity. Moreover, I have demonstrated that faith remains an important component of LGBT experiences after coming out. Not only do a majority of LGBT people report no change in the strength of their faith after coming out, but contemporary religious experiences are important influences on both LGBT and religious identities. Specifically, religious experiences that affirm LGBT identity help reduce religious conflict and increase the importance of one's sexual orientation and gender identity.

As I have explained in previous chapters, the religious forces that shape LGBT identity do not exist in a vacuum. By that I mean faith, spirituality, and religion are social constructs that are influenced by the cultural context within which they operate. In the United States, our pluralist liberal democracy has allowed religion to become a pivotal component of politics. It is therefore important to explore the motivation for collective religious behavior because much of the scientific literature I draw on in the next two chapters suggests that the practice of one's faith is the most important religious influence on political participation.

The general pattern for behavioral research among LGBT people assumes that LGBT people experience religious rejection (see Coley 2020) and the hurt this causes leads them to abandon and/or negatively evaluate religion, especially "organized religion," after coming out. That is certainly one valid experience that is represented in the data I have examined to this point. Furthermore, as I will show in this chapter, that experience represents one pathway to politico-religious activism for LGBT people. Namely, some LGBT people are motivated by discriminatory experiences to engage in political activism to educate society and to prevent discrimination in the future (see Cravens 2020). However, assuming all LGBT people practice their faith and politics under these circumstances reifies the notion that LGBT and religious identities can only exist in conflict and that after coming out religion only serves as a foil for LGBT people and their political activism.

By examining how LGBT people perceive faith as a component of LGBT politics and why LGBT people engage in collective religious behavior, we can build a clearer picture that moves beyond the conflict narrative and nuances our understanding of both LGBT faith and politics. Not only this, but it will then be possible to assess the similarities between secular and nonsecular behavior and specifically examine LGBT political participation and attitudes at the intersection of religiosity.

While many studies of LGBT religious behavior operate on the conflict narrative, other studies assume LGBT people practice their faith and engage with religious organizations after coming out explicitly to reduce identity conflict or alleviate guilt associated with being LGBT (see J. Anderson and Koc 2020). Such utilitarian approaches are also represented in political studies of LGBT people that argue that LGBT people prioritize tangible benefits (i.e., favorable economic policies) when determining which political party to support (see Schaffner and Senic 2006; Swank and Fahs 2013). In this scenario, LGBT people practice their faith and politics because they get something out of it. Still other studies recognize altruism as a potential motivator of both religious and social behavior (M. Bennett and Einolf 2017). People join religious groups or practice their faith in order to provide benefits to others, not necessarily themselves—although doing so may offer a purposive incentive to the faithful.

So, why participate? Is it altruism or utility? I begin this chapter with an analysis of survey data showing affective evaluations of religion and how religious LGBT people balance their religious and LGBT identities. Importantly, this balancing act often requires shifts in social behavior as some religious LGBT people attempt to protect themselves from LGBT social environments perceived as hostile to their faith. I then turn to a content analysis of responses to several open-ended questions that I posed to a convenience sample of LGBT people focusing on the role of religion in LGBT politics. Finally, I analyze *why* LGBT people engage in three types of collective behavior: religious, social, and political.

It is important to note that in the final analysis, I hold constant the LGBT focus of each type of collective behavior. That is, in the survey questions described in the final section of this chapter, the survey participants are asked why they engage with LGBT religious organizations, LGBT social organizations, and LGBT political organizations. I do this so that I can measure the differences across secular and religious forms of collective behavior. I will show that the motivation for collective behavior differs between secular and religious activities, but also that there are distinctions between each of the three types of collective behavior I analyze. I will also show that religious experiences can act as both a catalyst and a facilitator for political activism among LGBT people. In the next two chapters, I extend these analyses by exploring the effect of religion on political participation and attitudes through the lenses of political resource and identity theories.

"It's Complicated": Coming Out as Religious

In the previous chapter, I reviewed Coley's (2020) four archetypes for how LGBT people perceive and understand their LGBT and religious identities (see also Moon 2014). Recall, across one axis, Coley (2020) suggests LGBT people may hold "conservative" or "liberal" perceptions about the compatibility of their LGBT (or same-sex attraction or gender identity) and religious identities, and they may pursue "authoritative versus individualistic strategies" in terms of whom to trust about LGBT people and identity. Rather than following the reductionist *Will & Grace* paradigm, this nuanced view of LGBT religion shows how LGBT people potentially conceive of their place in heteronormative spaces but also (re)imagine religious spaces to make room for their equal participation. I can now examine what motivates LGBT people to engage in religious and political activity and ultimately how religion affects the political attitudes of LGBT people. I start with an overview of what LGBT people think about religion in the United States. That is, how do LGBT people perceive religion as a component of LGBT identity?

Defining "Welcoming" Religious Spaces

When probed about perceived conflict between religion and LGBT identity, several of the people I surveyed related personal anecdotes that suggest LGBT people are antagonistic toward religion and religious people, even if those people are also LGBT. For example, a white gay man from the western United States who was raised and currently identifies as Protestant recounted how "members of the LGBT community treat me with suspicion and even hostility" because he is a clergy person. Another white gay man from the Northeast who was raised and currently identifies as Protestant recounted a similar experience in a prominent gay neighborhood. In short, the man said, "Someone told me it was more acceptable to be out as a gay man than to be out (in the gay community) as a Christian."

In addition to coming out as LGBT, religious LGBT people must also consider how their religious identity will be accepted by the LGBT community. Social science tells us that groups often seek to establish boundaries around identities that clearly designate who is and is not a part of the group (Tajfel 1978). Such a project has clearly been undertaken by the various iterations of the homophile, gay liberation, lesbian feminist, and LGBT movements since the mid-twentieth century. In each case, group members viewed themselves as united by a common characteristic: homosexuality or same-sex attraction, binary male or female identity, for example. That characteristic became the basis for inclusion and exclusion. At times, lesbian women were excluded from the predominantly male homophile movement (Faderman 2015), transgender people were excluded from the predominantly gay and lesbian liberation movements (Warner 1999), and POC were largely excluded from both (Vaid 1995).

What of religion? As I explain in the Preface to this book, LGBT social and political life has been dominated by the *Will & Grace* paradigm, which depicts "LGBT" as predominantly male, white, upper-middle class, urban, and nonreligious. Common experiences with religious prejudice serve as the basis for excluding religious people from the identity group. The experiences of the survey participants I quote here are consistent with this history. Practically, this means some religious LGBT people feel excluded from LGBT spaces primarily because some LGBT people have been (and continue to be) excluded from religious spaces. The cross-pressure on religious LGBT people may have serious consequences for their social and political participation, and I will address this in more detail later. Now, it is important to understand just how pervasive antireligious prejudice is among LGBT people.

In order to better understand this dynamic, I asked several detailed questions. First, borrowing from a Pew Research Center (2013a) study, I asked the survey participants how friendly they perceived several major religious groups to be to LGBT people. Table 5.1 shows their responses.

As the table shows, most LGBT people view the major religious groups in the United States as unfriendly or neutral. Evangelical churches, the Catholic Church, and the Muslim religion are characterized as the most unfriendly toward LGBT people. The Buddhist religion is viewed as the friendliest, although only about one-quarter of the LGBT people I surveyed hold this view. Instead, a plurality or slight majority view the Hindu religion, the Buddhist religion, non-Evangelical and African American Protestant churches, and the Jewish religion as neutral toward LGBT people.

Further analysis shows distinct patterns across racial identities in the sample. For example, white LGBT people I surveyed are more likely to view non-Evangelical Protestant churches and the Jewish and Buddhist religions as friendly toward LGBT people. White LGBT people are also more likely to view Evangelical Protestant churches, the Catholic Church, and the Muslim religion as unfriendly toward LGBT people. Black LGBT people I surveyed are more likely to view Evangelical Protestant churches and the Catholic Church as friendly but the Jewish, Buddhist, and Hindu religions as unfriendly to LGBT people. Latinx LGBT people I surveyed are also more likely to view Evangelical Protestant churches as friendly as well as African American Protestant churches, the Catholic Church, and the Muslim and Buddhist religions (see Online Statistical Appendix XI).

Second, I asked the survey participants a series of unique questions to ascertain how they feel religious LGBT people are perceived by the broader LGBT community. The results are telling and stand in contrast to the views expressed in Table 5.1. Table 5.2 shows the distribution of responses to five

TABLE 5.1 PERCEPTIONS OF ORGANIZED RELIGION			
	Unfriendly	Neutral	Friendly
Non-Evangelical Protestant Churches	34	48	18
Evangelical Protestant Churches	59	33	7
African American Protestant Churches	41	45	13
The Catholic Church	64	27	8
The Muslim Religion	71	24	3
The Jewish Religion	41	44	13
The Buddhist Religion	26	50	23
The Hindu Religion	34	51	14
Source: Author data available from Cravens (2022). Notes: Row totals do not sum to 100% due to rounding. N = 1,100.			

TABLE 5.2 PERCEPTIONS OF RELIGIOUS LGBT PEOPLE				
	(Strongly) Agree (%)	Neither Agree nor Disagree	(Strongly) Disagree	Total Responses
I have been made to feel unwelcome in LGBT settings because of my religious identity.	10	20	61	786
I avoid socializing with other LGBT people who are not religious.	4	10	84	961
My religion is a point of contention with other LGBT people.	10	27	62	848
Other LGBT people judge me negatively because of my faith.	9	17	72	881
LGBT people are generally hostile to religious people.	14	25	60	1006

Source: Author data available from Cravens (2022).
Note: Row percentages do not sum to 100% due to rounding.

statements that I asked of the LGBT people who reported currently affiliating with some faith tradition (i.e., not atheist). Note, the strongly agree/agree and strongly disagree/disagree categories are collapsed in the interest of space.

As the table shows, most of the religious LGBT people I surveyed do not view LGBT people as unfriendly toward religion or religious LGBT people. In fact, a clear majority disavow this notion. Only one in ten survey participants have felt unwelcome in LGBT spaces because of their religion, and the same proportion report viewing their religion as a point of contention with other LGBT people. On the other hand, four in five say they do not avoid socializing with secular LGBT people, while seven in ten say they are not judged negatively by LGBT people because of their faith. While LGBT people are suspicious of religious institutions, that suspicion generally does not translate into hostility toward religious members of the LGBT community.

A white transgender man from the Midwest who was raised Protestant but now identifies as Jewish expressed these concerns when responding to a question about the relationship between religion and LGBT culture:

> I know that there is profound anger from a lot of LGBT folks towards religious *institutions* from the way that they were treated by these *institutions*. The relationship between LGBT folks and religion can be described as the Facebook "It's complicated" relationship designation. On the other hand, I know a lot of LGBT folks who are very involved in their religious activities. Most of them have been hurt too, but they haven't given up on their faith. (emphasis added)

The quote I chose to illustrate this dynamic is important because it comes from a white-identified respondent. As with evaluations of religious traditions, the experiences of LGBT POC are markedly different. Namely, the white LGBT people I surveyed are more likely than LGBT POC to agree with every statement in Table 5.2 except the last one. Specifically, Latinx LGBT people I surveyed are more likely than others to say they have been made to feel unwelcome in LGBT spaces because of their religion, that other LGBT people judge them negatively because of their faith, and that LGBT people are generally hostile to religious people. Black LGBT people I surveyed are more likely to avoid socializing with LGBT people who are not religious and to say that their religion is a point of contention with other LGBT people. Similar to Latinx LGBT people, LGBT people who identify as another racial identity are also more likely than others to say that LGBT people judge them negatively because of their faith and that LGBT people are generally hostile to religious people (see Online Statistical Appendix XII).

Taken together, the quantitative and qualitative survey data show that when LGBT people express hostility toward religion, it is largely toward the institutions that are used to oppress LGBT people. In fact, most of the LGBT people I surveyed view most of the major religious institutions in America with skepticism when it comes to their acceptance of LGBT people (see also Barringer 2019). Yet, this skepticism of institutions does not seem to translate directly into animosity toward LGBT people who are also religious. On the whole, the LGBT people I surveyed do not feel like LGBT social spaces are unwelcoming simply because one is religious.

Still, the LGBT POC I surveyed are significantly more likely to perceive LGBT people, in general, as hostile to religion and report changing their individual behavior to accommodate religious disagreement (i.e., avoiding socializing with LGBT people who are not religious). The fact that LGBT POC experience hostility in LGBT spaces because of their religiosity holds serious implications for their identity and political development. Specifically, Black and Latinx LGBT people I surveyed are more likely to view Evangelical churches as "friendly" to LGBT people. This likely reinforces Evangelical affiliation among the groups, which can, in turn, contribute to variation in political ideology as these institutions become or remain sources of political information (i.e., agents of political socialization) for LGBT POC after coming out.

Not only this but the most religious LGBT subpopulation (i.e., Black LGBT people) are also no more likely to attend affirming congregations or denominations than other LGBT people. The data suggest, then, that religious LGBT POC experience exclusion from secular LGBT spaces but do not make up for it with participation in religious LGBT spaces. LGBT POC, then, are potentially being denied the benefits of LGBT-affirming religion and LGBT affirmation in secular spaces, despite being the most religious LGBT population.

"Can There Be Balance?" Faith and LGBT Culture

To provide further detail on LGBT people's perspectives on religion, I analyze responses to two open-ended questions presented to a convenience sample of LGBT people as part of an online questionnaire administered in spring
2021.[1] The first question asked survey participants to describe the relationship between LGBT culture and religion (n = 120). The second question asked
survey participants to describe how their religious beliefs influences (if at all)
their participation in politics (n = 125). (See online methodological appendix for additional details about content analysis and survey questions. All
appendixes are available via Harvard Dataverse at https://doi.org/10.7910
/DVN/M87Q1V; for additional citation information see Cravens 2022b.)

After reading and coding the responses, several themes emerged that help
define (1) how LGBT people perceive religion as a component of LGBT culture and (2) how religion affects LGBT politics. For clarity, I show the basic
schema for understanding the responses in two tables. Table 5.3 shows the
pattern in how the LGBT people I surveyed understand religion as a component of LGBT culture. Of the 120 valid responses to the question (i.e., relationship between LGBT culture and religion), about one-third (31%) describe
a separatist dynamic between religion and LGBT culture. On the other hand,
two in five (60%) describe religion as at least compatible with LGBT culture,
although there are several variations on this theme, which I detail in Table 5.3.
Finally, fewer than one in ten (6%) responses were characterized as neutral.

Of the responses that view religion as a component of or compatible with
LGBT culture, a plurality of responses indicated agreement but gave no further details about the survey participant's reasoning. The remaining two-thirds
(62%) of affirmative responses represent five categories that condition the survey participant's affirmation. In a majority of these cases, the responses seem
to begin with the premise that religion can be harmful to LGBT people. This
suggests that many of the survey participants, even when acceding that religion is a component of LGBT culture, have potentially internalized negative views about religion. For example, most of the participants in this cat-

TABLE 5.3 IS THERE A PLACE FOR RELIGION IN LGBT CULTURE?			
Religion should be part of LGBT culture			
Yes, but:	Recognize contested history (20%)	Religion should do no harm (15%)	Faith, not religion (5%)
Yes, because:	Mutually supportive (13%)	Religion is always part of culture (9%)	
No, because:	Distinct experiences or Religion is opposed (43%)	Negative personal experi-ence with religion (23%)	
Neutral	Ambivalence (33%)		

egory suggest that there is space for religion in LGBT culture but because it is contested it is also precarious. By this I mean these responses concede that religion can be both beneficial and harmful to LGBT people, and religion used for abusive purposes is not a part of LGBT culture.

The following response from a gay man from the western United States who was raised Roman Catholic illustrates this point: "The relationship is one of tension. Religious leaders seem to feel that LGBT people are not religious. [The] LGBT community acts like LGBT people are not religious. In fact, we are both and reconciling the two is an ongoing work." For this and other responses in the category I define as "Yes, but": LGBT culture cannot be understood separately from the contested (i.e., sometimes negative) influence of religion. Although recognizing LGBT people are religious and have affected change in the American religious landscape, these responses also suggest LGBT culture is defined by conflict with dominant social institutions that are generally unwelcoming. LGBT culture, therefore, is the product of conflict. It is also a foundational identity, in that it is central to many of these respondents' sense of self. In short, these responses suggest, "Yes, faith can be a part of LGBT culture, but we cannot forget that it has been used to perpetuate oppression." To forget or otherwise obscure this lesson could jeopardize future LGBT cultural development by undermining the foundational position of LGBT identity.

The responses in this category also seem to balance optimism and pessimism about religious institutions. For example, another white gay man raised Protestant in the South said, "Religion has been a strong factor in the oppression of LGBT people in the United States and beyond. I don't happen to believe that is its destiny. I have seen many clergy and religious people join with nonreligious people in supporting our community." This balancing act, again, assumes that faith and LGBT culture can be integrated and that lessons learned from years of religious oppression of LGBT people can be applied to make LGBT religion a less intimidating, more culturally sensitive social project. The responses to *why* LGBT people join religious groups that I detail later seem to support this perspective.

Several participants conditioned their affirmative response (i.e., "Yes, but": column 2) on the fact that religion must not harm LGBT people if it is to be a viable component of LGBT culture. That is, they seemed to make allowances for religion in LGBT culture, but only if religion is not used to police others. These sentiments either took the form of overt condemnation of religious bigotry or were expressed in the view, highlighted in Chapter 3, that religion should be chosen, not compelled. For example, a white lesbian woman from the South who was raised agnostic offered the following: "I am more than happy for LGBT folks to be religious as long as they do not shame or attempt to change the sexuality or gender identity of others." Similarly, a white gay man from the West who was raised in no particular religious tradition said, "I am not inherently opposed [to religion in LGBT culture] and would not tell people what to believe, but patriarchal and cis-sexist beliefs are antagonistic to queerness. Religion does not necessarily have to support those things, though." Finally, an Asian American or Pacific Islander lesbian woman who identifies as Mormon in the western United States said, "As long as religion does not stop LGBT [people], it should be fine."

Like responses that recognize the contested history of religion and LGBT culture, the second category of responses in the "Yes, but" schema all but assume that religion will be used as an instrument to oppress others. For respondents in both categories, however, there is no space in LGBT culture for *that* form of religion. To these respondents, LGBT religion and culture is not compulsory but is freely chosen and practiced with the understanding that faith must first "do no harm."

Finally, affirmative sentiments (i.e., "Yes, but": column 3) were also conditioned on the premise that faith and/or spirituality are not the same as religion. As discussed in the previous section, these responses view religious institutions operated by bigoted individuals, rather than spirituality or faith, as the cause of religious oppression. The institutions, therefore, have no place in LGBT culture, but spirituality and/or faith is an integral component. For example, a white lesbian woman raised Roman Catholic in the Midwest said, "Sexuality and spirituality are not separate, nor do they need to be. Religion is not spirituality." Another white lesbian woman who identifies as Unitarian said, "Anything that seeks to speak to life, death, everything in between, and any/everything beyond, is bound to get some things right and some things wrong. 'Organized religion' has its own motives." Both responses imply faith and/or spirituality are important components of LGBT culture; however, religious institutions that are created by fallible human beings are more likely to reproduce prejudice than be beneficial to spiritual growth. This perspective, in particular, aligns with Coley's (2020) individualist notion of LGBT spirituality, while the fact that several of the responses were from lesbian women highlight the prevalence of the perspective among the group, which is consistent with previous work on the subject of religious individualism (see Wilcox 2009).

Some affirmative responses also detailed their reasoning without adopting the assumption that religion has been or must be in conflict with LGBT identity (i.e., "Yes, because"). The most common subset of these responses view religion and LGBT culture as mutually supportive in that it is possible to "learn from each other" or there is an "interplay" between the two. In addition, a subset of responses intimate religion is implicated in LGBT culture because religion permeates society and LGBT people are not immune from its influence simply because they are LGBT. For example, one white pansexual woman who identifies as Unitarian said, "[LGBT people] seek answers to life's question and religion has been there to give us reassurance and guidance *but* most religions are reflections of the culture they came from." This implies that religion is always a part of culture; however, it leaves room for the recognition that this could contribute to harm for those whom religious culture has constructed as nonconforming.

A considerable proportion of the responses suggested religion is not or should not be a component of LGBT culture (i.e., "No, because"). Interestingly, despite the difference in methodology between the two surveys I undertook, the proportion of responses in this category closely aligns with the proportion of survey participants in the representative survey sample who report experiencing religious and LGBT identity conflict (i.e., about one-third). About one-third (31%) of participants who indicated negative responses to the question identify as atheist or agnostic; however, many faith traditions are represented in this response category.

As Table 5.3 shows, the most common form of negative response views religion as either compartmentalized from LGBT identity or diametrically opposed to the existence of LGBT people. For example, a white lesbian woman from the Midwest who was raised and currently identifies as Roman Catholic said, "From my experience, it seems that the LGBT culture challenges the teachings and practices of religions and religious organizations. By and large, organized religions do not condone or support LGBT people or their lifestyles." Several others offered brief comments that religion and LGBT culture should not be "intermingled" or that they are "independent" or should not otherwise "influence each other." These responses suggest that religion and LGBT identity represent distinct experiences that can be understood separately, although the participants do not offer further details as to *why*.

For the second major category of negative responses (i.e., "No, because": column 2), survey participants appear to draw on personal experiences to identify why religion and LGBT culture should not be integrated. The responses in this category generally recount negative experiences either in young adulthood, prior to coming out, or even after coming out, that led them to view religion and LGBT culture as incompatible. For example, an aromantic white woman from the Midwest who was raised Roman Catholic said, "My experience with religion . . . was negative and oppressive—with the communities around me [in my youth] strongly anti-LGBT. That strongly shapes my lack of religious identity and leaves me suspicious about many religious institutions." Some responses in this category cite the "impact of believers," which suggests a negative experience with a person the survey participant understood to be religious. Others recount "shared trauma" experienced by many LGBT people who leave unwelcoming faith traditions. In each case, the responses convey the belief that LGBT culture has no place for religion, faith, or spirituality because of the potentiality for harm.

Finally, a small proportion of the responses could not be classified in either the affirmative or negative schema because they did not offer an explicit evaluation of religion and LGBT culture (i.e., "ambivalence"). Sometimes these participants simply offered "I don't know"; others were reluctant to generalize. For example, some responses emphasized the importance of personal choice in determining how much faith or religion should be integrated into LGBT culture, but the assessment came with no explicit endorsement of faith in LGBT culture or spaces. This aspect distinguishes these more ambivalent responses from the affirmative responses, which also suggests LGBT people can choose to integrate religion into LGBT culture provided it does not harm LGBT people.

Overall, the LGBT people I surveyed shared mostly positive evaluations of the potential for religion to be integrated into LGBT culture. Indeed, many offered personal anecdotes or examples to demonstrate how they or others they know were already engaged in this identity and cultural work. While most viewed the relationship between religion and LGBT culture as contentious, the responses still offered optimistic assessments for what LGBT religion could or should look like. Welcoming, affirming, nonconfrontational, altruistic, and consensual: these are the ideal values of queer religion as suggested by the LGBT people I surveyed. It should be noted, however, that very few participants offered their comments without any negative connotations or caveats.

Even though the responses cannot be generalized beyond the convenience sample from which they were collected, it is important to note the variety of religious experiences and affiliations represented in each response category. While many negative responses were shared by LGBT people who identify as atheist, even more came from people who identify with a faith tradition. Opposition to religion in LGBT spaces, then, cannot be said to originate solely from nonreligious LGBT people. Instead, resistance is more likely to come from the faithful who, in many cases, wish to take care of those in the LGBT community who have been spiritually, psychologically, or even physically wounded by religious bigotry and/or abuse.

In short, for many of the LGBT people I surveyed, faith appears to be a resource for LGBT identity development that they draw on throughout the formative years (pre–coming out) and into adulthood (post–coming out) and rely on as a source of strength and motivation for understanding their own identity but also for combating discrimination. Faith also appears to be an aspirational component of LGBT culture, representing what could potentially be "the best" in the human condition. However, for LGBT people, realizing "the best" necessarily comes with the understanding that many LGBT people have experienced "the worst" from their faith traditions. In the next section, I examine how this dynamic applies to LGBT politics.

"As Politically Active as a Church Is Allowed to Be": Faith and Political Motivation

Having established that most of the LGBT people I surveyed see a place for religion in LGBT culture, I now turn to an exploration of a critical component of LGBT culture (i.e., politics) and its intersection with religion. As I discuss in Chapter 1, politics and political mobilization have always been closely linked to the religious practices of LGBT people. Early LGBT religious leaders founded denominations that were explicitly political in both the secular and spiritual realms. Some viewed their political activity as an extension of their faith (see Perry 1974). Others came to politics through their faith, and still others focused on the "political" work of reforming their unaccepting denominations (see Coley 2020).

In this section, I share the results of a content analysis of responses to an open-ended question that asked survey participants to describe how their religious beliefs influence (if at all) their participation in politics. In the patterns of responses, it is apparent that like Perry (1974) and other LGBT religious leaders say, politics are an extension of faith. For some participants, the political activity they undertake and the attitudes they hold are directly related to religion—although this is not always a positive relationship. Still, most of the people I surveyed believe religion does influence LGBT politics, and, for many, religion inspires or facilitates political activism.

Table 5.4 shows the most common themes that emerged from the results. Of the 125 valid responses, more than half (55%) represent the view that religion and LGBT politics are related in some way. Slightly more than one-quarter (28%) represent the view that religion and LGBT politics either are not or should not be related. Fewer than two in ten (16%) could not be clearly classified within either schema.

TABLE 5.4 PERSPECTIVE ON RELIGION AND LGBT POLITICS	
How does religion affect LGBT politics?	
The two are related:	Catalyst -Proactive (14%) -Reactive (13%)
	Facilitator (26%)
The two are not / should not be related	Individualist (28%)

Responses that expressed the view that religion and LGBT politics are related generally fall into two categories. These responses characterize religion as either a catalyst or a facilitator of political behavior. Responses that characterize religion as a catalyst often point to religion as the source of the survey participant's interest in or beliefs about politics. For example, a white lesbian woman who was raised Protestant in the West said, "I believe that [becoming a Unitarian Universalist] shaped my initial entry into political activism/social justice as I was previously not involved in politics at all." This sentiment is shared across faith traditions, as exemplified by the following. First, a gay man who was raised Roman Catholic in the South offered the following characterization: "It is my faith that has molded my sense of justice, social welfare, peace. Who I vote for, which issues I support are decided by the moral code I have developed over the years. . . . Faith without works is hollow." Similarly, a white transgender man from the Midwest who was raised Protestant but currently identifies as Jewish said of their faith, "Judaism has an idea of 'tikkun olam'—'repairing the world.' Jews are supposed to do things to help the world and those who live in it."

The catalyst frame did not necessarily invoke LGBT politics in each instance. For some, the effect of religion on politics is broader than just the politics of LGBT identity. For example, a white bisexual genderqueer person who was raised Buddhist mentioned, "Being a vegetarian and being involved in animal rights activism has been an obvious connection between my religious views and my activism work." In each of the examples, the catalyst frame can also be characterized as proactive. That is, religion is viewed as the mechanism that activated the survey participant's political behavior. This is most clearly seen in the first example, when a change in religious affiliation is described as "shaping" the participant's "entry into political activism." For the most part, in each of the proactive catalyst cases, religion is described positively. Religion is also described as if it were a public good—something that mostly has the potential to benefit society as a whole by increasing political activity and making politics and society more representative. This is not the case for the other subset of responses that also describe religion as a catalyst for political behavior.

In the second subset of catalytic responses, which I label "reactive," survey participants describe how their interaction with anti-LGBT religious forces catalyzed their political activism. For example, a white lesbian woman who was raised agnostic in the South said, "I have never been religious, but my homophobic experiences with religious groups have made me more political and more likely to participate in LGBT-positive politics." Similarly, a biracial pansexual nonbinary person who currently identifies with earth-based spiritualities said, "My religion of my youth was homophobic. . . . I'm not part of any organization now. I have been extremely politically active since leaving the religion of my childhood."

Some survey participants also speak about broad "opposition to religious influence on public life" that motivates their "participation in politics." Others, including one Latinx gay man who was raised Protestant in the South, speak more directly about confronting the politics of conservative religion, saying, "I'm motivated in my opposition to religion to engage politically and blunt efforts by the Religious Right." In each instance, a negative experience or view of religion serves as a catalyst for political behavior, largely to prevent religious organizations (but, more specifically, religious conservatives) from gaining political power. Speaking directly to this dynamic, a white transgender Mormon man noted, "Religion mobilizes religious sensibilities of people in order to get their support to capture power." For this individual, religion only captures political institutions in "backward societies."

Some of the LGBT people I surveyed generally agree that religion affects LGBT politics but characterized the nature of the relationship as indirect (i.e., "facilitator"). That is, religion or faith did not directly cause attitudes or behavior to change among this group; however, it did provide space for political expression or otherwise facilitate political engagement. For example, several survey participants noted their congregation participated in Pride events or would encourage them to participate in other political activities. A white gay man who identifies as Protestant from the western United States detailed the many ways their church encourages engagement and conversation about politics: "We have a booth at Pride every year, and our pastor is there to talk with individuals who have been wounded by faith communities. My religious beliefs encourage me to advocate (by protesting, making phone calls, social media posts, voting) for others." In addition to attending Pride, a white lesbian woman who identifies as Roman Catholic from the South added members of their church collectively "write to our congresspeople in support of LGBT legislation."

Some responses made clear that their political activism predated their current religious affiliation and/or would exist even if they were not religious. These responses would generally acquiesce to the notion that religion facilitates political involvement, but would also note they would be involved in politics regardless of their faith. The example responses I provide, then, should not be construed to mean there is only a unidirectional relationship between religion and politics whereby political behavior stems from religious participation. Instead, the relationship between politics and religion is often bidirectional (Son and Wilson 2021), meaning religious participation can induce secular collective action (such as volunteerism or political activity), but secular volunteerism may also induce religious activism. As partisanship becomes an increasingly salient predictor of religious affiliation, this is even more likely to be the case (i.e., that LGBT people will identify as liberal Democrats and be drawn to more liberal, politically active religious groups; see Djupe, Neiheisel, and Sokhey 2018; Egan 2020; Margolis 2018a; 2018b).

Finally, while I discuss this more in the next chapter, the experiences of these LGBT people mirror what social scientists call political resource theory. As applied to religion, this theory suggests religious participation offers certain benefits (called civic skills) that translate into secular activities. As such, people who participate in religious activity are more likely to be politically active. Not only does religious participation develop civic skills that augment political participation; the theory also stresses that religious institutions act as recruitment mechanisms for politics. In this way, religious organizations provide both the means and the opportunity to be politically active.

The second major classification of responses to the question of how religion affects LGBT politics is characterized by the view that religion should not or does not have any effect (see Table 5.4, row 3). The predominant perspective in this category, which I label individualistic, is characterized by a personal commitment to not only keep religion and politics separate but to do so because one is also committed to not let religious institutions dictate everything that one believes. This is very similar to the individualistic religious approach to LGBT identity I describe in Chapter 4, which prioritizes individual study and thought about religion, sexuality, and gender rather than relying on the authority of one's religious leaders or institutions for guidance. For example, a white gay man who was raised Protestant but currently identifies with no particular faith tradition said, "I chose to ignore religion in politics. For if I have to have religion to make value-based judgments that affect politics, then I have no voice in politics."

Responses in this category may also reflect the perspective that religion is or should be compartmentalized from politics. For example, a white pansexual woman who was raised Catholic but currently identifies as agnostic said, "Personally, my religious upbringing did not impact my political views because I distanced myself from the religion so early on." This compartmentalization is similar to the separatism described in the previous section between religion and LGBT culture. In both cases, religion is seen as a separate sphere of influence that either should not or, from the perspective of the individual survey participant, does not affect how they view or engage in politics.

Like perspectives on LGBT culture, broadly, perspectives on religion in LGBT politics are multifaceted. Yet, there is enough consensus to suggest specific patterns of understanding among the people I surveyed. Specifically, most believe there is a place for religion in LGBT culture and that religion does affect LGBT politics. In either case, the malevolent potentiality of religion is never downplayed. While most of the responses are aspirational, they also reflect a shared reality that religion (understood as conservative, organized religious traditions or institutions) has been a source of harm and conflict for many LGBT people. While this appears to contribute to a vision for LGBT culture that excludes harmful religious traditions, it also appears to inspire a vision of LGBT politics that is motivated by the best components of religion (e.g., social justice, altruism) to combat the worst components (e.g., oppression, accumulation of political power by religious conservatives).

Religious and Secular Collective Action

Given these perspectives on the role of religion in LGBT culture and politics, what benefits do LGBT people actually get from collective social, religious, and political behavior? One of the goals of this study is to better understand LGBT political behavior and its relationship to religiosity. In the next chapter, I explore political behavior in more detail, but for now, it is important to understand in broader terms how LGBT people engage in collective action. By collective action, I mean individuals combining their efforts toward a common goal.

Social science generally recognizes religion as one form of voluntary collective behavior along with other secular forms of behavior, like social clubs or political or civic organizations, that represent American civil society (see Putnam 2000; Verba, Schlozman, and Brady 1995; Wald, Silverman, and Fridy 2005). Interestingly, studies of collective action suggest it is illogical for individuals to engage in such behavior, especially when the goal is to produce a public good—something that benefits everyone regardless of their membership status in the organization that worked to produce the good (Olson 1965). Why? Because most people are free-riders. That is, they benefit from the collective action of others without having to expend the resources to achieve the goal. Clean water or fresh air, for example, are public goods that cannot be denied to an individual just because they are not a member of the Sierra Club. So why do people join the Sierra Club or engage in other forms of collective action?

Generally, people engage in collective behavior because they receive certain benefits that can be denied to those who are not members of a specific group (Olson 1965). These benefits typically fall into three categories: material, solidary, and purposive. Material benefits are tangible incentives one receives for joining a group. Discounts, subscriptions, and so on are examples. For religious groups, especially exclusive traditions that claim to be the only "true" faith, a potential material benefit may also be eternal salvation. Both solidary and purposive benefits are cognitive incentives for collective behavior. If you are motivated to join a group because you want to be around like-minded people, then you are seeking solidary benefits. If you are motivated to join a group because participating gives you a feeling of helping others or fulfilling a purpose, then you are seeking purposive benefits.

As I explain in the next chapter, collective social and religious behavior is an important component of individual political mobilization because people who regularly engage in collective behaviors like social clubs and religious organizations are also more likely to engage in both collective and individual political activities (like joining a protest or voting, respectively). So, how often do the LGBT people I surveyed engage in collective social and religious behavior?

To answer this question, I asked the survey participants how frequently they participate in any LGBT social club or organization and how frequently they attend religious organizations for LGBT people. It is important to note that I specifically limit the scope of the behavior to social and religious organizations for LGBT people. This is so I can later compare the differences in motivation while controlling for any specific identity-related motivation. I detail LGBT political behavior in the next chapter and focus on social and religious behavior here.

Among the sample, about one-quarter (26%) report often attending an LGBT religious organization, while about one-third (31%) report sometimes attending. On the other hand, about two in five (41%) report never or only rarely attending an LGBT religious organization. Fewer LGBT people report frequently participating in an LGBT social club. Specifically, slightly more than one-third of the survey participants (38%) report often or sometimes participating in social clubs, while more than two in five (45%) say they never do and fewer than one in five (16%) only rarely participate.

Why Participate?

To better understand why the LGBT people I surveyed join religious groups that center LGBT experiences, I asked the participants to explain their motivations. Specifically, I presented the survey participants with a series of statements and asked them to indicate which, if any, were factors that influenced their participation in religious organizations for LGBT people. They were also able to suggest others, if none applied. Although varied, the responses represent many of the most common theoretical explanations for collective behavior, including material benefits, solidary benefits, and purposive benefits (see Olson 1965). Material benefits include resources, education, and emotional support. Solidary benefits include being involved with one's community, while purposive benefits include helping others. Table 5.5 shows the distribution of responses.

As the table shows, most of the LGBT people I surveyed who participate in LGBT religious organizations do so out of altruistic, rather than utilitar-

			Total
TABLE 5.5 WHY SURVEY PARTICIPANTS JOIN AN LGBT RELIGIOUS ORGANIZATION			
Reason	No (%)	Yes (%)	Total Responses
Helping to come to terms with my sexual orientation or gender identity	73	26	488
Getting an opportunity to learn about the LGBT community	64	35	488
Getting physical resources (e.g., medical care, legal or educational assistance)	81	18	488
Getting emotional support (e.g., counseling)	65	34	488
Getting an opportunity to be involved in my community	59	40	488
Getting an opportunity to help others	54	45	488
Getting help with discrimination	79	20	488
Alleviating guilt	90	9	488

Source: Author data available from Cravens (2022).
Note: Row percentages do not sum to 100% due to rounding.

ian, reasons. Specifically, two in five cite purposive or solidary benefits including opportunities to help others or to be involved in their community as the reason for their participation. This is consistent with the content analysis in the previous sections, which suggests many LGBT people view religion as a potential force for good in the LGBT community. Fewer than one in five cite material reasons such as physical resources for their participation. Material resources, however, may also include psychological benefits that accrue from participation, and, after applying this more expansive understanding of the concept, more survey participants appear to fall into this category. For example, more than one in five participants cite emotional support or education as reasons for their participation.

A significant proportion of participants also join religious organizations for LGBT people so they can come to terms with their sexual orientation or gender identity (26%). Recall from Chapter 2, this proportion is commensurate to the proportion of participants who report experiencing religious and LGBT identity conflict. In fact, a cross-tabulation shows that religious and LGBT identity conflict is significantly related to this particular motivation. Namely, more people than expected who experience conflict indicate they participate in religious organizations for LGBT people because they are trying to come to terms with their LGBT identity ($\chi^2 = 16.7$, p = .000). Relatively few of the people I surveyed join LGBT religious organizations to alleviate guilt; however, almost 10% do. Of the small proportion who offered different reasons (about 1%), the most common responses explicitly mentioned a desire to better understand or to "have a relationship with" God. Importantly, there are no differences in motivation for joining LGBT religious organizations when compared across racial identities in the sample.

Table 5.6 shows the distribution of survey responses when participants were asked why they join social organizations for LGBT people. In this case, the previous question prompt distinguishes "social clubs or organizations" from religious or political organizations (see online Methodological Appendix). Some distinctions between religious and secular social behavior emerge. First, participation in secular social groups is the most common form of collective behavior among the sample, with more than half indicating they engage in this form of behavior. Second, while roughly the same proportion of respondents cite material benefits as a reason for joining both social and religious organizations, a higher proportion of the people I surveyed appear to join social organizations to get cognitive or psychological benefits like emotional support or help coming to terms with their sexual orientation or gender identity. In addition, some respondents who indicated other reasons for joining LGBT social organizations specifically mentioned networking for business or job prospecting, psychological counseling, or organizations like Alcoholics Anonymous.

Third, more than two in five survey participants cite education about the LGBT community as a reason for joining an LGBT social club. Although higher than the proportion who join religious organizations for the same reason, it appears that both religious and social organizations serve an important educational purpose for out LGBT people. Fourth, both solidary and purposive benefits are important reasons to join social organizations among near-

TABLE 5.6 WHY SURVEY PARTICIPANTS JOIN LGBT SOCIAL ORGANIZATIONS			
Reason	No (%)	Yes (%)	Total Responses
Helping to come to terms with my sexual orientation or gender identity	65	34	766
Getting an opportunity to learn about the LGBT community	55	44	766
Getting physical resources (e.g., medical care, legal or educational assistance)	82	17	766
Getting emotional support (e.g., counseling)	61	38	766
Getting an opportunity to be involved in my community	52	47	766
Getting an opportunity to help others	52	47	766
Getting help with discrimination	78	21	766
Alleviating guilt	90	9	766

Source: Author data available from Cravens (2022).
Note: Row percentages do not sum to 100% due to rounding.

ly half of the respondents. Helping others and being involved in the LGBT community, then, are the predominant reasons why LGBT people join social groups, at least for the LGBT people I surveyed.

There are also racial differences in purposive motivation. Specifically, a cross-tabulation shows that more white LGBT people than expected identify the opportunity to help others as a motivation for joining LGBT social clubs, while fewer Black and Latinx LGBT people than expected identify this as a motivation (χ^2 = 10.1, p = .018). This is not to say that LGBT POC are not motivated by altruism in the same way as white LGBT people. Although the data do not allow for more specific analyses, it is likely that the variation reflects how the white survey participants define the LGBT community. That is to say, for many white LGBT people, the LGBT community reflects their whiteness. Motivation to join predominantly white social clubs is generally not high among LGBT POC, so joining predominantly white social clubs for the express purpose of prioritizing the needs of a predominantly white LGBT community would be counterintuitive. Instead of a critique of LGBT POC, this finding should be taken as a critique of predominantly white LGBT social groups that systemically exclude LGBT POC (see Bérubé 2001).

While involvement in the LGBT community is an important aspect of solidarity, several of the participants who indicated other reasons for joining social organizations also mentioned dating or finding a partner. This could reflect both solidary (finding like-minded partners) and material (companionship) motivations. Finally, about the same proportion of participants indicated that alleviating guilt was a reason they join social and religious organizations.

Table 5.7 shows somewhat similar results for why LGBT people I surveyed join or participate in political organizations for LGBT people. Solidary and purposive benefits, again, seem to be the most common reason why LGBT people engage in this form of collective behavior. In this case, most of the survey participants indicate collective political behavior provides an opportunity to help others and also to be involved in the LGBT community.

Material benefits are also important motivators for collective political action among the group, as more than one in five cite physical and emotional resources as reasons for engaging. Political activism also provides help with identity integration for more than one-third of the sample who report joining political organizations for the opportunity to learn about the LGBT community and about one-quarter join to help come to terms with their sexual orientation or gender identity. This appears to be especially important for LGBT POC who report help coming to terms with their sexual orientation or gender identity (χ^2 = 15.3, p = .002) and the opportunity to learn about the LGBT community (χ^2 = 10.9, p = .012) as motivators for joining LGBT political organizations at greater than expected frequencies.

			Total
TABLE 5.7 WHY SURVEY PARTICIPANTS JOIN LGBT POLITICAL ORGANIZATIONS			
Reason	No (%)	Yes (%)	Total Responses
Helping to come to terms with my sexual orientation or gender identity	75	24	633
Getting an opportunity to learn about the LGBT community	64	35	633
Getting physical resources (e.g., medical care, legal or educational assistance)	77	22	633
Getting emotional support (e.g., counseling)	75	24	633
Getting an opportunity to be involved in my community	51	48	633
Getting an opportunity to help others	47	52	633
Getting help with discrimination	73	26	633
Alleviating guilt	94	5	633

Source: Author data available from Cravens (2022).
Note: Row percentages do not sum to 100% due to rounding.

It is intuitive that political organizations would be a source of knowledge about issues facing the LGBT community; however, that LGBT POC rely on these organizations for identity integration work may also reflect perceptions of social or religious spaces as unaccepting, less diverse, or at the very least, not up to the task of identity work. While the data does not allow for more detailed explorations, it is clear that LGBT political organizations serve an important function for LGBT POC who want to learn more about the LGBT community or want to come to terms with their sexual orientation or gender identity. Even within organizations that recognize antiracism as a central component of LGBT political work, however, LGBT POC are still marginalized (see Ward 2008). LGBT political organizations, then, must be especially cognizant of the diversity inherent to the LGBT experience but also reflect this diversity in their leadership and policy priorities (see Strolovitch 2007).

Finally, of the relatively small proportion of participants who reported another reason for engaging in collective political behavior, the most common responses involved a mixture of solidary and purposive benefits. For example, several participants mentioned "speaking out on behalf of those [who are] unable" and "supporting those like-minded."

Before concluding, it is important to consider how the presence of identity conflict affects motivation for joining LGBT secular and religious groups. Specifically, how does religious conflict affect motivations related to identity integration? To better understand these relationships, I conduct a series of cross-tabulations focused on the response choices about LGBT identity development. More than helping others or even becoming better educated about the LGBT community, people who experience religious conflict are more likely to join LGBT organizations because they want help coming to terms with their LGBT identity.

Specifically, the results suggest more people than expected who experience conflict between their religious beliefs and LGBT identity report joining all three types of organizations because they want help coming to terms with their sexual orientation or gender identity. Similarly, more people than expected who experience conflict report joining all three types of organizations because they seek or get emotional support (e.g., counseling). Finally, while conflict is also associated with joining social organizations to learn more about the LGBT community, there is no relationship between conflict and joining religious or political organizations for educational purposes. Furthermore, conflict is not significantly related to joining any organization because of solidary benefits (see Online Statistical Appendix XII).

Based on these results, it is apparent that LGBT people join both secular and religious organizations because they provide opportunities to both give and receive physical and emotional support. The most common reasons for joining these groups are purposive or solidary rather than for material benefits that respondents might receive because of their participation. Some LGBT people do seek out collective action because they can get material benefits (including counseling services and help with material needs like financial support). This appears to be most common for participation in political organizations, however. It may be that like Schaffner and Senic (2006), the people I surveyed included tangible policy benefits in their reasoning for joining these organizations.

It is also apparent that many LGBT people join both secular and religious LGBT organizations because of the identity integration support they provide. For many who experience identity conflict, LGBT organizations provide an opportunity to help bridge the perceived gap between their religious and LGBT identities after coming out. In fact, a disproportionate number of those who experience conflict join all forms of LGBT organizations because they seek out help with coming to terms with their LGBT identity. LGBT POC I surveyed join political organizations for a similar purpose. Perhaps because religious and social organizations are generally centered on white LGBT people, political organizations (especially if they are founded on intersectional or queer organizing principles; see DeFilippis and Anderson-Nathe 2017) might offer LGBT POC more space to participate. Although I did not ask about the racial diversity of the LGBT political organizations, it may also be that the results here reflect the importance of political organizations led by and reflective of LGBT POC. Along with providing needed political support, these organizations also offer refuge for religious LGBT POC who struggle with identity conflict.

All LGBT service organizations should recognize that a higher proportion of volunteers are likely from backgrounds that contribute to religious and identity conflict and prepare their service strategies accordingly. Politically, this means that LGBT people who experience conflict might be overrepresented among the membership of LGBT organizations, which may affect the values and service strategies of those organizations. Depending on *how* LGBT people who experience conflict view the role of religion in LGBT culture and community life, it could be that religion is devalued, especially in secular LGBT organizations. This latter scenario could contribute to the perspective of LGBT organizations as nonreligious, despite the significant proportion of LGBT people in the United States who see religion as an important component of LGBT culture and politics. While several national LGBT political organizations have launched initiatives in recent decades targeting religious communities (e.g., Human Rights Campaign's Project One America, National LGBTQ Task Force's Practice Faith, Do Justice program), like the early work of the Council on Religion and the Homosexual, these programs largely focus on educating non-LGBT people.

Conclusion

LGBT people generally view religion as a legitimate component of both LGBT culture and politics. Although LGBT people largely view all religions as unfriendly (or neutral, at best) toward LGBT people, on average, religious LGBT people do not view the LGBT community as hostile toward their faith. In fact, many religious LGBT people are critical of conservative religious traditions that have oppressed LGBT people and express their beliefs that faith should be inclusive, welcoming, and noncompulsory if it is to be a component of LGBT culture.

The data from this chapter show, however, that the experience of LGBT culture is different depending on the social location, especially related to race, of the individual. LGBT POC, especially religious Black and Latinx LGBT people, appear more reticent to join secular LGBT spaces than white LGBT people. In fact, Black LGBT people I surveyed are more likely than others to alter their social behavior in response to religious prejudice. Namely, Black LGBT people I surveyed are more likely to avoid secular LGBT spaces altogether, while LGBT POC, generally, are more likely to report hostility toward religion from other LGBT people.

These differences likely translate into the variation I observe in motivation for joining specific types of groups or organizations. For example, LGBT POC are more likely to report joining LGBT political organizations to get help coming to terms with their LGBT identity and to learn more about the LGBT community. Political spaces, rather than religious or other secular social spaces, are places for LGBT POC to find help and support when racism, religious bigotry, or hetero- and cis-sexism erect barriers to participation in other forms of collective behavior.

Differences in religious socialization also translate into variation in social behavior after coming out. Specifically, LGBT people who experience religious and LGBT identity conflict are more likely to join LGBT organizations (of all types) because they are seeking help coming to terms with their LGBT identity. Taken together with the lessons from the content analysis in this chapter, religious LGBT organizations have an important role to play in post–coming out identity development.

Studies of LGBT religious congregations have found that these religious groups are more likely to develop in areas that exhibit the most need (see Kane 2013), for example, in places where conditions are the "most hostile" to LGBT people. Indeed, the history of LGBT-led congregations and denominations suggest that these institutions were organized precisely because their leaders were expelled from their leadership positions in other denominations and they believed their faith compelled them to act to create a more just society for LGBT people (see Perry 1974). Many of the LGBT people I surveyed shared this sense of social and political obligation. For some, negative experiences with conservative religious institutions led them to advocate for LGBT rights. For others, however, faith led them to act politically as advocates for LGBT rights. These catalytic faith experiences sometimes come with attitudinal (e.g., a shift in policy preferences) as well as behavioral changes. The commonality is that faith inspires their politics. Others share a sense of social and political obligation, but for them faith is a facilitator for action. It is not the direct cause of their activism, but it allows for political expression either by recruiting them to participate or giving them time, space, or resources to engage.

In the next chapter, I take up these perspectives in detail. I situate these experiences within the body of social science generally referred to as political resource theory. I contend that religious LGBT people are more politically active than nonreligious LGBT people. However, the survey data I have collected allow me to test a more specific assertion that religious participation that occurs in the context of LGBT affirmation is even more impactful for political engagement. In the penultimate chapter, I use identity theories to describe how religious affiliation and engagement with affirming faith communities affect political attitudes among LGBT people. I will revisit the detailed account of the benefits LGBT people receive from participating in both secular and religious LGBT organizations in this chapter as I test the assertion that LGBT-affirming religious experiences represent a distinct socializing process from secular LGBT collective behavior.

6

"Faith Without Works Is Hollow"

Religion, Resources, and Political Mobilization

On a hill at the Fair
Stood an old rugged cross
Atop of a parachute frame;
And beneath that old cross
MCC'ers with zest
Sold hot dogs cooked o'er a Coleman flame.

So a "thank you" to all those who helped,
For our booth was the talk of the town;
Thanks for shopping, and set-up, and sales,
And for propping when the wind would blow us down.

—A hymn of thanks to commemorate Portland
Gay Pride Day by Mary Klepser (1979)

For one week in early 1981, a group known as SOS-San Francisco (SOS-SF), an Evangelical Christian organization born out of the 1970s Jesus movement in California, brought a reported 1,500 missionaries into the streets of the city to hang promotional posters, play music, and "witness to them about Christ" (SOS Ministries, n.d.). The *them* SOS-SF seemed to target with their evangelism was San Francisco's large LGBT community. Although this was a time shortly before the first cluster of what would be identified as AIDS cases emerged in California, and even though the group swore no ties with prominent Evangelicals like Anita Bryant or Jerry Falwell,[1] the LGBT community saw the incursion of SOS-SF as an extension of the work of those anti-LGBT personalities because the literature they distributed prominently featured images of San Francisco's gay neighborhood, the Castro, and it was reported that some had "announced their intention to wage war on our community" (A. Bennet et al. 1981).

By mid-1981, Rabbi Allen Bennet of Congregation Sha'ar Zahav, Ken Kammann of Dignity (the LGBT Catholic advocacy group) in the Bay Area, the Reverend Jim N. Dykes of the MCC of San Francisco, and the Reverend Jane

Adams Spahr of MCC and Presbyterians for Lesbian/Gay Concerns (which later merged with More Light Concerns to become More Light Presbyterians) authored a letter to both "legitimate religious leaders and communities" and to the LGBT community addressing the "moral war" that had been declared in their city (A. Bennet et al. 1981). The words of this letter, the mobilization that it and the religious leaders of San Francisco undertook that summer, and the tepid response from some members of the LGBT community demonstrate the strengths and weaknesses of faith as a tool of political mobilization and highlight the contributions of this chapter to the story of LGBT politico-religious activism.

In their letter, a jeremiad against political and social violence toward LGBT people, the authors encourage LGBT people not to lose their faith because of the actions of those opposed to LGBT equality. "We appeal to you," they implore, "not to turn from faith in God due to the manifest corruption of some who dishonor that name God by their words and acts" (A. Bennet et al. 1981, 9). Instead, they view social activism as both the heritage and mission of their faith and at the same time situate their claim to LGBT equality within the American pluralist tradition. In a pledge to the religious opponents of LGBT equality, they offer "our prayers and supplications to God that . . . you may repent from your hatred and turn from your blasphemy of God's name." At the same time, they commit to respect their "divinely given human rights . . . to believe, to assemble, to teach and to persuade free from social or legal interference," but also to "meet your hatred with our love, your fear with our hope, your ignorance with God's wisdom . . . within any and all forums of this still free society" (A. Bennet et al. 1981, 9). At the end of the letter, the authors appear to offer a warning framed in the context of the Nazi pogroms and persecution of LGBT people: "We shall not wait passively for others to destroy us," they resolve. "If your hatred and fear bring forth their vile results, if you do attempt to break our community, drive us into hiding, and hunt us down, then with God's help we shall call upon our people to defend themselves."

In August, SOS-SF intended to hold a large rally; however, on the day of the event, they were heavily outnumbered by counterdemonstrators—many activated through religious networks (O'Loughlin 1981). Congregants from Glide Memorial Church led the counterdemonstrators in song. Rabbi Bennet represented the Council on Religion and the Homosexual at the event, while "San Francisco's answer to the Carmelites of Old," the Sisters of Perpetual Indulgence, a troupe of drag performance artists who conducts charitable work and satirizes religion by dressing as nuns, "shed some of their grace on the event" (O'Loughlin 1981). According to reporting from the time, the "basis for opposition" to SOS-SF and other so-called traditional morality groups was "both political and religious." One counterdemonstrator is quoted as saying explicitly, "They [SOS-SF] try to put a wall between God and gay, as if you can't know God if you're gay" and that similar political activity standing up to religious prejudice could have made a difference for Jews, LGBT people, and other minorities prior to the rise of Nazism (O'Loughlin 1981).

In the end, the SOS-SF rally dispersed after two hours as their permit required. But the rally had been disrupted, counterdemonstrators were mobilized, and more than two thousand people were reminded of the power of religion to influence LGBT politics. As Rabbi Bennet and the other clergy wrote in their letter,

> We must realize now, in the face of our opponents' hatred, that it is not our comfort that is at stake. It is not our prosperity. It is not even just our freedom. Our very lives are at stake. . . . We must use this so-called "moral war" as an opportunity to re-affirm our love for one another and to renew . . . our efforts to free ourselves and our world from every oppression. (A. Bennet et al. 1981, 1)

Not all religious LGBT people agreed with the strategies advocated by Bennet and the LGBT ministers. Whereas the original letter putting the Moral Majority on notice for its violence against LGBT people also left open the possibility for LGBT people to "defend themselves," intimating violence could be met with violence, some religious LGBT people took issue with this particular form of activism and used religious examples to denote a more prudent path for LGBT people to follow. For example, in a response printed in the *More Light Update* of August 1981, the newsletter for Presbyterians for Lesbian and Gay Concerns, a concerned letter writer uses the examples of Mahatma Gandhi and Dr. Martin Luther King Jr., Belfast—then in the midst of the Troubles—and "the Middle East" to postulate that a more faithful response to religiously motivated violence would be for the LGBT community to "outstretch a loving hand to help others instead of holding a nonunderstanding fist ready to strike like a blow against our confused or deceived brother" (Williams 1981).

No matter the response, faith helped shape the context of the debate over LGBT people and rights—informing issue positions but also framing the identity groups involved. Faith also laid the groundwork and defined the rules for political mobilization in response to perceived threats. Finally, as the quote at the beginning of this chapter illustrates (along with findings from the previous chapter), faith communities also give people the opportunity and resources to act collectively, for example, by staffing a booth at the local Pride festival or buying hotdogs to support a local religious or political organization. These are common features of religion in American politics. The focus of this chapter is to apply the existing theories of religious resources and mobilization to LGBT religious experiences and form a picture of how faith both frames political issues and politically mobilizes LGBT people.

Using data from my survey of LGBT people, in this chapter I will show religion, especially affirming religiosity, motivates political behavior. In the next chapter, I show the effects of religion on LGBT people's political attitudes suggests that religious socialization, even in affirming environments, has a different—more conservative—effect than socialization in secular LGBT communities. In both cases (i.e., political activism and attitudes), I demonstrate that religious practice, belief, and religious changes associated with coming out are powerful influences on LGBT politics.

Yet the effects of religiosity extend beyond issues and behaviors that directly affect LGBT identity. Attending Pride events and supporting LGBT rights policies, but also voting, running for office, and beliefs about guns, immigration, and the role of government, are all affected by religiosity. In this and the next chapter, I show that the effect of religiosity can be both direct and indirect. Sometimes, as with political participation, the effect of frequent religious participation and the affirming nature of the religious community is direct; however, as with political attitudes, the cultivation of belief systems that value LGBT identity is more important than even frequent religious participation. In this way, the effect of affirming participation can also be transmitted by cultivating cognitive resources that value LGBT identity.

While the United States is remarkable for its religious pluralism, de jure discrimination against non-Christian (and minority Christian) faith traditions remains a dominant theme of the American politico-religious experience, as has the use of religion to justify discrimination on the basis of other non-normative identities. Despite this, a myriad of religious beliefs and practices persist in the United States (Chaves 2011).

While religious identity is important, it is the practice of religion that has the most profound consequences for American political behavior. Two theories, political resource and resource mobilization, based in political science and sociology have primarily guided inquiry into the effect of religiosity on political behavior within the American pluralist context (McCarthy and Zald 1977; Verba, Schlozman, and Brady 1995). Numerous studies of multiple faith traditions using these theoretical frameworks suggest that participation in religious practices allows for the accrual of skills and resources that easily translate into secular political activity. Not only that, but contact with and participation in religious institutions help frame political debates and often serve as recruitment structures for particular political positions (Djupe and Grant 2001; Fetner 2008; Harris 1999).

Religious pluralism also fosters denominationalism, or the cultivation of sects and congregational variation within broader religious traditions

(Greeley 1972). Importantly for political behavior, these denominations often serve as the foundation for social identity development (Ammerman 1987). Religious organizations serve as agents of socialization that help congregants define and contextualize their lives and experiences in relation to the broader society. Religious traditions also establish the boundaries of identity, determining who is or is not accepted as a group member. Because each represents distinct, but intersecting, social identities, sexuality, gender, and race also interact with religiosity in important ways that contribute to variation in political behavior. Sometimes, religion reinforces cultural or ethnic distinctiveness (Chen and Jeung 2012); however, it may also be used to exclude those who do not conform to the tradition's paradigm of morality, such as LGBT people (Taylor and Snowdon 2014).

Because of this heteronormative construction of religiosity, LGBT people have been excluded from behavioral theories of religion and politics, while religious LGBT people have been excluded from behavioral theories of LGBT politics. In the following sections, I describe in detail the theoretical frameworks that structure the present inquiry into LGBT politico-religious mobilization. I then return to analyses of survey data to demonstrate how faith, particularly religious affirmation, affects the political activism of LGBT people based on the model I described at the end of Chapter 4. I conclude the next chapter with a reevaluation of that model and update it based on the findings I present in this chapter.

Religion as Political Resource

Although some early behavioral scientists acknowledged religion as an important cultural experience that contextualizes politics, it was not until the 1980s that social and political behavioralists began to appreciate the value of religion as an explanatory variable within the American political context (Wald and Wilcox 2006; Wald, Kellstedt, and Leege 1993; Wald, Silverman, and Fridy 2005). The lack of attention was variably contributed to doctrinal complexity, unfamiliarity with the subject matter, and outright prejudice; however, there has since developed a distinguished body of literature that treats the subject of religiosity as a legitimate influence on political outcomes (Jelen 1998; Woodberry and Smith 1998).

The complex nature of religious experience can quickly confound quantitative researchers, and social scientists have not always been careful to accurately conceptualize and model religious phenomena (Woodberry and Smith 1998). In political science, religiosity has been shown to affect political outcomes differently depending on how religiosity is measured. In their study of American political behavior, for example, Wald, Kellstedt, and Leege (1993, 121) are careful to disentangle "church involvement" from other aspects of religiosity, including "religious belief, denominationalism, private acts of devotion, and the salience of religious identity." Furthermore, political behavior is a broad concept that encompasses numerous electoral and non-electoral activities, including voting, donating money, volunteering, and protesting. Other behaviors may implicate affective or cognitive processes, such as attitudes toward specific policies or candidates and political knowledge. While institutional engagement may predict political participation, specific religious beliefs or denominational affiliations may better account for the relationship between religiosity and political attitudes (Gay and Ellison 1993).

The political effects of religion are often modeled in this way—that is, as a function of religious activity and/or religious identity. In political science, behavioral research has primarily focused on the application of two theoretical frames to interrogate and explain how religion influences the political attitudes and behaviors of adherents: political resource and identity theories. Each operates under heterosexist assumptions about the relationship between religiosity and sexuality that are complicated by the study of religious LGBT people. Specifically, each theory assumes identity congruence and integration (i.e., that one believes they are accepted by their faith and that their faith is not a source of internalized identity conflict).

As sociology embraced religious studies before political science did, it is intuitive that the discipline's primary frame for understanding religious effects on politics is derived from sociological theory (Wald and Wilcox 2006; Wald, Silverman, and Fridy 2005). One of the most influential theories with implications for political science is McCarthy and Zald's (1973) resource mobilization theory. Derived from the rich social movement theory tradition, resource mobilization theory attempts to model collective political behavior by examining the factors necessary for social movement organization success (McCarthy and Zald 1977; Tarrow 1998; Tilly 1978; Wald, Silverman, and Fridy 2005).

Building on Olson (1965), McCarthy and Zald (1973; 1977) argue that professional social movement organizations are more likely to overcome the collective action problem and become effective agents of political and social change. Professionalized organizations are more successful because of the resources that flow between the organizations and their constituents. According to McCarthy and Zald (1973; 1977), collective identity alone is not enough to ensure that social movements succeed. An organization's issues are more likely to appear on the national political agenda and be acted on when organizations have access to economic resources and professional networks. Further, in an application of the resource mobilization theory to local political contexts, Williams and Demerath (1991) analyze religious and political tensions in Springfield, Massachusetts. In this case, the authors recognize the "moral authority" that religious organizations "command" as a resource in political debates over local economic development policies. Stemming from an American "separation ethos" that placed religious organizations outside of the "world of interests," this moral authority helped local religious organizations garner media attention and force issues onto the political agenda, the authors argue (Williams and Demerath 1991, 425).

While most sociological studies focus on collective action and social movement mobilization, the resource paradigm has been adapted to the study of individual political behavior in the field of political science. Verba and Nie (1972, 13), for example, postulate the "standard socioeconomic model of participation." This model suggests individual economic factors—notably one's job, education, and income—are the most important determinants of political participation. Those with more resources are better equipped to overcome the informational, temporal, and economic barriers to political engagement. In this model, disposable time is just as important as disposable income. The schedule flexibility afforded to the upper-middle class and affluent, as well as the financial stability, result in more opportunities to be politically active.

Verba, Schlozman, and Brady (1995) build on this resource-based approach to articulate their "civic volunteerism model" of political participation (see also Brady, Verba, and Schlozman 1995). This important work further applied the resource model to political participation, but also to American social and religious activity. While emphasizing economic resources, it is their assertion that "people do not" participate in politics either "because they can't; because they don't want to; or because nobody asked" (Verba, Schlozman, and Brady 1995, 269). Referencing social movement theory, the study concludes political participation is a function of individual resources, but also of organizational "engagement and recruitment" (Verba, Schlozman, and Brady 1995, 269).

Voice and Equality advanced the study of political behavior not by reexamining the resource paradigm but by suggesting that individuals who engage in civic, social, and religious organizations accrue resources that support or motivate political activity. For the study of religion and politics, Verba, Schlozman, and Brady (1995) provide a framework for understanding how religious activity affects political behavior (see also Cassel 1999; Pollock 1982).

Religiosity and the Development of Civic Skills

According to Verba, Schlozman, and Brady (1995, 204), individuals who engage in "voluntary organizations and churches" accrue "civic skills" that increase both the likelihood of participating in politics as well as overall feelings of political efficacy. Verba, Schlozman, and Brady (1995, 204) define civic skills as "the communications and organizational abilities that allow citizens to use time and money effectively in political life." Such skills include effective verbal and written communication as well as organizational abilities. The implications for religious participation are clear. Active involvement in a voluntary religious organization likely allows opportunities to communicate with other parishioners (or in Evangelical denominations with nonbelievers), plan or organize meetings and events, or otherwise develop skills that improve communication and organizational abilities. In a democratic political system founded on individual participation, these skills translate into secular work like political organizing.

In addition to civic skills, other studies suggest participation in organized religious activity fosters civil values such as a sense of civic duty and/or obligation (Macaluso and Wanat 1979). From this perspective, participation in "formal" religious organizations "sanctifies" civil obligations and conveys to congregants a sense of obligation to "assume the duties of citizenship in return for the benefits it bestows" (Macaluso and Wanat 1979, 160). Importantly for a broad theory of religious participation and political engagement, the hypothesized relationship between religious activity, civic obligations, and political participation extends beyond Christian denominations. In their study of data collected from the Muslim American Public Opinion Survey, Dana, Barreto, and Oskooii (2011), for example, find Muslims who regularly attend mosques are more likely to "identify as American Muslims rather than by national origin," believing mosques "encourage Muslims to integrate into U.S. society." Furthermore, Dana Barreto, and Oskooii (2011) find a positive relationship between Muslim religiosity and political participation (see also Ayers and Hofstetter 2008). Across religious traditions, throughout the course of one's life, religious participation in America places individuals in "a milieu" of people and messages supportive of civic duty that foster the value in congregants (Macaluso and Wanat 1979, 161).

Along with civic values, other studies suggest a relationship between church attendance and another cognitive resource: political efficacy (Houghland and Christenson 1983). External political efficacy generally refers to "the belief that the social and political system will be responsive to change efforts," while internal efficacy refers to the belief that one is capable of understanding politics and successfully contributing to change efforts (Thomas et al. 2017, 214). Theories of the relationship between religion, efficacy, and political behavior suggest efficacy is a mediating variable between religiosity and participation. That is, efficacy is cultivated by social interactions that occur in religious settings, which, in turn, motivates political activity (see Schwadel et al. 2016). As with civic skills, religious participation is thought to build efficacy as congregants are asked to take part in various activities that allow them to see the benefit of their participation within their communities. Because efficacy is a by-product of social capital, it is not surprising that it is more pronounced among individuals with social networks that incorporate numerous co-religionists (Schwadel et al. 2016). Recent research suggests the mobilizing power of religious participation comes through recruitment more so than the cultivation of civic skills (Djupe and Gilbert 2006; Djupe and Grant 2001). At the very least, the distribution of civic skills often reflects structural barriers to religious participation, such as heterosexism or racism (Friesen and Djupe 2017).

Religiosity and Political Recruitment

Although Djupe and Grant (2001) question the direct relationship between civic skills acquired through religious participation and political activism, they nevertheless recognize the important role of religious organizations in recruitment. That is, in addition to civic skills, religious organizations serve as mobilizing structures, encouraging political participation among members. In this way, religious organizations also respond to "nobody asked" in reference to why people typically do not engage in political activity (Verba, Schlozman, and Brady 1995, 269).

In the United States, religious and nonprofit organizations designated as tax-exempt under the Internal Revenue Code are prohibited from engaging in certain explicit kinds of political activity—directly contributing money or endorsing a single political candidate, for example. These organizations may still serve as political recruitment structures, however, by providing information or opportunities for congregants to engage with the community or political leaders and by framing political events (Chaves 2004; Gamson 1992).

Furthermore, some denominations value political engagement more than others, and different forms of social and political activism are generally related to variations in theology (Beyerlein and Chaves 2003; Chaves 2004; Kellstedt and Smidt 1993). In addition, research has shown recruitment is more likely to occur in congregations where political activism is characteristic of the broader community's culture (Brown and Brown 2003; Cavendish 2002). Even with these caveats, American political history is replete with examples of religious organizations recruiting or cultivating political activists. While I recounted one such example at the beginning of this chapter, an additional example helps illustrate political resource and identity theories while also contextualizing the development of LGBT politico-religious activism.

Recruitment: Activating the Grassroots Religious Right

I reviewed some of the Religious Right's history in Chapter 1, but it is important to recognize that in addition to policy-based appeals (e.g., encouraging congregants to use their religious beliefs to inform policy preferences), the Religious Right often engaged in a number of specific strategies to recruit both voters and candidates primarily through local networks (Green et al. 1996). Wilcox and Sigelman's (2001) study of voting guides, for example, demonstrates that when electoral information is made available in a place of worship before an election and when religious groups encourage people to vote, their intended purpose was often realized. Specifically, white Evangelicals and Black Protestants were more likely to receive this form of recruitment contact and were more likely to be politically active than their religious peers. While recruitment by religious institutions seems to augment turnout, other literature suggests local, unique efforts, rather than broad national mobilization strategies, may be a better explanation for changes in turnout among Evangelical Christians in the 1990s and 2000s (see Claassen and Povtak 2010).

In this vein, Bullock and Grant (1995) describe how conservative Christian candidates for public office relied on fellow congregants as campaign workers and also how ministers were recruited to stand for election in the 1994 congressional midterms in Georgia. Bullock and Grant (1995) suggest both that religious institutions help recruit and support candidates through volunteerism and that local conservative Christian institutions serve as powerful deterrents to potential candidates who do not share the values of the dominant religious institutions in their communities (for similar effects of the development of LGBT identity, see Barton 2012 or review Chapter 3 and Chapter 4). Guth (1996, 316) also recognize that clergy can enhance the "political relevance of religion" among Evangelical congregants by highlighting elections and particular political issues, such as abortion, poverty, and even defense policy, in their sermons.

Finally, many of the leaders of the Religious Right came to power through the novel use of technology, especially cable and satellite television. Jerry Falwell, a cofounder of the Moral Majority, broadcast services from the Thomas Road Baptist Church in Lynchburg, Virginia, to millions of American homes weekly. Many others soon followed, using broadcast media and novel distribution methods such as direct mail campaigns, whose recipients were largely drawn from church membership rolls across the country (Fetner 2008).

Many studies of the Religious Right note the mobilizing effect of religious media consumption on conservative Christians. While there is also a saturation effect that limits the utility of these recruitment methods, research shows religious organizations can successfully use emerging and existing mass communications technologies to recruit and politically activate members (see Fetner 2008; Guth et al. 1996; Jelen and Wilcox 1993). Notably, some research suggests that rather than "supplant" traditional religious participation, religious media consumption "supplements" the effects of traditional religious participation on political attitudes and behavior, especially among Evangelical denominations (Guth 1996).

Taken together, the efforts of national religious organizations and local conservative Evangelical Protestant congregations contributed to the mobilization of religious congregants across the country throughout the 1970s to the first decade of the twenty-first century. Further, the work of these groups helped crystallize a countermovement to the burgeoning LGBT rights movement built on a social identity of shared conservative religious convictions that can be reinforced through religious participation. In this way, religious organizations not only recruit political participants and provide civic and organizational skills to help navigate secular political institutions but also provide a social identity that helps consistently frame political events and cognitive skills that enhance congregants' ability to participate in complex political processes.

How do these lessons apply to LGBT politics? Before discussing the results from analyses of survey data, it is important to review theories of LGBT politics that reinforce the important role of socialization and identity-based organizations in defining group membership, cultivating cognitive resources, and political recruitment.

LGBT Politics: Activism and Liberalism

LGBT people are one of the most politically liberal and politically active groups in American politics (Cravens 2020). Several theories have attempted to explain why LGBT people are so distinct in their political endeavors compared to heterosexual and cisgender people. The most common explanations are selection, conversion, and, similarly, embeddedness (see Cravens 2020 for a more detailed explanation of each). While there are distinctions between the theories, they are all fundamentally arguments in favor of political socialization theory. That is, each theory argues that socializing events, whether one's childhood upbringing (selection) or relationship with LGBT people and organizations after coming out (conversion and embeddedness), result in more liberal political beliefs because LGBT people who are raised in accepting environments and/or who have close connections with LGBT people after coming out know more about the marginalized status of LGBT people in society and hold political positions that favor social and civil equality. Furthermore, supportive networks place LGBT people in communication with movement elites who help frame issues, while social, political, and, potentially, religious organizations help LGBT people engage politically on behalf of their preferred political outcome or candidate.

According to these theories, not only should LGBT people have distinctive political behavior as compared to non-LGBT people, but, as I explained with religion in Chapter 3, coming out should be an inflection point, after which political behavior changes for a substantial proportion of LGBT people. An analysis of the survey data I collected lends some support to this notion. Specifically, I asked survey participants how their political beliefs, interest in politics, and political activism changed after they came out. Fewer than one in ten reported becoming more conservative (5%), less interested in politics (6%), or less politically active (3%) after coming out. On the other hand, between one-quarter and one-third reported becoming more liberal (29%), more interested in politics (34%), or more politically active (25%) after coming out. Like the previous analysis of religiosity, however, it is obvious that a majority of LGBT people do not experience any political changes after coming out as LGBT. These findings are similar to other studies of LGBT political changes after coming out (see Egan, Edelman, and Sherrill 2008).

While interesting, and consistent with the idea that LGBT people embed within liberal political networks after coming out that ultimately affect their political attitudes and behaviors, what the underlying theories do not specify is whether or not religious socialization—either before or after coming out—is a process distinct from secular socialization. Surprisingly, few quantitative studies of LGBT political behavior have accounted for these religious effects (see Cravens 2018; 2021 as examples). To be clear about the potential sources and effects of LGBT political attitudes and behavior, it is important to disentangle religious and secular socializing experiences and examine the effect of religious socialization before and after coming out (as I have done to this point). I am also interested in any potential variation between affirming and nonaffirming religiosity. Specifically, while religiosity might be a source of political resources and identity development and maintenance, affirming religiosity offers many of the same identity-based benefits for LGBT people that socialization in secular LGBT organizations might also offer. In short, then, I am curious if secular and religious socialization have similar mobilization and identity cultivation effects on LGBT politics or if those benefits only accrue to LGBT people whose religion affirms their LGBT identity and religiosity. I begin with a broader evaluation of political resource theory as it applies to LGBT religious experiences. In the next chapter, I delineate these experiences (i.e., secular vs. religious) and examine their effects on measures of both political attitudes and activism.

How LGBT People Participate in Politics

Before examining specific relationships, it is important to describe the ways the LGBT people I surveyed engage in politics and/or political activism. That is because the various forms of political engagement come with different barriers to entry. It may be relatively easier to attend a Pride rally than to run for political office, for example. Resources and religious identities might, therefore, be more important to some behaviors than others. Recognizing this variation, I asked the survey participants a series of questions about how they engage in politics and political activism. Some behaviors, like attending a Pride event, implicate, specifically, their LGBT identity. Others, like writing letters or voting, may not directly implicate LGBT identity, but identity may still be a motivating factor. By examining such a variety of behavior, it is possible to ascertain the boundary conditions that define when and how religious socialization, belief, identity, and participation affect politics and political activism within the group.

Table 6.1 shows how frequently survey participants engage in each of six solidary activities. Three behaviors are associated with financial activism and three behaviors are associated with volunteerism. While most of the people I surveyed have not given to a politician or political organization because they support LGBT rights, the majority do engage in other forms of financial activism, like boycotts or patronage, based on a company's position on LGBT rights. Similarly, most of the people I surveyed do not participate in voluntary social organizations or attend rallies; however, a majority attend LGBT Pride events relatively frequently.

Table 6.2 shows how frequently survey participants engage in seven electoral behaviors or political behaviors directly related to electoral politics. Similar to Table 6.1, in most cases, the people I surveyed do not frequently engage in behavior that requires additional time or money, such as working for a political campaign, attending political rallies, contacting elected offi-

TABLE 6.1 FREQUENCY OF SOLIDARY POLITICAL ACTIVISM				
	Never (%)	Rarely	Sometimes	Often
Bought a certain product or service because the company that provides it is supportive of LGBT rights	21	16	46	15
Decided NOT to buy a certain product or service because the company that provides it is not supportive of LGBT rights	27	13	31	26
Donated money to politicians or political organizations because they are supportive of LGBT rights	53	13	21	11
Attended a rally or march in support of LGBT rights	45	18	24	11
Attended an LGBT Pride event	32	15	31	21
Attended religious organizations for LGBT people	64	15	14	6
Participated in an LGBT social club or organization	45	16	27	10

Sources: Author data available from Cravens (2022). Last two items are also discussed in Chapter 5.
Notes: Row percentages do not sum to 100% due to rounding. $N = 1,100$.

TABLE 6.2 FREQUENCY OF PARTICIPATION IN ELECTORAL POLITICS				
	Never (%)	Rarely	Sometimes	Often
Vote in a general election	14	15	7	63
Attempt to persuade others to vote for a candidate or party	36	23	24	15
Attend political events or rallies	57	15	22	5
Work or volunteer for a political campaign	70	10	15	4
Donate money to political organizations or candidates	61	16	16	5
Contact elected officials to express my opinions	55	19	17	7
Run for political office	93	2	3	1
Source: Author data available from Cravens (2022). Notes: Row percentages do not sum to 100% due to rounding. N = 1,100.				

cials, or running for office. However, a majority of the people I surveyed vote frequently and attempt to persuade others to vote for a particular candidate or party, on occasion.

These are not exhaustive lists of political behaviors; however, they do give a reasonable indication of the types of voluntary social, political, religious, monetary, and electoral behaviors that LGBT people undertake. In the following sections, I examine the relationship between these behaviors and the measures of socialization I have previously identified. I first examine how socialization prior to coming out is related to political behavior. Then, I examine how contemporary religiosity effects political activism after controlling for important cofounding variables like outness and the strength of LGBT identity.

Faith, Socialization, and Political Participation

How do social and religious experiences before coming out affect the political behavior of LGBT people later in life? Notably, I test two different forms of political activism: activism that is explicitly connected to LGBT identity and activism that is not. It is reasonable, then, to expect two different patterns of relationships. Namely, political activism that is explicitly connected to LGBT identity is more likely to be affected by socializing messages about LGBT people than electoral activism. If this is the case, it is reasonable to assume that positive socialization related to LGBT identity likely makes it easier to engage in activism on behalf of that identity later in life. However, as I describe in Chapter 3, at the same time LGBT people are receiving messages about LGBT identity, religious socialization may also occur. When religious socialization is also the source of messages about LGBT people, whether positive or negative, it can significantly affect LGBT identity development. But, it is also reasonable to expect that the benefits of positive messages about LGBT people for political activism will extend across religious groups in the study.

To test these assumptions, I model a series of regression estimations focusing on the two forms of political activism. As I detail in Online Statistical Appendix XII, I construct two normalized indexes of political activism from the responses to the statements in Table 6.1 and Table 6.2. (All appendixes are available via Harvard Dataverse at https://doi.org/10.7910/DVN /M87Q1V; for additional citation information see Cravens 2022b.) One index measures LGBT activism (e.g., how frequently the survey participant takes part in various activities related to LGBT identity, like attending Pride, marching, joining clubs), and one index measures electoral activism (e.g., how frequently the survey participant takes part in various activities related to electoral politics like voting, campaigning, contacting elected officials). Because these are scale measures, I use regression estimation to construct four equations that model the relationships with key independent variables. I control for the same independent variables as I do when modeling the effects of socialization on the importance of LGBT identity in Chapter 3. The full models are shown in Online Statistical Appendix XII.

The results provide several important insights. First, positive socialization in the form of messages about LGBT people, alone, does not appear to affect either form of political activism. However, consistent with the political resource model, positive socialization in concert with specific faith traditions (i.e., measured through an interaction term) is associated with both forms of political activism that I measure. Survey participants who identify as "born again" prior to coming out are, on average, about 32% less politically active than those who did not identify as "born again." However, for each additional positive source of information about LGBT people someone raised "born again" received, their activism is predicted to increase by about 13%. LGBT people who identified as "born again" before coming out are less likely to engage in all forms of LGBT political activism except attending religious groups for LGBT people. They are also less likely to vote and attend political rallies. However, the trend reverses in every case for those who received positive social messages about LGBT people before coming out. In short, while those who were raised "born again" might be less likely to engage in LGBT and electoral activism after coming out, positive pre–coming out socializing experiences can, potentially, be enough to reverse this trend.

Notably, this pattern is repeated for electoral activism among those who identified as Catholic or with no particular religion before coming out. The LGBT people I surveyed who were raised Catholic are less likely to attempt to persuade others to vote for a candidate or party, less likely to donate money to political causes, and less likely to contact elected officials, compared to

Protestants. Those who identified as nothing in particular before coming out are less likely to vote and contact elected officials. However, receiving positive social messages about LGBT people before coming out seems to reverse these trends (see Statistical Appendix XII).

Second, the effects on political participation of specific religious socializing events like attending a religious school and undergoing a religious rite are mixed. On average, the LGBT people I surveyed who participated in a religious rite as a child are more likely to engage in economic boycotts and more likely to vote. Attending a religious school appears to have no significant relationship to other forms of political activism, however. Similar to the positive effect of LGBT social messages just described, experiencing positive social messages about LGBT people prior to coming out is also associated with an increased likelihood of political participation among both those who did and those who did not undergo a religious rite. The positive effects, however, are concentrated among those who are already the most politically active. That is, regardless of whether or not one underwent a religious rite, positive social messages are associated with increased political activity among the survey participants who "sometimes" or "often" vote or engage in economic boycotts but not among those who "never" or "rarely" participate in these activities.

What does this mean? First, the results appear to support the resource hypothesis. Undergoing a religious rite suggests a person has committed to religious education and is established within a religious community. The resource hypothesis asserts these connections are determinants of political participation, and, indeed, this appears to be the case among the LGBT people I surveyed. Second, the results also suggest positive socializing messages about LGBT people alone are not enough to affect political activism; however, positive socializing messages about LGBT people do appear to mediate the effects of religious socialization on both LGBT identity development and political activism. When the effects of religious socialization are negative, such as when LGBT people develop identity conflict, for example, positive socializing messages appear to attenuate the effects. When the effects of religious socialization are positive, such as when LGBT people who undergo a religious rite are also more likely to vote, positive socializing messages appear to augment the effects—in this case, by increasing the likelihood that those who did not accrue religious resources in their youth participate in politics as much as those who did benefit from a religious upbringing.

A third important insight from the results is that, as with LGBT identity, coming out later is associated with decreased LGBT activism. That is, LGBT people who come out later are less likely to engage in every measure of solidary activism I identify. There is no similar blanket effect on electoral activism; however, coming out later is associated with a decreased likelihood of running for political office. As I describe in Chapter 3, this is likely a consequence of religious socialization that sets boundary conditions on the importance of LGBT identity. That is, LGBT people who come out later have less time to develop an independent LGBT identity and feel closer connections to communities other than those centering LGBT people. For LGBT people who were religious before coming out, their religious community, rather than the LGBT community, likely retains importance after they come out. As I show in the next chapter, this also has important effects on the political attitudes of LGBT people.

Similarly, changing religious affiliations after coming out is associated with an increase in LGBT activism but appears to have no relationship to electoral activism. This lends further evidence to the claim that the LGBT people I surveyed who did switch their religious affiliation after coming out did so in order to support their LGBT identity development. That change, then, makes it more likely that they engage in LGBT activism. The results, however, show this relationship extends to participation in economic boycotts but not more visible forms of LGBT political activism such as attending political rallies or Pride events. Furthermore, changing religious affiliations after coming out appears to sacrifice an important political resource—voting. Some of the LGBT people I surveyed who changed their religious affiliation after coming out are less likely to vote than those who did not change their religious affiliation. Specifically, a change in religious affiliation after coming out is associated with about a 10% decrease in the likelihood of voting among those who vote most frequently.

This leads to an important question that I address in the next section. Namely, must LGBT people sacrifice the positive participatory benefits of religion when they change their religious affiliation after coming out? Furthermore, do religious experiences after coming out exert similar socializing effects on political behavior as positive messages received prior to coming out? Finally, are the religious effects on political activism different for those who participate in affirming religious communities?

Contemporary Religion and Political Participation

In Chapters 3 and 4, I detail models predicting the relationships among socialization before coming out, religious socialization after coming out, and political activism. Specifically, I show that receiving positive social messages about LGBT people before coming out is associated with increased importance of LGBT identity later in life. In Figure 4.4 (Chapter 4), I hypothesize that importance of LGBT identity will be associated with political participation (or activism) after coming out. I also hypothesize that regardless of one's social environment before coming out, affirming religious experiences after coming out will also be associated with political activism, just as it is associated with importance of LGBT identity.

To test these hypotheses, I again model political activism among the LGBT people I surveyed (see Online Statistical Appendix XIII). Figure 6.1 shows the relationship between the primary independent variables of interest and LGBT activism. In the figure, the names of coefficients used in the model are on the y-axis and the circles represent the point estimates for each coefficient. That is, the estimated value of the LGBT activism index given the average value of the coefficient and holding all other variables in the model at their mean values. The horizontal lines radiating from each circle represent the 99% (darker) and 95% (lighter) confidence interval for each point estimate. If the confidence interval crosses the vertical line, then the effect of the variable on LGBT activism is not statistically significant. The placement of the point estimate on either side of the vertical line shows whether the effect of the variable is positive or negative—that is, whether there is a positive or negative relationship between the variable and LGBT activism.

As the figure shows, both religiosity and religious affirmation have a positive relationship with LGBT activism, as does the belief that being LGBT is not a sin. Specifically, each additional religious behavior that the LGBT peo-

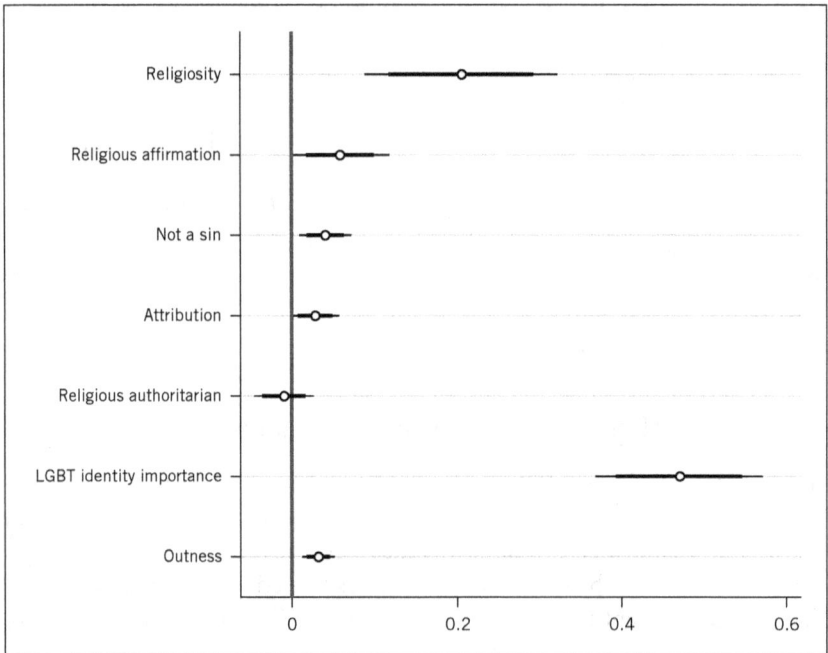

Figure 6.1 Religious and Identity Effects on LGBT Activism. *n* = 694. (*Figures based on Model 2 in Statistical Appendix XIII; 95% and 99% confidence levels shown.*)

ple I surveyed engage in (e.g., praying *and* attending religious services) is associated with about a 20% increase in the LGBT activism index. In addition, religious affirmation has an independent positive effect on LGBT activism, although the magnitude is smaller (a one-unit increase on the affirmation index is associated with about a 2% increase on the LGBT activism index). The more affirming an LGBT person's spiritual community, then, the more likely the person is to participate in solidary activism.

Importantly, the alternate regression model in Online Statistical Appendix XIII estimated with interaction terms shows that religiosity and religious affirmation have their own independent positive effects on LGBT activism. That is, the effect of one does not vary in relation to the effect of the other. In other words, the benefit of religiosity to LGBT activism is not contingent on affirmation from one's spiritual community. Nor is the benefit of affirmation to LGBT activism contingent on one's religiosity. To put it simply, being part of an affirming religious community has its own independent, positive effect on LGBT activism. Religiosity and religious affirmation, then, are both important spiritual factors that augment LGBT activism. But, are the benefits of affirming religious communities limited to LGBT activism?

To answer this question, Figure 6.2 shows the interactive effect of religiosity and religious affirmation on the probability that a survey participant

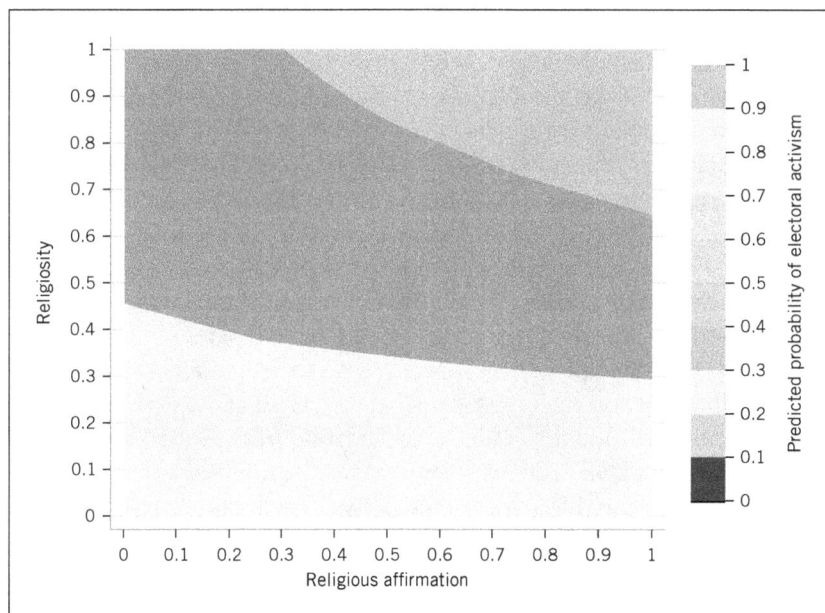

Figure 6.2 Effect of Affirming Religiosity on Electoral Activism. *n* = 694. (*Figures based on Model 4 in Statistical Appendix XIII.*)

frequently engages in the variety of behaviors measured by the electoral activism index. The figure is constructed from the regression equation modeled in Online Statistical Appendix XIII (Model 4) and controls for other important demographic, religious, and LGBT identity measures. The x-axis represents values on the religious affirmation index and the y-axis represents values on the religiosity index. As the key on the right of the figure shows, the various shades represent predicted probabilities of electoral activism given specific values on each index.

As the figure shows, across the range of possible values on the religious affirmation index, there is no change in the probability of electoral activism. That is, the probability of participating in electoral politics stays constant at pr(activism) = .2 regardless of the value of the religious affirmation index alone. Unlike the relationship with LGBT activism, religious affirmation has no independent effect on electoral activism. Religiosity, however, does have an independent positive effect on electoral activism. Namely, an increase from the lowest to the highest value on the religiosity index is associated with about a 10% increase in the probability of engaging in electoral activism (pr(activism) = .3). The interactive relationship between religiosity and religious affirmation is depicted by the change in probability from the bottom left corner of the figure to the top right corner of the figure. Namely, a change from the lowest to the highest possible value on both indexes is associated with about a 20% increase in the probability of engaging in electoral activism.

Taken together, the results appear to answer one of the central questions of this study. Namely, the benefits of religiosity to LGBT activism accrue equally to religious LGBT people regardless of how affirming their individual religious denomination or congregation is. However, the benefits of religiosity to electoral activism appear to accrue more to religious LGBT people embedded in affirming religious communities. The results also suggest important nuances to this statement that I will expound in the next section, but, for now, we are left with the question "Why?" Why is the positive relationship between religious affirmation and electoral activism conveyed (or mediated) through religiosity but the same cannot be said for LGBT activism?

Results from the qualitative survey responses help make sense of these findings and offer some potential explanations. First, LGBT activism directly implicates LGBT identity, and so participation in a spiritual community that centers one's LGBT identity likely makes the kinds of activities represented in the LGBT activism index more salient. Furthermore, religious communities that center and affirm LGBT identity are also more likely to offer opportunities to participate in such events. Indeed, recall from Chapter 5, when asked to reflect on the relationship between their religious beliefs and politics, several survey participants representing Protestantism, Catholicism, and Judaism mentioned that their congregations participate in their local

Pride celebrations by sponsoring a booth or marching in the local parade. Other LGBT people I surveyed mentioned that their religious community encouraged them to engage in electoral activism, like corresponding with elected officials, but even then, this recruitment often occurred in the context of campaigns for specific LGBT legislation. In these instances, electoral activism appears to be an externality that comes about as the result of LGBT-specific political mobilization in affirming spiritual environments.

Second, the findings do not suggest that affirmation is unimportant to electoral activism. On the contrary, the results suggest affirmation is activated through private and public devotion. That is, affirmation alone does not provide the resources necessary to politically mobilize. It likely lays the foundation for action, but political mobilization takes additional work. In this case, frequent attendance and regular religious participation help put the principles of one's faith into practice. Recall the response of a gay man who was raised and currently identifies as Roman Catholic: "It is my faith that has molded my sense of justice, social welfare, peace. Who I vote for, which issues I support are decided by the moral code I have developed over the years. . . . Faith without works is hollow."

The relationships depicted in Figures 6.1 and 6.2 suggest broad associations between religiosity, religious affirmation, and political activism. The detailed regression models in Online Statistical Appendix XIII bear out these relationships across all the measures of political activism. Namely, the benefits of religious affirmation for political activism are most pronounced for political activities that directly implicate LGBT identity, including attending rallies and Pride events, joining LGBT religious organizations, and donating money to LGBT organizations. Religious affirmation also has a positive relationship with campaigning for political candidates. The benefits of religiosity, and the multiplicative benefits of religiosity and affirmation, are also broadly applicable. Specifically, in only four out of fourteen political behaviors I measure—participating in economic boycotts for LGBT causes, attending LGBT rallies, and attempting to persuade others to vote for a candidate—religiosity is not associated with participation. In all other cases, including voting and running for office, religiosity is associated with increased political activism among LGBT people.

Reducing the Barrier for Entry

One of the nuances to this story of religious mobilization is the fact that much of the predicted change in political activism occurs among the least politically active people I surveyed. That is, when religiosity and affirmation are significantly related to political activism, the effect is often concentrated among those who say they "never" participate. For example, Figure 6.3 shows

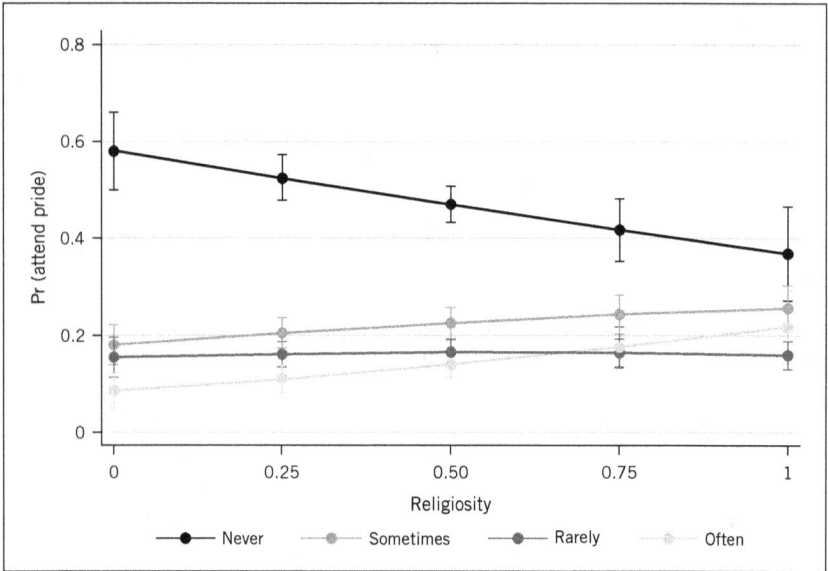

Figure 6.3 Effect of Religiosity on Participation in LGBT Pride Events. *n* = 694.
(*Figure based on ordered probit regression estimation with pride attendance as dependent variable. Full model is shown in Statistical Appendix XIII; 95% confidence levels are shown.*)

the effect of religiosity on frequency of Pride event attendance. Each circle represents a point estimate, or the predicted value of the participation variable (attending Pride) given increasing values on the religiosity index. The four lines represent the four potential responses to the question.

The three lines at the bottom of the figure represent the likelihood that a survey participant reports attending an LGBT Pride event "rarely," "sometimes," or "often." As the figure shows, the slope of the lines indicates a positive relationship between religiosity and the probability of attending Pride events rarely, sometimes, or often. The line at the top of the figure, however, shows a clear negative relationship. As the figure shows, this line represents the probability of "never" participating in LGBT Pride events. The relationship can be interpreted to mean, then, that as religiosity increases, the probability of never attending Pride events decreases. For clarity, increasing values on the religiosity index from the lowest to highest possible values is associated with about a 10% increase in the probability of rarely, sometimes, or often attending an LGBT Pride event. However, the same increase in religiosity is associated with about a 20% decrease in the probability of never attending an LGBT Pride event.

For this, and almost all other measures of activism, the results suggest that religiosity offers a way to reduce the barrier to entry for first-time political activists, making it easier for the least engaged to do something. In short, religiosity appears to offer a path toward activism for those who would otherwise not be engaged. This relationship holds not just in LGBT activism but in every case in which religiosity is a significant predictor of political activism, except one. Only in relation to voting does the pattern change and the positive effect of religiosity accrue to those who vote most frequently.

The effect is also similar for affirmation and for specific beliefs like attribution or the belief that being LGBT is not a sin. In each instance when the variables achieve a significant relationship with activist behaviors, the model estimations show the effect of the variables on the behavior is generally a pronounced decrease in the likelihood of never participating. The results are consistent with qualitative findings from Chapter 5. Recall, for example, the experience related by a white lesbian woman who was raised Protestant in the West: "I believe that [becoming a Unitarian Universalist] shaped my initial entry into political activism/social justice," they said. Continuing, "As I was previously not involved in politics at all."

Taken together, these findings bring clarity to the nature of the relationships among religiosity, LGBT identity, and political participation. Although not definitive, the results are consistent with the idea that religiosity, religious affirmation, and positive religious beliefs about LGBT people can offer a mechanism for LGBT people who may otherwise not be politically engaged to become more active participants in American politics.

Voting and Running for Office

Voting and running for elected office are foundational to a representative democracy. Because LGBT people are underrepresented in American political institutions, it is important to determine what effect, if any, religiosity might have on the problem of representation. Notably, the results suggest religious affirmation does not have a significant effect on either voting or running for office. Religiosity, however, has positive effects on both. Figure 6.4 shows the effect of religiosity on the probability that survey participants vote in general elections. Again, the small circles represent point estimates, or the predicted value on the participation variable (voting) given increasing values on the religiosity index, and the four lines represent the four potential responses to the question on voting behavior.

The three lines at the bottom of the figure represent the probabilities that the survey participants will vote never, rarely, or sometimes. The line at the top of the figure represents the probability of voting often. As religiosity increases, the probability of voting often increases while the probability of voting less frequently decreases. Specifically, an increase from the lowest to highest value on the religiosity index is associated with about a 15% increase in the probability of voting often in general elections.

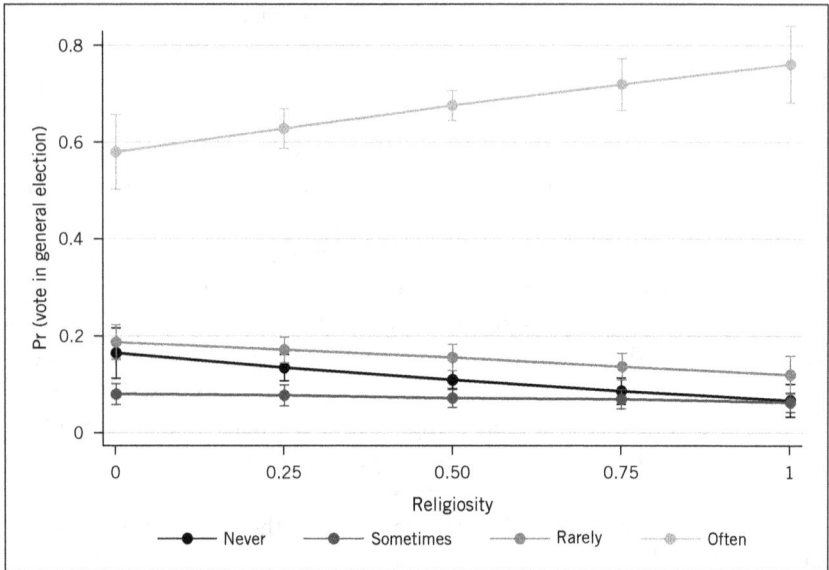

Figure 6.4 Effect of Religiosity on Voting in General Elections. *n* = 694. (*Figure based on ordered probit regression estimation with voting as dependent variable. Full model is shown in Statistical Appendix XIII; 95% confidence levels are shown.*)

Similar relationships exist between specific beliefs about LGBT identity and voting. The belief that being LGBT is not a sin and the belief in attribution are both associated with an increased probability of voting often but decreased probabilities of voting less frequently. On the other hand, the results suggest non-Christians and those who identify with no particular religious tradition are less likely than Protestants to vote frequently.

Finally, there are several other important relationships to note among the people I surveyed. Namely, Black and gay survey participants are significantly more likely to vote frequently than white and lesbian survey participants, respectively. On the other hand, transgender people I surveyed are significantly less likely to vote frequently compared to cisgender people. Traditional resources like income and education are also associated with voting, but LGBT people with children I surveyed are less likely to vote frequently, as are older LGBT people I surveyed.

It is likely that these results reflect the structural barriers to voting that are prevalent in the American electoral system. Voter ID laws negatively affect voters of color, urban residents, and young voters, who are less likely to possess photo identification when required (Kuk, Hajnal, and Lajevardi 2022). Similarly, transgender people whose government-issued identity documents reflect the sex they were assigned at birth are frequently disenfranchised

(Adibi 2020). Religiosity alone cannot overcome all barriers to political engagement, but as the evidence marshaled here shows, it can be a significant resource for LGBT people who otherwise might not be able to participate.

Before relating the effect of religiosity on running for office, there is an important statistical problem to address. Running for office is a relatively rare event among the LGBT people I surveyed. Specifically, more than 90% of the sample report never having run for elected office. This finding is, itself, important but not altogether uncommon. That is, a small proportion of the general population typically stand for election, so it is intuitive that a small proportion of the LGBT population stand for election.

For the purposes of statistical analysis, however, making predictions with such a small sample of actual cases where the survey participants report running could introduce bias into the predictions. So, to correct for this, I estimate an alternate regression model using a statistical program that weights the results to account for the low likelihood of running for office among the survey participants (King and Zeng 1999). To do this, I must collapse the four response categories (never, rarely, sometimes, often) into two. In this case, the new variable takes on a value of 1 if survey participants have rarely, sometimes, or often run for office and a value of 0 if they have never run for office.

The results are generally similar but easier to interpret. Namely, a one-unit increase in the religiosity index (e.g., attending religious services *and* praying frequently) is associated with about an 89% increase in the likelihood of running for office at least rarely. One other religious source of variation in activism warrants discussion. Among the LGBT people I surveyed, atheists appear significantly less likely to run for office. Although this may be an artifact of a small sample size, it is also possible that atheism represents a barrier to electoral office that LGBT people feel would be difficult to overcome.

Recent social scientific research provides important context to this finding and suggests social processes and not statistical error are responsible for the finding. First, a 2022 report from the U.S. Secular Survey, which is a project of the group American Atheists, found that LGBT people are especially likely to hide their atheism or lack of religious affiliation because they experience religious discrimination more frequently than other groups of atheists in the United States (see U.S. Secular Survey 2022). Second, political research shows that LGBT candidates typically run in districts that are politically liberal with fewer religious conservatives (Haider-Markel 2010). However, other research shows that electability is a major concern for voters when evaluating LGBT candidates (Magni and Reynolds 2021). If atheism is viewed as an additional electability concern in addition to being LGBT, it could significantly alter voters' calculus. LGBT people who are also atheist and want to run for office could perceive this situation as a barrier and choose not to stand for election.

Conclusion

The findings presented here highlight both individual and systemic ways religiosity can affect LGBT political behavior. While reducing the barrier to participation at the individual level, religious affiliation (or lack thereof) may still act as a structural barrier to specific forms of electoral activism, like running for office. This is consistent with research highlighted earlier that suggests conservative Christian hegemony in certain areas discourages political candidates from other faith traditions from running for office (e.g., Bullock and Grant 1995). Not only this, but public policy founded on religiously inspired opposition to attribution also structurally disadvantages LGBT people in the American electoral system. Specifically, transgender people who live in states with strict voter ID laws that also proscribe amending sex markers on identity documents such as birth certificates may be ultimately barred from voting.

The structural barriers religion may impose on political activism also represent reasons why some LGBT people engage in politics. Namely, some LGBT people get involved in politics because of negative experiences with religious conservatives. Others get involved in politics because they hope to prevent religious conservatives from accumulating political power. Recall from Chapter 5 the experience of one white lesbian woman who was raised agnostic in the South, who said, "My homophobic experiences with religious groups have made me more political and more likely to participate in LGBT positive politics."

At the individual level, religiosity also affects how and why LGBT people engage in politics. LGBT people are one of the most politically active groups in American politics. Even among this active group, though, religion makes a difference in activism. First, religion is a political resource for LGBT people. Specifically, practicing one's faith is associated with increased political activism among the LGBT people I surveyed. As in Verba, Schlozman, and Brady (1995), the findings here suggest religiosity can be a democratizing force as the positive participatory benefits of religiosity extend to LGBT people regardless of the affirming nature of their faith. That is, LGBT people need not be engaged in a faith tradition that fully affirms their LGBT identity in order to take advantage of the resources for political participation that religion offers to congregants.

However, affirming faith is most important for activism on behalf of LGBT people. The religious cosmology affirming faith traditions create and transmit to their members does affect how their members engage with the broader LGBT community. Those who participate in affirming traditions are more likely to attend Pride events and rallies in support of LGBT rights and to donate money to LGBT causes. Since affirming religiosity is also associated with importance of LGBT identity, it is likely that affirming faith is both a resource for activism and a mechanism for identity maintenance among LGBT people. In the latter sense, affirming religiosity helps LGBT people maintain ties with the LGBT community, thus reinforcing the salience of identity-related activism opportunities. This is consistent with the qualitative results in the previous chapter that show the second-most common reason LGBT people cite for participating in LGBT religious organizations is because they want an opportunity to be involved in their community.

That is not to say that practicing an affirming faith does not affect other forms of political behavior, like electoral activism. Although the models I reviewed in this chapter show no direct relationship between religious affirmation and electoral activism (as I measure it), when LGBT identity coincides closely with an electoral outcome (i.e., an openly LGBT candidate is on the ballot or an LGBT rights measure is up for a vote), it is likely that the identity salience conveyed by participation in an affirming tradition will increase the likelihood of electoral participation. Furthermore, the measures I use here do not speak to the religious activism that LGBT people undertake within specific congregations or denominations. In both events, it is likely that affirming faith inspires and facilitates activism to push religious and political institutions to be more welcoming to LGBT people. Regardless of affirmation, however, on average, religiosity—measured as a function of both internal and external devotion—provides a consistent political resource for LGBT people, making religious LGBT people more likely to engage in electoral politics than nonreligious LGBT people.

Importantly, the effects of religious socialization on political activism can extend across the lifespan. LGBT people who indicated some amount of commitment to a faith tradition in their pre–coming out years by participating in a religious rite are also more likely to be politically active later in life. Their political activism is augmented (made stronger) if they also received positive socializing messages about LGBT people before coming out. This highlights the effect of identity integration on political engagement in that one's religious upbringing may have detrimental effects on later political engagement, but the connection to one's LGBT identity associated with early positive socialization outweighs the negative effects of experiences that might otherwise keep LGBT people from political activism. Specifically, I found this among LGBT people who identified as "born again," Catholic, or as nothing in particular before coming out. After accounting for positive LGBT socialization, negative trends in political participation appear to reverse among these groups. This suggests the increase in identity salience and importance that accrues to LGBT people who were raised in accepting social environments, even if they affiliate with a faith tradition that is typically hostile to LGBT identity (like "born again" Evangelicalism), translates into political activism later in life.

This clarifies why LGBT people who were not raised in positive social environments and later experience religious and LGBT identity conflict are also *more* likely to engage in LGBT activism than LGBT people who do not experience conflict. Namely, LGBT people who experience conflict likely participate in LGBT activism because they are seeking socializing experiences that help integrate their faith and LGBT identity. This is borne out by the results in Chapter 5 that show LGBT people who experience conflict are significantly more likely to join a host of LGBT secular and religious groups for help with this kind of identity maintenance. Unlike those who were raised in positive environments, LGBT people who experienced negative socialization early in life seek positive experiences later. Importantly, experiencing religious affirmation after coming out can help diminish identity conflict, increase the importance of one's LGBT identity, and further increase the likelihood of engaging in LGBT activism.

While faith is a resource for political activism, the final questions I pursue in this book are about the effect of religion on political attitudes and whether secular socialization effects LGBT politics in the same way as religious socialization. Rather than political resource theory, social science suggests that political socialization theory better explains the effect of religion on political attitudes. This is because religion is as much an identity as any other identity we may hold. LGBT religious people, by definition, identify as religious. This means their religious identity likely frames the world they live in (including what they think and know about politics and how they engage in politics), just like their LGBT identity. Like all socially constructed identities, religious identities erect boundaries, set limits, and distinguish between groups. In the case of religious identities, the boundaries are largely based on cognitive understandings of morality. Because religion is fundamentally conservative—that is, values tradition and seeks to maintain social order—it is likely that the LGBT faithful operate under different attitudinal constraints than LGBT people who are not religious. In the final analytic chapter of this book, I examine this dynamic and compare how religious and secular socialization affect LGBT politics.

7

"My Politics Are My Religious Beliefs"

Faith and Political Attitudes of LGBT People

The last time the CCES asked respondents if they favored or opposed same-sex marriage was in 2016. At the time, two-thirds (64%) of the full sample favored allowing same-sex couples to marry, while about one-third (34%) registered opposition. Not surprisingly, there were pronounced differences in support depending on the religious affiliation of the respondent. Specifically, those who identify with a faith tradition are less supportive of same-sex marriage than those who do not identify with a faith tradition. This is a common feature of religious affiliation in American politics. Those who identify with a faith tradition often hold different, usually more conservative, attitudes than those who are unaffiliated, especially if the attitude reflects an issue that religious groups have taken a position on because they believe their faith compels them to do so (on same-sex marriage, see Cox, Navarro-Rivera, and Jones 2014).

Looking only at LGBT respondents in the 2016 CCES data, opinions about same-sex marriage are far more lopsided. Among this group, greater than nine in ten (92%) support same-sex marriage. Even then, a similar pattern emerges. The small number of opponents are more likely to affiliate with a faith tradition. Fewer religious LGBT people than expected registered support for same-sex marriage in 2016, while more religious people than expected registered opposition to the policy ($\chi^2 = 239.8$, p = .000). A similar pattern emerged among LGBT people and their attitudes toward abortion in 2016 based on CCES data.

Admittedly, this is a blunt analysis, but it highlights an important aspect of LGBT religion and politics. Namely, even when it comes to LGBT rights, the political calculus undertaken by religious LGBT people seems to weight sexuality and gender identity differently in comparison to religion. It would be unfair to say that one identity is or should be more important than another. However, understanding what makes religion important and how that affects the political attitudes of LGBT people is the final task of this book.

What LGBT People Think about Politics

Having examined the effects of religiosity on political activism, I now turn to an examination of the effects of religiosity on political attitudes among LGBT people. When studying what affects political attitudes, it is important that researchers do not rely solely on measures of ideological self-identification (i.e., asking survey participants to self-identify how liberal or conservative they are) because to do so would obscure important differences (e.g., between social and economic liberalism; see Bonilla-Silva 2018). To that end, Table 7.1 shows the distribution of responses to several survey questions measuring attitudes about the role of government, economic egalitarianism, LGBT rights, abortion, gun control, immigration, and vote choice in the 2020 presidential election. Most of the statements are from previously validated behavioral indexes, meaning researchers have previously demonstrated the questions indeed measure the concepts they purport to represent (e.g., egalitarianism). For clarity, strongly agree/agree and strongly disagree/disagree are reported in the same column of Table 7.1.

As the table shows, the LGBT people I surveyed are generally supportive of economic egalitarianism but have somewhat mixed opinions about government interventions to achieve it and mixed opinions on gun control. They are also generally opposed to abortion restrictions and supportive of immigrants to the United States. Majorities of the people I surveyed support LGBT civil rights to public accommodations and in the context of a private business owner's willingness to refuse service to LGBT people. In addition, nearly two-thirds (61%) of the LGBT people I surveyed voted for Joe Biden in 2020. These findings are consistent with the relatively small proportion of the sample who report being ideologically conservative (12%) or identify as a Republican (11%) as compared to the majority who report being ideologically liberal (52%) or identify as Democrat (55%). While almost one-third of the LGBT people I surveyed report being neither liberal nor conservative in their ideological orientation (32%), slightly more than one-quarter (28%) identify as neither Democrat nor Republican or as an Independent.

In the following sections, I examine how religious socialization and contemporary religious beliefs, behaviors, and affiliations affect political atti-

TABLE 7.1 DISTRIBUTION OF POLITICAL ATTITUDES			
	(Strongly) Agree (%)	Neither Agree nor Disagree	(Strongly) Disagree
Role of Government			
The government should try to ensure that all Americans have such things as jobs, health care, and housing	86	8	4
The free market can handle today's complex economic problems without government being involved	28	36	34
Egalitarianism			
Incomes should be more equal because every family's needs are the same	45	25	27
Incomes should not be more equal because everybody's contribution to society is not equally important	26	30	41
LGBT Rights			
There should be a strictly enforced law requiring businesses to serve persons regardless of their sexual orientation	77	13	7
There should be a strictly enforced law requiring businesses to serve persons regardless of their gender identity	79	12	6
Transgender people should be able to use public facilities consistent with their gender identity	71	19	8
Abortion, Gun Control, and Immigration			
There should be no restrictions on the ability of a woman to get an abortion	64	14	20
Government should do more to protect the rights of gun owners in the United States	33	24	41
Immigrants to the United States burden the country because they take American Jobs	19	19	60
Source: Author data available from Cravens (2022). Notes: Row percentages do not sum to 100% due to rounding. $N = 1,100$.			

tudes. As I have described, religious beliefs help establish a cosmology within which one finds meaning and through which one interprets contemporary events—including questions of political importance. Furthermore, participation in religious organizations, which are "crucible[s] of public opinion" (Olson, Cadge, and Harrison 2006, 356), solidifies denominational affiliations, effectively defining identity-based in- and out-groups, and cues from religious authorities frame political debates (Kellstedt and Green 1993; Roof and McKinney 1987). I begin the analyses in this section with an investigation of socializing experiences and then turn to the effect of contemporary religiosity on political attitudes. Throughout, I pay special attention to the role of affirming religiosity in the milieu of factors that influence political orientations, ideologies, and vote choices.

Faith, Socialization, and Political Attitudes

In previous chapters, I show that social and religious experiences before coming out affect political activism later in life. In this section, I ask the same question of political attitudes. To test the relationship between religious experiences prior to coming out and cotemporary political orientations, I again model several regression estimations using responses to the statements in Table 7.1 as dependent variables. The full models are shown in Online Statistical Appendix XIV (all appendixes are available via Harvard Dataverse at https://doi.org/10.7910/DVN/M87Q1V; for additional citation information see Cravens 2022b). Overall, the results show mixed effects, which is not surprising given the variety of attitudes I analyze in this study. Still, some patterns do emerge that warrant discussion. First, although the results are mixed, the pattern of attitudinal effects does suggest that positive socialization likely occurs in the context of affluence, resulting in differential effects on attitudes about social and economic issues.

It is intuitive to think that survey participants who received positive messages about LGBT people grew up in more politically liberal environments and, therefore, hold more politically liberal attitudes later in life, but the data only partially support this assertion. Specifically, survey participants who received positive socializing messages about LGBT people before coming out are more supportive of legal protections for LGBT people, are more supportive of gun control, and also value immigrants to the United States. However, survey participants who received positive messages about LGBT people before coming out are less likely to support "government involvement" in economic markets and are more likely to agree that incomes should not be more equal.

Second, religious socializing experiences have greater effects on social, rather than economic, attitudes. For example, LGBT people who identified as atheist before coming out are more likely to agree that incomes should be more equal, but the only other religious variable that affects economic attitudes among the people I surveyed is whether or not the participant changed their faith tradition after coming out. Even then, the relationship was only significant in two out of four models using economic attitudes as dependent variables. On the other hand, religious socializing experiences appear to be the most consistent predictors of attitudes toward "social" issues like LGBT legal protections, abortion, gun control, and immigration.

Specifically, LGBT people who identified as atheist before coming out are more likely to agree that transgender people should be allowed to use public accommodations that are consistent with their gender identity, are more likely to oppose restrictions on abortion, and are more likely to support gun regulations, compared to LGBT people who identified as Protestant. In addition, LGBT people who identified as "born again" before coming out are significantly less likely to support abortion rights, more likely to oppose gun regulations, and more likely to agree that immigrants to the United States "burden" the country. Furthermore, LGBT people who changed their religious affiliation after coming out are more likely to support legal protections for LGBT people, support transgender people's right to public accommodations, support abortion rights, and disagree that immigrants to the United States "burden" the country.

Third, in some cases, where LGBT people are raised can affect their political attitudes later in life. Namely, compared to LGBT people who lived in the southern United States before coming out, LGBT people I surveyed from the Northeast are more supportive of abortion and gun control, while LGBT people raised in the western United States are less likely to agree that immigrants "burden" the country.

Finally, only two models show significant variation in attitudes across race. Specifically, Latinx LGBT people I surveyed are less likely than white LGBT people to agree that immigrants "burden" the country, while Black LGBT people I surveyed are less likely than white LGBT people to agree that people should be able to use public accommodations that are consistent with their gender identity.

Because of the sample size, it is difficult to fully disaggregate; however, alternate regression estimations[1] in Online Statistical Appendix XIV show that religious opposition to public accommodations among Black LGBT people in the sample is concentrated among those who had no particular faith tradition before coming out. This group is significantly less supportive than those raised unaffiliated from other racial groups. Religious affiliation, then, may offer a moderating influence on this particular attitude. On the other hand, alternate regression estimations suggest religious affiliation is not a significant source of variation in support for immigrants to the United States among Latinx LGBT people I surveyed. Rather, Latinx identity appears to be the most important early socializing influence on this attitude. I will return to and emphasize the importance of racial and religious identity intersections in the coming sections.

Ideology, Partisanship, and Vote Choice

Views about specific economic or social issues are important to understand; however, they do not provide a complete picture of political attitudes. As Greene (2002) notes, like other forms of identity, political identities have multiple components. In addition to specific policy preferences, ideology is also often measured as self-reported conservatism or liberalism, through partisan identity, and even by vote choice. What, if any, effect does socialization have on these aspects of political behavior? To answer this question, I estimate three regression equations using a scale measure of self-reported ideological liberalism, a dichotomous Democratic Party identity measure, and a dichotomous indicator representing self-reported vote for Joe Biden (the Democratic Party nominee) in the 2020 presidential election as dependent variables. The full models are specified in Online Statistical Appendix XV.

Several important observations emerge from the analysis that merit discussion. First, LGBT people who received positive messages about LGBT identity before coming out are less likely to identify as ideologically liberal. This is consistent with the findings I reported in the previous section in regard to positive socialization and conservative economic attitudes, but it also highlights the notion that positive socialization can have complex effects on political attitudes. On the one hand, if positive socialization about LGBT people occurs in economically privileged environments, positive socialization may also be an indicator of generational wealth or affluence, and such economic measures are often associated with conservative economic attitudes (Page, Bartles, and Seawright 2013). On the other hand, LGBT political research shows a connection between perceptions of privilege and conservative political attitudes (Cravens 2021). Specifically, LGBT people who believe their identity is privileged or accepted by society hold more conservative political opinions because they have no incentive to change a social or political system that they perceive as beneficial. Receiving positive social messages in one's youth may contribute to a sense of identity acceptance and, consequently, ideological conservatism later in life.

Indeed, this scenario is consistent with the second important observation from the data. That is, coming out later is associated with ideological conservatism. Each additional year the LGBT people I surveyed did not come out is associated with about a 2% decrease in the likelihood that they identify as a Democrat later in life. This builds on my discussion in Chapter 3 and lends additional evidence to the notion that coming out later allows time for other identities (especially religious identities) to consolidate. That leaves less time for new socializing experiences centering one's LGBT identity and less room for LGBT identity as an important component of one's sense of self. This data suggests these experiences also have political consequences in that ideological liberalism and Democratic partisanship are not as likely to develop, either, when LGBT people come out later in life.

The results also show there are no denominational variations in ideology, partisanship, or vote choice based on the survey participant's faith tradition before coming out. This does not mean that religious socialization is not important to ideological development, however. A third important observation is that changing one's religious affiliation after coming out is associated with ideological liberalism. The LGBT people I surveyed who changed their religious affiliation after coming out are about 95% more likely to report voting for Joe Biden in the 2020 presidential election than participants who did not change their religious affiliation after coming out.

This is important because it helps contextualize the politics of the coming out process. As I explain in the previous chapter, changing one's religious affiliation after coming out is associated with LGBT activism. It is also associated with ideological liberalism. Furthermore, as I describe in Chapter 3, LGBT people who come out later or receive positive messages about LGBT people early in life are less likely to change their religious affiliation after coming out. For most of the people I surveyed, then, the decision to change their religious affiliation after coming out is likely driven by the social and political conservatism of the faith tradition in which they were raised. That the change is also associated with liberalism and especially with a Democratic vote choice suggests changing religious affiliations after coming out, at the very least, gives LGBT people room to develop their political beliefs outside of conservative religious constraints.

Finally, there are notable demographic differences, especially in vote choice, that I explore further in the following sections. On average, Black and Latinx LGBT people are more likely to report voting for Joe Biden than white LGBT people I surveyed. The results also indicate Black LGBT people I surveyed are more likely than whites to identify as Democrats. Conversely, bisexuals in the sample are less likely to report voting for Biden and less likely to identify as Democrats than lesbians. Because these differences may also be explained by other indicators (e.g., strength of LGBT identity, outness), I return to a discussion of race and sexuality-based variation in partisanship and vote choice in the following sections.

Contemporary Religion and Political Attitudes

The effects of socialization on political attitudes, ideology, partisanship, and vote choice are important to understand. Yet, because socialization represents a series of events that can occur throughout one's life, and because contemporary religious experiences help frame contemporary political debates as well as provide resources to act politically, it is also important to examine how contemporary experiences shape political attitudes. Again, I am primarily concerned with the interrelationships between religiosity, affirming religious beliefs and practices, and political attitudes. To better understand these interrelationships, I follow the same methods I have outlined in previous sections and model regression equations using specific attitudes as the dependent variables (see Table 7.1). Because contemporary partisanship and ideology are correlated with political attitudes, I include measures of each as controls. The full models are shown in Online Statistical Appendix XVI.

I will address the denominational patterns first and then examine how religiosity affects political attitudes. In the previous section, I showed that LGBT people who identified as "born again" before coming out hold more conservative views on issues like abortion, gun control, and immigration later in life, while LGBT people who identified as atheist before coming out hold more liberal views on the same issues. The examination of contemporary effects on these same political attitudes shows similar patterns in all but one case. Namely, LGBT people who identify as "born again" after coming out are more supportive of public accommodations for transgender people[2] compared to LGBT people who do not identify as "born again." What does this say about the lasting effects of socialization within a religious tradition largely shown to be unaccepting of LGBT people?

The data show that about 84% of the LGBT people I surveyed retain their "born again" affiliation after coming out. About 5% of "born again" identifiers did not previously identify but did after coming out, and about 9% did previously identify but did not after coming out. The vast majority of "born again" identifiers represented in the model estimations in Online Statistical Appendix XVI, then, have identified as such throughout their coming out process. For them, coming out seems to shift the political calculus around issues related to LGBT identity. In other words, coming out as LGBT—and potentially experiencing hetero- and cis-sexism firsthand—appears to increase identity salience enough to change their perspective on LGBT rights. Such a scenario is consistent with the conversion hypothesis of LGBT liberalism (see Cravens 2020; Egan 2012).

The data also suggest a similar relationship among LGBT Catholics. Non-Christians are also more supportive of LGBT rights, specifically gender identity–based legal protections, than Protestants; however, there is no relationship between pre–coming out affiliation and support among this religious group. Still, even after controlling for other factors including religiosity, religious affirmation, religious individualism, identity conflict, political ideology, and partisanship, these three religious groups are more supportive of LGBT rights than others I surveyed. For Catholics and those who identify as "born again," the reason appears to be related to coming out.

Finally, other demographic characteristics, such as income, education, age, having children, race, and place of residency, all show some significant effect on political attitudes among the LGBT people I surveyed. For example, LGBT people with children are more likely to oppose gun control and believe that immigrants "burden" the United States. Yet, older LGBT people I surveyed are more economically and socially liberal than younger LGBT people in the sample. Having children is a significant socializing event that recent life-course research suggests shapes both religious and political beliefs (see Margolis 2018a). Studies of heterosexuals, for example, show that having children sometimes shifts behavior in that people who have children often seek out religious communities because of their powerful socializing effects. However, since political identities coalesce earlier in adulthood, the choice of which religious community (if any) to join is usually influenced by preexisting political opinions. In these situations, though, Republicans join religious communities at higher numbers than Democrats (Margolis 2018a). Having children among this sample, then, may be indicative of such a life-course change that explains the relationship to conservative social attitudes.

Given the range of attitudes I measure, the variation in significant demographic indicators is not surprising. What is important to recognize are the similarities and differences that emerge between models of early and later socializing experiences. For example, in models of early socializing experiences, the results show that Black LGBT people—especially those raised religiously unaffiliated—are less likely to support public accommodations for transgender people. However, in models that control for a robust variety of contemporary religious indicators, there appears to be no significant racial variation in these attitudes. It is likely, then, that the religious and LGBT socialization Black LGBT people I surveyed underwent from pre- to post–coming out periods in their lives changed attitudes among the group so that they are no more or less liberal than any other racial group.

On the other hand, from the pre- to post–coming out period, Latinx identity remains a significant predictor of support for immigration. In post–coming out models, Latinx LGBT people I surveyed are also more likely to support gun control and support LGBT civil rights protections than any other racial group. In this case, racial identity remains a powerful determinant of political attitudes, even after undergoing significant religious and LGBT socializing experiences (i.e., coming out).

In most instances, more than where one lived before coming out or moved after coming out, more than one's sexuality, gender, or race, even more than one's early religious affiliation, later secular and religious socialization and the beliefs about LGBT people and religion that one cultivates throughout the coming out process greatly affect how LGBT people think about political issues. Early religious experiences can have lasting effects, yet the beliefs about LGBT people one cultivates through social interaction before coming out and the beliefs about LGBT people and religion one cultivates through social interaction after coming out—more than just religious experiences—seem to better explain variation in LGBT political attitudes later in life. I explore this idea more in the next two sections before offering a final model of LGBT religion and politics gleaned from all of the findings from this study.

The Sacred and the Sexual? Comparing Religious and Secular Effects on Attitudes and Activism

In this section I contextualize the attitudinal and behavioral findings presented so far by highlighting the distinctive effects of affirming religiosity and affective orientations about the compatibility of religion and LGBT identity (i.e., beliefs about religious affirmation). Namely, after controlling for self-reported liberalism and Democratic partisanship, as well as other potential confounding variables, in models of political behavior, religious participation especially in affirming spaces augments political activism. In the case of political attitudes, however, affirming religiosity, measured as religious devotion, participation, and the opportunity to participate, are not significant sources of variation. Instead, as I suggest in the previous sections, among the LGBT people I surveyed, specific beliefs about the compatibility of religion and LGBT identity are significant sources of variation in political attitudes.

In other words, participation in religious activities, personal religious devotion, and the opportunity to participate in religious communities represented by attending affirming congregations increase the likelihood that LGBT people will participate in politics, but the effect of these experiences on attitudes is indirect. In short, the effect of affirming religious participation on political attitudes seems to be transmitted through the cultivation of supportive religious beliefs, including the belief that being LGBT is *not* a sin, the belief in attribution, and the belief that God accepts LGBT people. Each of these are often associated with progressive or liberal political opinions; however, authoritarian beliefs about religion (i.e., that religious institutions are an authoritative source of information about LGBT identity) are generally associated with less progressive or conservative opinions.

This pattern holds in relation to attitudes about the provision of government services, support for LGBT legal protections and equal access to public facilities by transgender people, as well as attitudes about abortion rights, gun control, and immigration. In nearly every case where the models show statistically significant relationships with political attitudes, belief that LGBT and religious identities are compatible are associated with progressive or liberal opinions.

This suggests the effect of affirming religiosity on political attitudes is to increase political liberalism; however, the effects are not transmitted directly through participation in affirming congregations. Instead, the effect of affirming religiosity on political attitudes among LGBT people is transmitted through the cultivation of affective and cognitive orientations that help LGBT people not just integrate religious and LGBT identities but also increase religious individualism (i.e., the idea that one single faith tradition is not the source of truth about LGBT identity). This also helps to explain why changing one's religious affiliation after coming out is also sometimes associated with progressive or liberal opinions. Changing affiliations suggests that beliefs about the authority of the tradition in which one was raised over one's life and identity has been reduced.

This is important given the dominant theories of LGBT political behavior view social and political organizations as sources of political liberalism as much as they are sources of political mobilization (see Cravens 2020; Egan 2012). The results, here, suggest that the effect of secular and religious organizations on LGBT political attitudes may not be the same. However, the models in Online Statistical Appendix XVI cannot fully test this assertion. To do so, the models must account for survey participants' engagement in both secular and religious organizations.

Table 7.2 shows the truncated results of a linear regression model that compares the effects of secular and religious participation on the political attitudes of the LGBT people I surveyed. In this case, the dependent variable in both models is an index generated by averaging responses to each of the questions in Table 7.1. The responses are reverse coded as necessary, and the

TABLE 7.2 COMPARING EFFECTS OF RELIGIOUS AND SECULAR PARTICIPATION ON LIBERAL POLITICAL ATTITUDES		
	Model 1	Model 2
Variable	β (S.E.)	β (S.E.)
Religious change	-	-
Current Affiliation		
Catholic	-	-
Another Christian	-	-
Non-Christian	-	-
Atheist	-	-
Nothing Particular	-	-
"Born Again"	-	-
Religiosity	−.083** (.033)	-
LGBT Activism	.064** (.027)	-
God Accepts		-
Not a Sin		.035*** (.007)
Attribution		.032*** (.007)
Religious Authoritarian		−.018** (.009)
Religious Affirmation	-	-
Religious Conflict	-	-
LGBT ID	.096*** (.032)	.072** (.031)
Outness	-	-
Notes: n = 682. Models estimated with robust standard errors. *** p ≤ .01; ** p ≤ .05		

index is normalized so that it ranges from 0 to 1, where low values are associated with more ideologically conservative attitudes and high values are associated with more ideologically liberal attitudes.

The results of two models are shown in the table. In Model 1, I include measures of religious participation (religiosity) and religious affirmation. I also include the measure of LGBT activism I describe in Chapter 6. Along with measuring activism, this indicator shows the extent to which the LGBT people I surveyed are engaged in social and political communities for LGBT people (minus the measure of participation in LGBT religious organizations). Important to this comparison, then, the models include measures of secular and religious LGBT participation. To test the assertion that I make earlier in this section (i.e., the effect of religious affirmation on political attitudes is transmitted through particular beliefs), I include in Model 2 the measures of belief about religious and LGBT identity compatibility, including the belief that being LGBT is not a sin, attribution, that God accepts LGBT people, and religious authoritarianism. For clarity, I only report coefficient estimates that achieve statistical significance at the 95% confidence level or above. The full model is shown in Online Statistical Appendix XVII.

Based on the results in the table, I come to two important conclusions: First, religious and secular organizations appear to convey different effects on political attitudes of LGBT people. As the table shows, in Model 1, the sign associated with the coefficient estimate for religiosity is negative, while the coefficient estimate for LGBT activism is positive. That means the effect of religiosity on political liberalism is negative, while the effect of LGBT activism is positive. In short, a one-unit increase in religiosity (e.g., attending church and praying frequently) is associated with about an 8% decrease in liberalism as measured by the index. On the other hand, a one-unit increase in LGBT activism (e.g., attending Pride and donating money frequently) is associated with about a 6% increase in liberalism. There is no significant effect between the affirming nature of a survey participant's religious congregation or denomination and liberalism, nor is there an interactive effect with religiosity, meaning religiosity—whether affirming or not—when measured alone is associated with attitudinal conservatism. The converse is true of LGBT activism.

The results suggest, then, that religious and secular participation likely socialize LGBT people differently. Regular religious participation, even in settings that affirm LGBT identity, is still fundamentally religious (i.e., centers religious experiences, teachings, theologies, and dogmas). This means moral and social (if not civil) obligations are likely framed differently in religious and secular settings, with religious views on individualism, individual rights, personal responsibility to society, views on life and conception and gender roles taking their cues from theology. When internalized, these views take precedence over other claims to the same moral and social positions. This potentially explains why those who are "born again" hold more conservative views on gun control and immigration but not on public accommodations for transgender people. In the latter case, LGBT identity claims to the moral and social attitudes appear to win out, while in the former case, religious claims on moral and social attitudes take precedence. While coming out is an important factor that alters the development of political attitudes, it does appear limited to issues of LGBT identity. This is consistent with recent research on how personal experiences can be used to shift attitudes around these kinds of moral issues, including LGBT rights and abortion (see Harrison and Michelson 2017, for example).

From Model 1 to Model 2 in Table 7.2, I control for the belief that God accepts LGBT people, that being LGBT is not a sin, the belief in attribution, and religious authoritarianism. After controlling for these measures, the significant effects of both religious and secular participation disappear. The second conclusion I can draw from these results, then, is that the effects of religious participation, participation in affirming religious communities, and participation in secular LGBT organizations are moderated by these variables. In short, the effects of participation are only indirect. Beliefs about LGBT people as compatible with religious-based moral and social claims have a direct effect on attitudes in that they are related to political liberalism. On the other hand, the belief that religious institutions are authoritative sources of information about LGBT identity also have a direct effect on attitudes, but it is associated with political conservatism.

The latter beliefs are almost certainly the result of religious socialization; however, the former may not be conveyed only through LGBT religious groups. That is, LGBT people may learn or refine these beliefs by engaging with secular LGBT groups too. I further tease apart this relationship in the next analysis, focusing on political behavior. For now, I can assert that beliefs that view LGBT people as compatible with religious-based moral and social claims are developed and reinforced through participation in both religious and secular LGBT organizations, although some LGBT people reach these beliefs after rejecting religion altogether. These liberalized attitudes about LGBT identity, which have developed through both religious and secular socialization, are also predictors of other liberal political opinions, which are shown in Table 7.2.

The results in this chapter suggest religious and secular organizations may convey different values that influence political attitudes in the opposite directions. This is important because it also suggests that secular and religious LGBT organizations may socialize LGBT people differently. On the one hand, LGBT organizations convey traditionally liberal values. On the other hand, religious organizations, even if they affirm LGBT participation, convey traditionally conservative values.

To further clarify how religious and secular engagement affects LGBT political activism, I revisit the models of electoral behavior in Chapter 6. Specifically, I use the same model described in the previous section with the LGBT activism index (without the indicator for religious participation) as a predictor of electoral activism. The model includes the religiosity index as well as measures of religious affirmation and other controls described in previous sections. The full model is also shown in Online Statistical Appendix XVII. Table 7.3 shows the truncated results of the regression models.

Unlike the models of political attitudes discussed previously, the results in Table 7.3 show that both secular and religious participation positively affect electoral activism. This suggests participatory resources accrue not only to religious LGBT people but also to those who engage in secular organizations and activities. Even though religious and secular socialization results

TABLE 7.3 COMPARING THE EFFECTS OF RELIGIOUS AND SECULAR PARTICIPATION ON ELECTORAL ACTIVISM		
	Model 1	Model 2
Variable	β (S.E.)	β (S.E.)
Religious change	-	-
Current Affiliation		
Catholic	-	-
Another Christian	-	-
Non-Christian	-	-
Atheist	-	-
Nothing Particular	-	-
"Born Again"	-	-
Religiosity	.139*** (.037)	.149*** (.038)
LGBT Activism	.341*** (.027)	.335*** (.037)
God Accepts		-
Not a Sin		-
Attribution		-
Religious Authoritarian		-.
Religious Affirmation	-	-
Religious Conflict	-	-
LGBT ID	-	-
Outness	−.013** (.006)	−.013** (.006)

Notes: n = 682. Models estimated with robust standard errors.
*** $p \le .01$; ** $p \le .05$

in attitudinal differences, the same cannot be said about political engagement. Even after controlling for specific religious beliefs about the compatibility of LGBT and religious identities (i.e., from Model 1 to Model 2), the positive relationships maintain. Not only this, but the cognitive and affective understandings about LGBT identity and religion that directly affect political attitudes have no significant effect on electoral activism. This is consistent with the findings from Chapter 6, but it also shows that it is most likely organizational, not cognitive, resources that religious participation provides that boosts the political engagement of LGBT people.

In short, religious participation provides LGBT people with organizational resources and recruitment opportunities that augment electoral participation. This happens in much the same way for secular and religious LGBT organizations. Recall from Chapter 6, however, that affirming religious participation is especially important for solidary activism, or LGBT-specific activism. As I explain in the conclusion to this chapter, this does not mean religious affirmation has no bearing on electoral activism. LGBT people who attend affirming congregations are, by definition, entitled to more opportunities to participate than those who attend congregations that ban them from membership or leadership positions, for example. Furthermore, LGBT people who engage in affirming religious practices likely do accrue cognitive resources that both facilitate identity integration and increase the likelihood of engaging in other (secular) solidary behaviors.

An examination of political attitudes shows, however, that religious and secular participation offer two distinct forms of socialization to LGBT people. On the one hand, secular socialization appears to convey political frames that contribute to attitudinal liberalism. On the other hand, religious socialization (even if it occurs in affirming spaces) appears to convey political frames that contribute to attitudinal conservatism. The fundamentally religious nature of the latter is likely the best explanation for this distinctiveness. Yet, just because religious LGBT people are likely exposed to conservative attitude frames as part of their religious socialization does not mean they are absolutely more conservative than nonreligious people. The relationship is nuanced by the extent to which religious LGBT people internalize positive messages about their religious and LGBT identities and how much authority they vest in their religious tradition.

Ideology, Partisanship, and Vote Choice Revisited

Before drawing this chapter to a close, it is important to revisit the relationship between religiosity and the measures of ideology and partisanship and to assess how the pre–coming out relationships change or maintain after controlling for contemporary experiences. To do this, I estimate models using the same dependent variables (self-reported ideology, partisanship, and vote choice in the 2020 election) but control for contemporary religious experiences. The full models are shown in Online Statistical Appendix XVIII.

According to the results, neither religious belief, religious affiliation, nor change in religious affiliation directly affect partisanship among the sample. Democratic partisanship is best explained by the strength of one's LGBT identity. Specifically, a one-unit increase in LGBT identity importance (explained in Chapter 3) is associated with about an 800% increase in the likelihood that a survey participant identifies as a Democrat. Because the strength of one's LGBT identity is affected by positive socialization as well as affirming religiosity and affirming religious beliefs, it would be inaccurate to say religiosity does not affect partisanship. Instead, the effects are indirect through religiosity's influence on the strength of the survey participants' LGBT identity. Liberalism and racial identity are also important predictors of partisanship, but these too have indirect relationships with religiosity.

Self-reported ideological liberalism and 2020 vote choice are both partially explained by the pattern I describe in the previous section (i.e., specific beliefs about religious authority and LGBT identity compatibility with religion rather than religious participation), although religiosity did affect vote choice in 2020. Specifically, LGBT people who changed their religious affiliation after coming out are more liberal than those in the sample who did not change their religious affiliation, but there is no relationship between affiliation change and vote choice in 2020. Instead, atheists are about 4% more likely to report voting for Joe Biden in 2020 compared to Protestants.

The results also provide additional evidence to support the assertion that religiosity motivates participation among LGBT people, but not liberalism. Namely, religiosity alone is associated with a reduced probability of voting for Joe Biden. A one-unit increase in the religiosity index (e.g., praying *and* attending religious services frequently) is associated with about an 87% decrease in the probability that a survey participant voted for Joe Biden in 2020. In comparison, the belief that God accepts LGBT people and the belief in attribution are associated with about a 47% and a 55% increase in the probability of voting for Joe Biden, respectively. The belief in attribution is also associated with self-reported liberalism. In short, religiosity alone appears to provide the resources necessary to engage in political activism but also appears to frame political issues in less progressive (and more conservative) terms. Attendance at LGBT-affirming religious congregations also does not appear to convey policy liberalism in the same way as participation in secular LGBT organizations. Instead, internalizing affirming beliefs (e.g., being LGBT is not a sin) appear to be the necessary precursor to liberal political ideology development among religious LGBT people.

Conclusion: The Faith Factor in LGBT Politics

In this and the previous chapter, I divided discussions between political activism and political attitudes. That is not only because each represents distinct components of political life; it is also because two different bodies of scientific research have accumulated that attempt to explain each separately. One goal of this study is to determine whether LGBT religious experiences fit within the paradigms established by each body of literature, or somehow bridge the two by developing both resources for political activism and a political identity that shapes political attitudes and opinions.

One question I have attempted to answer is whether or not religiosity affects political participation among LGBT people in the same way that it does among non-LGBT people. Political resource theory suggests that regardless of sexual orientation or gender identity, religious participation produces resources that easily translate into secular political endeavors. The model I outline in Chapter 4 expresses this relationship, and the findings from the survey data I collected and discuss in this chapter are consistent with both existing theory and the assertions in my model. Namely, religiosity, measured as frequency of private and public devotion, such as attending religious services, but also prayer, meditation, and scripture study, is associated with political activism in two forms.

First, religiosity and religious affirmation (participating in a religious congregation and/or denomination that affirms LGBT identity) are both associated with solidary political activism on behalf of LGBT people, such as attending Pride events and volunteering for LGBT organizations. Because religious affirmation is a measure of both acceptance and increased opportunity to participate in one's faith tradition, it is likely that when LGBT people have increased opportunity to engage with organized faith communities, they receive identity affirmation (internalizing positive notions about their faith and LGBT identity) and resources to engage politically on behalf of that identity.

Second, religious affirmation appears to have no independent effect on electoral activism, such as voting, running for office, or contacting politicians. Religious participation, however, does have a positive effect; and the effect is amplified by the increased opportunities to participate in one's religious community afforded to LGBT people by affirming congregations and denominations. More than abstractly providing resources, the data reviewed in the previous chapter show that religious affirmation reduces the barrier for entry to political activism among LGBT people since it increases the likelihood of both voting and running for political office, but also solidary activism like attending Pride events are predicted to occur among the least politically active.

The model of political behavior I outline in Chapter 4 does not account for the effect of religion on political attitudes among LGBT people largely because it is assumed that affirming religious experiences will have the same effect on political attitudes as other LGBT socializing experiences that occur after one comes out as LGBT. However, the data in this chapter provide important context for the limits of LGBT socialization and nuance what we know about the effects of religion on LGBT politics. These findings require that I revisit the model in Figure 4.4 (Chapter 4) to add new paths describing the relationship between religiosity and political attitudes among religious LGBT people. Specifically, in this chapter, I show that participation in religious organizations and participation in secular LGBT organizations have different effects on political attitudes.

As Figure 7.1 shows, the behavioral and attitudinal components of "affirming religiosity" must be deconstructed and understood separately, especially with regard to their effects on political attitudes. Alone, affirming religiosity appears to have no direct effect on political attitudes; however, LGBT people who internalize positive beliefs about the compatibility of LGBT people and religion are more likely to hold progressive views on a number of issues, including abortion, immigration, LGBT rights, and the role of government. On the other hand, religiosity without affirmation is associated with conservative attitudes, including opposition to Democratic candidates (like Joe Biden) for political office. As it relates to political participation, religios-

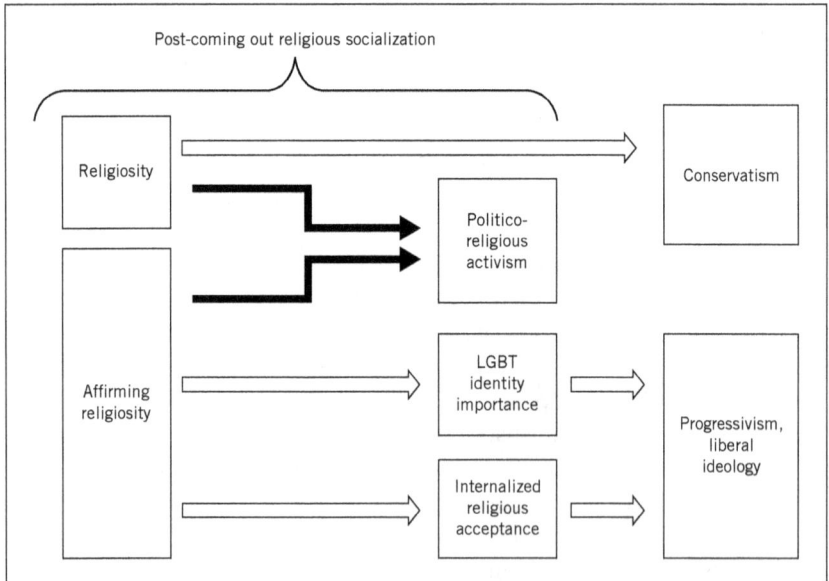

Figure 7.1 Paths to Political Activism and Attitudes for Religious LGBT People

ity is associated with electoral activism and, in combination with participation in affirming religious communities, is also associated with LGBT solidary activism.

The findings are consistent with the political resource theory of political participation in that religious participation, and the expanded opportunities for LGBT people to participate afforded by affirming religious congregations and denominations, increase the likelihood that LGBT people will be politically active. The findings also bridge identity and political resource theories by recognizing that the effects of affirming religious congregations on LGBT political attitudes (and vote choice) are a function of internalized beliefs about the compatibility of LGBT and religious identity and that without these affective orientations, the main effect of religious participation on political attitudes is to increase ideological conservatism.

Because the relationships in the statistical models are not always significant, this suggests the effect of religiosity on attitudes is also conditional on the issue context. In other words, like everyone else, religious LGBT people may consider how their faith teaches about a particular issue when forming an opinion. In addition, the emphasis on coming out in LGBT politics means that LGBT identity (or experiences that happened as a result of coming out, like discrimination) may be a more important determinant than religiosity in some circumstances—for example, when I demonstrated that those I surveyed who identified as "born again" before coming out were the least supportive of LGBT rights, but those who identify as "born again" after coming out are actually more supportive of LGBT rights than others in the sample.

In short, the results show that religious LGBT people experience cross-pressures to conform stemming from religious and LGBT socialization. On the one hand, religious socialization, especially without any positive LGBT social context, appears to evoke ideological conservatism—mostly in the form of resistance to government services and opposition to social progressivism. In this case, religious authority appears to be central to LGBT people's conceptions of themselves and their politics. The belief that one's faith is an authoritative source of information about LGBT identity is a strong indicator of ideological conservatism. As I discuss in Chapter 3, this is especially true for Protestants and those who identify as "born again," but it is represented among other traditions as well.

To this point, a white pansexual woman from the western United States who was raised Catholic but currently identifies as agnostic shared the following when asked about the contested place of religion in LGBT culture:

> I think religion generally impacts conservatism and many other elements of political contributions, particularly single-issue voting. . . .

I think religion would have definitely played a bigger role in my political views had I remained in the faith for longer.

In contrast, a white lesbian woman from the western United States who was raised Methodist shared the following perspective on the individualistic approach to religion and its relation to politics:

I do not pretend to know what the "truth" is about religion, other than to believe there is no "right" way to believe, other than in respect and understanding, whether in agreement or disagreement. My politics (beliefs about interacting with the world) are my religious beliefs. Higher power is not important to me. Only following a caring and loving path, which requires action and interaction.

Deference to religious authority, then, in addition to frequent religious participation and devotion, are key to understanding religious cross-pressures on LGBT politics. When religious institutions are given deference, the result for political attitudes is likely the development of ideological conservatism. When LGBT people pursue a more individualized approach to religious authority, the result for political attitudes is likely the development of ideological liberalism.

On the other hand, LGBT socialization, including within affirming religious communities, appears to evoke ideological liberalism. The inclusive religious cosmologies that LGBT people construct, however, must be internalized to affect attitude formation. In this case, participation in religious communities—either affirming or nonaffirming—makes it easier to participate in political activism. But, participation in affirming religious communities, specifically, increases LGBT identity salience and makes it easier to engage in solidary activism on behalf of LGBT people. Yet, the effect of religious (and secular) participation can be explained by specific beliefs about the compatibility of religious and LGBT identities. Affective changes associated with affirming religious participation (but also with participation in secular LGBT organizations) that demonstrate that LGBT people have internalized the notions that they are not inherently damaged or morally corrupt, that the divine does not condemn them, are by-products of affirming religious participation but also the likely source of liberal attitude formation among religious LGBT people after they come out.

Conclusion

Yes Gawd! How Faith Shapes LGBT Politics

After nine months in the United States at the beginning of the eighteenth century, Alexis de Tocqueville offered the following assessment of American politics: "Upon my arrival [in America] . . . the religious aspect was the first thing that struck my attention; and the longer I stayed there, the more did I perceive the great political consequences resulting from this state of things" (quoted in Kramnick 2007, 247, 251). If Tocqueville had visited only fifty years earlier, his observation may have been markedly different. In fact, at the time of the signing of the Declaration of Independence, only about 17% of the colonial population were members of a church or local congregation (Finke and Starke 1992; Starke and Finke 1988). In acknowledging the lack of what Finke and Starke (1992, 39) call religious "commitment" among the colonials, Tocqueville also notes the connection between religious pluralism and American governmental structures, remarking, "I do not know whether all the Americans have a sincere faith in their religion . . . but I am certain that they hold it to be indispensable to the maintenance of republican institutions." Continuing, "If it [religion in America] does not impart a taste for freedom, it facilitates the use of free institutions" (quoted in Kramnick 2007, 249).

While it is widely claimed that American religious pluralism undermined traditional European religious hierarchies and reflected the democratization of the American political system, it was not immediately understood that pluralism would be the nation's guiding principle with regard to religion (Eck 2001; Pottenger 2016). The dominant Christian denominations could count on government support during the colonial period, a corollary to the lack of religious "commitment" among Revolutionary Americans, according to Finke and Starke (1992). Even Constitutional disestablishment was not enough to fully enable a "free market religious economy," as Massachusetts continued to collect church taxes until 1833 while North Carolina retained religious oaths for public officials that excluded non-Protestants until Reconstruction (Diner 2004; Finke and Starke 1992, 58–59). Although an arduous process, the disestablishment of religion is the biggest distinction between the American and European politico-religious experiences (T. Smith 1965).

As Tocqueville observed, disestablishment democratized American religion. At the congregation level, disestablishment and a general federal ambivalence to the internal machinations of American religious congregations led many religious communities to adopt a majoritarian perspective where "individual members," rather than the clergy, "would have the power to shape religious practice" (Diner 2004, 56). As Samuel Hill (1980, 5–6) notes, this has meant "religious" issues have been "forced into the open." As religions vie for popular (rather than governmental) support, "resolution of [religious] issues" in America has become "a rather public affair" (Hill 1980, 6). In this way, disestablishment and subsequent democratization of religion fits nicely into the Madisonian extended "sphere of country" in which competition between factions within society makes it "less probable that a majority of the whole will have a common motive to invade the rights of other citizens" (Madison 1787). Religious organizations, like other social interests, are forced to contend for members, resources, and, at times, the attention of policy makers.

For all this pluralistic fervor, however, Christianity has been (and remains) hegemonic in American national political culture. From the colonial period, Christian religiocentrism has "presupposed the baptism, thus Christian identity, of all citizens" (Hill 1980, 5). Once combined with revivalist zeal in the nineteenth century, the Christian-dominated religious "free market" would contribute to the spread and fractionalization of American Christianity and the oppression of other faith traditions and people deemed immoral that continues into the present age (Finke and Starke 1992; Pottenger 2016).

National expansion carried the dominant religious beliefs and practices of the colonists across the continent in the form of new laws and social conventions throughout the nineteenth century. While some colonial Christians favored "tolerance" toward Indigenous faith traditions and the faith traditions of those brought to the continent via immigration or enslavement, evangelism and conversion best characterized the majority strategy well into the twentieth century (Johansen 2016, 47). Even after formal sponsorship ended, Christian theology was well represented in the public policy decisions of both the state and federal governments (Eck 2001). Indeed, "'no state church' has meant anything but 'no church at all'" (Hill 1980, 5).

As Hill (1980, 35) notes of the period, "bringing [the Protestant Christian] God's sovereignty and will to bear on the public order was as much a suitable response as yielding one's heart to his grace and redemptive work." In the occupied Native American territories, Native religious practices were banned while immigration and naturalization laws stemming from religious bigotry have variously limited migration of Catholics, Jews, Muslims, and all "Asian" immigrants (see Mann 2016; Morone 2003). In law, "non-sectarian" came to mean "all Protestant religious viewpoints could be accommodated" (Diner 2004, 59). Public schools and orphanages, charged with sheltering and teaching children, for example, existed "as much to indoctrinate" Jewish, Catholic, and nonreligious children "in Protestant piety," according to Diner (2004, 59).

At various times, national expansion, immigration, conversion, schism, nationalism, and fundamentalism have each tested the American commitment to pluralism (J. Smith 2010; Sorin 1997; Warner and Wittner 1998). As Eck (2001, 31) quips of the American national motto, *E Pluribus Unum*, it clearly does not mean "From many religions, one religion." Despite the assumptions of the popular melting pot metaphor, the United States is a country of diverse cultural expression as racial and ethnic minority populations have long resisted social and political "assimilation" and religious traditions have multiplied, each contributing their own "commitment to the common covenants of citizenship" (Eck 2001, 31; Gabriel 1972; Warner 1998). Alongside Indigenous and European Christian traditions, many other faith traditions, as well as reimagined forms of dominant Christian traditions, have persisted, developed, or thrived—usually despite persecution (Sorin 1997; Warner and Wittner 1998).

Like Indigenous religious practices in the United States, many faith traditions, including Buddhism, Hinduism, Judaism, Islam, Sikhism, Jainism, Voodoo, Paganism, and minority Christian faiths and sects, have been scrutinized and subjected to social and legal discrimination by an ethnocentric Euro-Protestant political (and immigration) system (Eck 2001; Warner and Wittner 1998). As this book shows, LGBT people have contributed an important dynamic to this tale of pluralism. Since the advent of the modern gay liberation movement in the 1950s, LGBT people and their allies have reimagined and democratized both the religious and political landscapes of the United States to create inclusive spaces for sexual and gender minorities (see Faderman 2015; Taylor and Snowdon 2014; Thumma and Gray 2005; White 2015). Whether through reform efforts to create LGBT-affirming denominations, supportive organizations unsanctioned by denominational hierarchies, spirituality not associated with institutional religion, or even religious disassociation, LGBT people pursue multiple strategies to either integrate their LGBT identity with their religious identity or protect it from discordant religious traditions.

The place of LGBT people in American religion has been contested by those who would seek to restrain the existence of LGBT people in other civil, political, and social aspects of American life. Since the 1970s, general hostility toward LGBT people has given way to more positive attitudes (Garrettson 2018), and the American public now recognizes that most religious traditions contribute to negative attitudes toward LGBT people (Cox and Jones 2010). Yet conservative white Protestants still contest LGBT rights, and public policy debates often frame LGBT civil rights against heterosexuals' religious liberties. Denominations are splitting to make room for full participation of religious LGBT people (see M. Anderson 2020), and congregants, especially younger congregants, are leaving their faith traditions explicitly because of institutionalized homo- and transphobia (Cox, Navarro-Rivera, and Jones 2014). Underlying the entire contemporary political environment, however, is the erroneous assumption that LGBT people cannot be religious and that LGBT people do not support religious civil liberties.

Contrary to these assumptions, as I have shown throughout this text, a majority of LGBT people affiliate with a faith tradition, and religiosity among the group is similar to that of younger heterosexuals (Sherkat 2016). Religiosity among and faith communities inclusive of LGBT people represent the growing diversity of American religious experiences. Furthermore, religion is a powerful motivator of social and political behavior. Religious LGBT people regularly confront discriminatory social and political regimes, demanding the United States fully realize its promise of religious pluralism and democracy (Coley 2020). It should now be clear that studies of LGBT religion inform our understanding of American religious diversity, but also the conditions under which religiosity shapes political outcomes in majoritarian societies.

How, though, does faith shape LGBT identity and politics? In short, faith shapes LGBT identity and politics through socialization both before and after coming out. Religion provides a cosmology through which LGBT people attempt to understand who they are and their place in the world. The conditions many faith traditions place on LGBT inclusion, however, also create boundaries on LGBT people and their ability to integrate their faith, sexual orientation, and gender identity. Faith also shapes LGBT identity and politics through the provision of resources that augment political participation, particularly after coming out as LGBT. By way of concluding this text, I will review important results that support both claims and then synthesize the findings into two important lessons for American politics. Specifically, I will highlight how LGBT people are aspirational about faith—a finding that challenges the social construction of LGBT people as monolithically unreligious—and that affirming faith traditions are good for democracy.

Religious Socialization, LGBT Identity, and Politics

The data from this study make clear that faith communities are powerful agents of socialization that shape LGBT identity and politics both before and after coming out. Early in life, faith communities help define the boundaries of acceptable social behavior. As I show in Chapter 1, many faith communities understand LGBT identity through the lens of behavior. That is, many American denominations deny attribution, or the notion that same-sex attraction and gender diversity are innate characteristics. The denial of LGBT identity as a misguided moral failing brought about through strict (albeit misinformed) interpretations of religious texts, serves as the basis for the social construction of LGBT people as inherently unreligious. This is the case because many conservative religionists believe that choosing to be LGBT is tantamount to choosing to reject the divine. Strong messages of acceptance and rejection early in life have lasting effects. This is true even before LGBT people come out. For example, this study lends evidence to the idea that LGBT people raised in conservative Protestant and especially Evangelical communities are likely to delay coming out because these LGBT people first seek to establish their lives outside of their faith communities for fear that being out among their co-religionists will lead to their emotional and physical ruin. After coming out, variation in LGBT identity, political activism, and political attitudes can be traced back to either social or religious affirmation. Furthermore, the extent of one's religious individualism—that is, whether one accepts or rejects the notion that a single faith leader or doctrine has all the answers about LGBT identity—is a strong predictor of both LGBT identity and identity conflict.

LGBT people who receive positive social messages about their sexuality and gender prior to coming out have a stronger attachment to their LGBT identity later in life. Not only this, but LGBT people who receive positive social messages before coming out are also less likely to change their religious affiliation later in life. On the flip side, LGBT people who receive negative social messages prior to coming out are more likely to experience conflict between their faith and LGBT identities later in life. Among the LGBT people I surveyed, those who attempted to change their sexual orientation or gender identity through conversion therapy are also disproportionately drawn from the group who experiences conflict.

Positive religious socialization, then, is representative of a supportive social environment less constrained by hetero- and cisnormativity. This environment likely helps LGBT identity formation by fostering identity integration or at least allowing LGBT people to question hetero- and cisnormativity without as much fear of reprisal. Interestingly, such an environment also helps secure one's religious affiliation—making it less likely LGBT people will abandon or change their religions after coming out.

Later in life, the identity integration that stems from early acceptance helps LGBT people with identity maintenance and reifies lessons learned early in life about religious and LGBT identity compatibility. After coming out, positive social messages about LGBT people represented by LGBT religious organizations can overcome negative effects of religious trauma by further reducing identity conflict. Importantly, the effects of positive socialization apply even to those raised in religious traditions, such as Evangelicalism, perceived as the most hostile to LGBT identity. This is because social institutions like affirming LGBT religious organizations (and secular LGBT organizations) help LGBT people understand and internalize positive information about their LGBT identity and locate their place in society. Cosmologies that affirm LGBT identity, revere and honor sexual and gender diversity, and locate LGBT people within the divine will are strong socializing mechanisms for LGBT people who have traditionally been left out of liturgy, ritual, and observance. Overall, the social connections and cognitive resources that accrue to LGBT people in affirming faith communities make it easier to come to terms with being LGBT. In fact, many of the LGBT people I surveyed turn to both religious and secular LGBT organizations explicitly for these purposes (i.e., getting help coming to terms with their LGBT identity). LGBT people who do not have these connections may find it more difficult to mitigate identity conflict, especially if they were raised in an unwelcoming or prejudiced environment.

That is not to say that all LGBT people in nonaffirming faith traditions are destined for despair. Numerous studies of LGBT religious people in nonaffirming traditions recognize that they can adapt to survive, but also that they do affect institutional change over time (see Coley 2020; Taylor and Snowdon 2014; Thumma and Gray 2005). In fact, some LGBT people choose to stay in nonaffirming congregations so that they can spur reform and provide a more supportive environment for future LGBT people. Others who experience the constraints of racism, classism, or geography may lack access to affirming congregations and therefore stay in nonaffirming congregations out of necessity. These LGBT people also show a deep commitment to their faith and demonstrate the resilience that faith can provide, even if it must be practiced within a nonaffirming community.

This study also helps clarify the religious socialization (and its effects on politics) of LGBT POC. First, my research confirms what other studies have found with respect to religiosity among LGBT POC (see, for example Battle, Pastrana, and Daniels 2010; Battle, Pastrana, and Harris 2017). Namely, LGBT POC I surveyed are more religious than white LGBT people. This is especially true for Black LGBT people in both samples I recruited. Moreover, LGBT

POC are more likely to view Evangelical and Catholic churches as friendly. This is potentially because these traditions are overrepresented in the group's upbringing. Moving beyond what other research has shown, LGBT POC I surveyed are more likely to report hostility from the LGBT community because of their faith. Because of this hostility, Black LGBT people I surveyed are more likely to change their behavioral patterns to avoid social interactions with nonreligious LGBT people. These experiences necessarily produce differences in socialization. LGBT POC I surveyed, for example, come out earlier than white LGBT people and are more likely to join LGBT political, rather than religious or social, organizations when seeking help coming to terms with their LGBT identity.

Furthermore, among the LGBT POC I surveyed, positive social messages received before coming out appear to have limited effects on religious changes after coming out. Regardless of a positive pre–coming out social environment, LGBT POC I surveyed are less likely than white LGBT people to change their religious affiliation after coming out. This is likely because LGBT POC experience both heterosexism and racism from hetero-cis society and both racism and religious discrimination from the LGBT community. This is likely also because LGBT POC, especially Black and Latinx LGBT people I surveyed, are more likely to view religious institutions and leaders as sources of authority in their lives than are white LGBT people. For all of these reasons, LGBT POC are not as likely to change their religious affiliation and remain active in religious communities after coming out.

However, a religious upbringing and religiosity later in life do not translate into internalized homophobia for LGBT POC. Coming out may not change religious beliefs for LGBT POC as much as for white LGBT people, but attitudes about LGBT civil rights are roughly similar. In fact, coming out appears to be uniquely responsible for shifting attitudes toward transgender accommodations among the Black LGBT people I surveyed. Regardless of racial identity, coming out is a powerful agent of socialization after which both white and LGBT POC experience attitude changes that reflect an "updated" sense of relation to the LGBT community and a similar supportive shift toward LGBT-specific policy concerns. This is not to say that homo- and transphobic religious institutions are not a source of conflict for LGBT POC. For some, they can be a barrier to coming out. But many religious LGBT POC in this study seek out secular opportunities to learn about the LGBT community and for help coming to terms with their LGBT identity. For LGBT POC, it appears religious communities offer racial identity support and maintenance strategies while secular LGBT communities may be more likely to offer LGBT identity support and maintenance strategies.

The effects of socialization on political attitudes can be long lasting as LGBT people who benefited from positive socialization early in life hold more liberal social attitudes later in life. The research seems to show, however, that positive socialization may have happened disproportionately among economically advantaged LGBT people. This results in different effects on economic attitudes, but it also means that positive information about LGBT people early in life may be an issue of access that cannot solely be solved by changing people's minds. Young LGBT people must also have a way of getting or receiving positive information. In the digital age, this places a particular onus on social and digital media to provide spaces for LGBT identity and spiritual development. This is problematic, however, given the failure of social media to provide for the needs of LGBT people (see Diaz 2022 for an example).

Despite this limitation, one major finding stands out. Evidence from this study suggests that after coming out, secular LGBT socialization does not function in the same way as religious LGBT socialization when it comes to political attitudes. This is because religious socialization happens in the context of a defined faith tradition that delineates the religious responsibilities of congregants. In certain situations, one's religious obligations can supersede other considerations, like ties to one's LGBT identity or partisanship. For the LGBT people I surveyed, this happened with respect to social attitudes about topics like gun control and abortion among those who identify as "born again." However, coming out is a powerful socializing event in its own right. The same "born again" identifiers who hold conservative abortion attitudes, for example, also favor transgender accommodations in public spaces. As I explain in Chapter 7, in the latter case, LGBT identity claims to the moral and social attitudes appear to win out, while in the former case, religious claims on moral and social attitudes take precedence. Even though coming out is an important factor that alters the development of political attitudes, it does appear limited to issues of LGBT identity and/or civil rights.

The effects of religious socialization on political participation later in life are also subtle. Positive social environments can facilitate political action because one develops a sense of connection to LGBT identity and responsibility to the LGBT community, or because one experiences trauma that inspires activism to prevent future traumatic events. I explain the latter case in the next section. Contact with affirming religious communities indirectly affects electoral activism because it increases the likelihood that LGBT people will engage in solidary activism—like attending Pride events, marches, and so on. As I explain in the next section, these activities provide resources that translate into further political activism in the electoral arena.

Yet, LGBT people need not be embedded in faith communities for religion to affect identity and political development. The nature of the American political and religious systems means religion perennially overlaps with politics. The increasing access of religion to American social institutions means religion has a hand in shaping those institutions, even if it is only indirect. As many of the survey participants shared, religion is part of American culture, and LGBT people are not immune from its effects just because they are LGBT—or because they disaffiliate with religion at times. Instead, the faith of others often establishes the conditions under which LGBT people must engage in politics (see Fetner 2008; Stone 2012). Indeed, several of the LGBT people I surveyed indicated they engaged in political activism either because they experienced religious homo- or transphobia or because they want to prevent those who abuse faith for personal and political gain from accumulating political power.

Faith as an LGBT Political Resource

To this point, few studies have examined the connection between religion and political behavior among LGBT people (see Cravens 2020; 2021). The dominant theories that seek to explain how faith affects political engagement among the group rely on the assumption that one's faith tradition is generally amenable to one's participation in the tradition (i.e., being a member, holding a leadership position, being allowed to volunteer, or just being welcomed by a congregation). The long and contentious history of LGBT inclusion in American religious communities shows that the major American denominations have not always been welcoming to openly LGBT people. However, the push to democratize religious and political spaces led by the LGBT rights movement during the twentieth century resulted in both political change and welcoming religious spaces that, for the first time, afforded openly LGBT people many of the same opportunities to exercise their faith that had always been afforded to non-LGBT and closeted people. Along with the core question of how faith shapes political activism, this study also examines a tangential question: Does affirming faith affect politics the same way as nonaffirming faith?

The results of this study show that LGBT people who actively participate in a faith tradition are also more politically active than LGBT people who do not participate in a faith tradition. Faith, therefore, appears to function as an organizational resource for LGBT people to engage in electoral politics in much the same way that it does for non-LGBT people. I detail why this is important for democracy in the next section; however, the main findings of this research demonstrate that religious participation largely functions to reduce barriers to participation by facilitating political engagement. Not only this, but the primary beneficiaries of religious participation are the least politically active LGBT people in my samples.

This study offers some of the most comprehensive analyses of LGBT-affirming faith experiences yet conducted. From the rich data I collected, I can make two important points about the effect of affirming faith on LGBT politics. First, regularly practicing in an affirming faith tradition does appear to hold special significance for solidary political activism among LGBT people. Namely, affirming religiosity has a direct effect on solidary political activism—activism undertaken on behalf of the LGBT community. Affirming religiosity, especially religious traditions that have fully integrated or centered LGBT identity in their cosmologies, seem tailor-made for this kind of political work. Many of the LGBT people I surveyed share experiences about their religious community's commitment to attending local Pride events or speaking out on behalf of local and national LGBT policy issues. These solidary behaviors help educate non-LGBT people as well as LGBT people struggling to come to terms with their sexuality and/or gender identity. In fact, most of the LGBT people I surveyed who participate in affirming faith traditions seek out LGBT religious organizations explicitly for solidary benefits. For most, then, faith facilitates political participation, although, for a significant number of LGBT people, it was a change to an affirming faith that also introduced them to politics.

The second point about the effect of affirming faith on LGBT politics supported by the data in this study is that affirming faith has an indirect effect on electoral activism. Even though there is not a direct connection in statistical models between measures of religious affirmation and electoral activism, it is clear that the expanded opportunities to participate in religious activity afforded to the LGBT people I surveyed who are embedded within affirming faith communities by definition means they have more opportunities to accrue political resources than LGBT people who do not attend affirming congregations. If you are barred from membership or leadership positions within your church, as is the case for LGBT people in many prominent Christian denominations, then you cannot readily accrue organizational resources. However, organizational resources do not only accrue through participation in the formal institutions of a religious denomination. As numerous studies have shown, religious LGBT people who work within nonaffirming denominations often do their work in groups not sanctioned by the denomination (Coley 2020). Kinship International (Seventh-Day Adventist), Dignity USA (Roman Catholic), and others whose work is known by their respective denominations may not be formally recognized as official institutions of the church. Still, as the data in this study show, participation in these organizations can help build capacity for both religious and political reform by opening opportunities for LGBT people to be engaged.

It is important to note that socialization can also explain the development of political resources, particularly cognitive resources that emphasize liberal democratic norms and values. Although not all religious groups do this, many inspire both civic duty and political efficacy, key cognitive resources that are associated with political participation (see Houghland and Christenson 1983; Macaluso and Wanat 1979). Recall from Chapter 5, I classified some of the responses about the relationship between LGBT politics and religion as proactive catalytic because they reflect the respondents' experiences learning (often at an early age) that their religion values social engagement, and that was crucial to their understanding of politics later in life. Far from the separatist Christian fundamentalism that dominated much of the American religious landscape at the turn of the twentieth century, many of today's religious groups—across denominations and ideological orientations—appear to understand the utility of social activity for both political and proselytizing purposes (e.g., Marsden 1980; Swartz 2012). Many denominations encourage their members to be engaged in their community and world. This kind of civic learning, when engaged early and frequently, can have a lasting impact on congregants' willingness and ability to engage in politics throughout their life (e.g., Erikson and Tedin 2015; Neundorf and Smets 2017).

Finally, related to political resource theory, an important contribution of this study is the finding that religious and secular participation appear to convey similar resources for electoral but not solidary activism. This is consistent with existing social capital theory (see Putnam 2000; Putnam and Campbell 2010). However, this study shows that LGBT-specific social groups are an important precursor to solidary activism. Specifically, the data here show that people who participate in either secular or religious LGBT organizations appear to develop similar organizational skills and are exposed to similar recruitment structures that increase the likelihood of electoral activism. After controlling for both secular and religious participation, however, several cognitive orientations related to LGBT identity and religion remain significant predictors of solidary, but not electoral, activism. Because these cognitive resources about the compatibility of religious and LGBT identities (i.e., being LGBT is not a sin, God accepts LGBT people, and LGBT identity is inherent) are most likely to come from religious, rather than secular, socialization, this lends evidence to the conclusion that religious LGBT organizations perform a unique socializing function. In this case, religious LGBT socialization after coming out helps build cognitive capacity for religious and LGBT identity integration, which increases the likelihood of future solidary activism.

In addition to elucidating how faith shapes LGBT identity and politics, the findings from this work can be synthesized into two important lessons for American politics. These lessons not only dispel incorrect assumptions about LGBT people of faith but also demonstrate the potential of LGBT faith communities to shape the future of American democracy.

LGBT People Are Aspirational about Faith

In their evaluations of faith as a component of LGBT culture and politics, the LGBT people I surveyed are generally optimistic about the role faith can and should play in the lives of LGBT people. This is in stark contrast to the history of conservative Christian social, religious, and political organizing in the United States, which, as I show in Chapter 1, has largely constructed LGBT people as unreligious. It should be clear at this point that the social construction of LGBT people as unreligious is a myth perpetuated by opponents of LGBT rights to make it easier to dehumanize them and deny their civil rights claims in the public sphere.

It should also be clear at this point that LGBT people are not unreligious. They do not sacrifice their spirituality when they come out as LGBT. Like other social groups, there are LGBT atheists, agnostics, and those who identify as religiously unaffiliated. However, there is also a rich tapestry of faith that runs through the LGBT community. LGBT people are represented in almost every faith tradition in the United States. Even though some denominations have attempted to shred that tapestry and cut out those LGBT people through excommunication, shunning, schism, and bigotry, they have not been successful. The American pluralist tradition and the indominable LGBT spirit have proved too powerful to suppress. In the past half a century, once solidly oppositional faith traditions have opened their doors to LGBT members and leaders. Even though some traditions continue to resist, there are still LGBT people within those traditions working to bring about changes that will allow for full participation and welcoming fellowship.

Pluralism and LGBT determination have also pushed the boundaries of faith by creating spaces (not just reforming old ones) specifically for LGBT people. Many of the LGBT people I surveyed recognized the sometimes traumatic experiences religious LGBT people endure; however, most still believe religion can be a source for good, healing, support, and community. They make clear, though, that this assessment is dependent on faith being non-confrontational, welcoming, and consensual for LGBT people. Many LGBT-serving denominations have embraced this ethos and, because they were founded by LGBT leaders, center LGBT people in their tradition. The MCC is probably the largest, but there are other smaller congregations in many American cities with LGBT leadership that practice these principles.

Importantly, threads from that rich tapestry of LGBT religion frequently intertwine with politics. Historically, this has taken the form of demonstrations like the response to SOS-SF I shared at the beginning of Chapter 6, protests, participation in marches, and more. In other historical examples, the founders of LGBT religious organizations have discussed how much their faith informs their politics (see Faderman 2015; Perry 1974). Indeed, Los Angeles Pride owes its start to the efforts of religious LGBT people who began the Christopher Street West parade in June 1970 to commemorate the one-year anniversary of the Stonewall Riots in New York City (see *Call Me Troy* 2007). Following these patterns, most LGBT people I surveyed believe religion can be a force for good in politics, although, again, they recognize the shared traumatic history of religious oppression that has shaped the lives of many LGBT people. Faith inspires social action both to provide for the public good through positive social change focusing on improving the lives of LGBT people and, for a substantial proportion who entered politics to prevent conservative Christians from obtaining too much political power, to provide for the public good by maintaining America's disestablishment ethos.

Not all LGBT people are religious, nor are they all optimistic about the role of religion in American politics or LGBT culture. However, the results from this study show that most LGBT people have not internalized the negative constructions perpetuated by conservative religious activists over the last several decades. Many non-LGBT people, too, have rejected the assumption that LGBT people are not eligible for full fellowship in America's religious institutions. As I discuss in Chapter 1, public opinion polling in recent years shows that as many as seven in ten American millennials believe that religious groups are alienating young adults by being too judgmental about gay and lesbian issues, specifically (Cox, Navarro-Rivera, and Jones 2014). Most religious Americans, in fact, are changing their views on LGBT public policy issues, although survey data is lacking about Americans' perspective on religious affirmation. Some of the most recent data available (albeit from 2008) suggests a positive trend in attitudes toward LGBT affirmation among American Protestant clergy; however, at that time a majority of ministers still believed their churches should not ordain LGBT people (see Jones and Cox 2008). Yet, as of 2019, the only religious group in the United States that still predominately opposes LGBT rights is white Evangelicals, who represent an increasingly diminishing proportion of the American population, but a group whose political influence retains outsized reach (see Greenberg et al. 2019).

Affirming Faith Is Good for Democracy

This study makes clear that religion, especially faith that respects and affirms the diversity of identities inherent in the world, provides a resource to marginalized people that they can draw on to act politically to secure their rights and liberties. It ensures that marginalized groups' voices are heard, but the cross-pressures associated with religious values means they do not always speak with one voice. Some have interpreted this as a weakness of religion with respect to LGBT politics (see Mecca 2009); however, it can also mean that America's pluralistic intentions are secured as multiple competing voices are given room to speak. Regardless, a religious culture that welcomes LGBT people in full participation reflects a social and political culture that does the same. Furthermore, it reflects a political environment that provides opportunities to increase political participation among marginalized groups who are underrepresented in electoral politics. In short, the development of LGBT-affirming religious denominations and congregations is a sign of both a healthy pluralistic religious environment and a healthy democracy.

As I explain in Chapter 6, faith is a mobilizing force whose electoral benefits extend to LGBT people even if their LGBT identity is not fully affirmed by their religious community. However, affirming faith makes it more likely that LGBT people will engage on behalf of the group, taking risks and making public statements about LGBT marginalization, working to make the world better for others. Participation in a faith tradition reduces barriers to LGBT political participation, and the LGBT people who engage politically do so on behalf of marginalized people. Not only this, but as I also show in Chapter 6, the benefits of religious participation are most pronounced among those who are the least politically active. LGBT people who never vote, for example, are significantly more likely to vote in the future if they regularly practice their faith.

These benefits of affirming faith and the idealized vision of queer faith are expressed by survey participants in both samples I evaluated. In Chapter 5, the LGBT people I surveyed said "queer religion should be welcoming, nonconfrontational, consensual, and socially transformative." In Chapter 6 and Chapter 7, the statistical analyses show the LGBT people I surveyed who experience faith in this way also put those beliefs into practice by engaging in religious, political, and socially transformative activism.

LGBT faith fits within a long history of American religious pluralism. Although their faith has often been denied and the group constructed as unreligious, LGBT people of faith persist. The percentage of Americans who affiliate with a faith tradition is decreasing (see Pew Research Center 2022). One reason for the decline in affiliation is because young people reject faiths that discriminate against LGBT people (Cox, Navarro-Rivera, and Jones 2014). As the LGBT population in the United States increases, religious institutions in America—which have always been reliant on public support (see Hill 1980)—must carefully consider their response. Will they perpetuate a prejudicial myth that LGBT people cannot be religious, or will they embrace and welcome LGBT people? It is clear that American religious institutions that ignore LGBT people or continue to discriminate against them risk losing both LGBT and non-LGBT parishioners (see Coley and Cravens 2022).

Regardless of the response of America's faith traditions, LGBT people will continue to exercise their faith. Faith, even when not explicitly affirming of LGBT identity, will also continue to be a resource for LGBT people in their struggle to shape a more welcoming society. The reciprocal relationship between faith and LGBT identity development described in this book means that religion will also continue to shape the lived experiences of LGBT people. More affirming faith traditions ultimately reflects the construction of a multicultural democracy that embraces diversity and values the contributions and participation of all people. Fewer affirming faith traditions reflects the opposite, a society that limits the benefits of faith and citizenship to a select few who match a cisheterosexist prototype. Importantly, this book shows that LGBT people—and, specifically, LGBT people of faith—have agency and power in the political and religious processes that will determine America's future.

Notes

INTRODUCTION

1. The edited volume by Mecca (2009) contains a manifesto, first published in 1976, from the Philadelphia-based group Gay Pagans and Atheists that details a politicized argument for this kind of post–coming out transformation. The manifesto critiques organized religion, and even "gay church apologists" in the United States, not only for the negative treatment of LGBT people but also for chauvinist, classist, and racist misdeeds perpetuated throughout Western history.

Interestingly, contemporary research suggests disassociation with a religious tradition after coming out is not enough to completely eliminate the psychological stress experienced when one believes one's religious and sexual identities to be incongruent. In fact, depending on the data source, 10% to 25% of LGBT people who identify as atheist or agnostic also report conflict between their religious beliefs and sexual identity (Cravens 2018). The internalized effects of religious-based homo- and transphobia, then, often extend well into an individual's openly LGBT life, even if they no longer affiliate with any religious tradition.

2. While "it is difficult to know what people mean when they say they are spiritual but not religious," Chaves (2011, 41) suggests "the most obvious interpretation is that such people consider themselves to be generally concerned with spiritual matters but are not interested in organized religion." The trend among the general population toward a "spiritual but not religious" affiliation, it is suggested, is occurring because "nonreligious people are more likely to say they are spiritual, not because people are less likely to say they are religious" (Chaves 2011, 40).

3. I have attempted to mitigate many of these methodological biases by designing and testing a unique survey instrument (which I describe in Chapter 3). The nature of survey research creates limitations (of time and space, for example), however, which mean that not all biases are eliminated. Related to Christian religiocenrism, for example, I attempt

to measure religious participation using not just questions about church attendance or scripture reading but also meditation—attempting to balance both private and public devotional practices that vary across faith traditions. Although not perfect, my methodology represents the best way to undertake this study given the many constraints associated with LGBT and religious survey research I detail in this section of the Introduction.

CHAPTER 1

1. The 2020 general conference of the UMC was postponed due to the coronavirus pandemic. The proposal to split the denomination was tabled until the next general conference, scheduled for 2022. Prior to that meeting, some conservative Methodist congregations formed their own denomination—the Global Methodist Church—arguing that it was the inevitable conclusion of the 2020 protocol. The move, in particular, seemed to rankle the more liberal and moderate factions of the general conference, who pulled their support for the plan in 2022 (Miller 2022). With the conservative factions outnumbered, the denomination could finally support full inclusion of LGBT people; however, the issue has not been decided as of this writing.

2. Oldfield (1996) also identifies nationalism as a "subcultural trait" of Evangelicalism. Although not discussed here, the idea that America (as the "city on a hill") is the example of Christian morality for other nations also has a relationship to the perpetuation of anti-LGBT prejudice. In addition to fomenting a closer relationship between conservative Evangelicalism and white Christian nationalism, as the LGBT movement accrued policy successes in the United States, many Evangelicals turned their attention to "shining the light" on regions of the world whose cultures align with Evangelical theology. Leading American Evangelicals, for example, have been instrumental in the creation of the World Congress of Families, an international nongovernmental organization founded by a professor at the conservative Christian Hillsdale College to promote the strict heteronormative and patriarchal view of the family that lobbies against LGBT rights internationally. In a 2007 "manifesto," the group's founder and former executive vice president declared, "The complementary natures of men and women, both physically and psychologically, are evident throughout the course of human history and in every society. Deviations from natural sexual behavior cannot truly satisfy the human spirit" (SPLC 2020). See also Baptiste (2014) and Federman (2014).

3. Premillenarianism is a form of eschatology (the branch of theology concerned with death and the soul). This pessimistic belief, popular among many twentieth-century Christians, derives from biblical pronouncements about the Second Coming of Christ. In this view, the faithful will be "raptured" seven years before the actual Second Coming. During the intervening period of "tribulation," those "left behind" will struggle against satanic forces unleashed on the world before Christ returns to vanquish all evil and establish a thousand-year reign of peace on Earth. Many fundamentalists at the turn of the twentieth century interpreted this as a mandate to avoid social and political entanglements (be heavenly minded). It is often contrasted with postmillenarianism. This more optimistic belief, popular among many nineteenth-century Christians, suggests the Second Coming will occur at the end of a thousand-year period of peace in which Christianity becomes the guiding principle of all mankind. Many believers interpreted this as a mandate to reform society in the image of Christian morality to speed the Second Coming. Many Evangelicals are not theological fundamentalists, and throughout the twentieth century they blended the pessimism of the former eschatology with the political mandate of the latter.

4. Collectively, W. Dorr Legg referred to these institutions as "the Four Horsemen of the Gay Apocalypse" (Faderman 2015). The reference evokes the figures mentioned in the final book of the Christian Bible, "Revelation" or the "Apocalypse of John," which are responsible for unleashing various cataclysms on the earth in the period before the final judgment of humanity. The biblical riders symbolized Conquest, War, Famine, and Death, and were mounted on white, red, black, and pale horses, respectively. It is unclear if Legg meant to imply the animosity between LGBT people and religion was ineradicable; however, that Legg would equate "religion" with such destructive imagery reveals the profound distrust of the institution, its leaders, and its adherents among some early LGBT activists.

CHAPTER 2

1. In 2016, 369 respondents who identified as transgender also identified as lesbian, gay, bisexual, or as another sexual orientation. In 2017, 184 respondents who identified as transgender also identified as lesbian, gay, bisexual, or as another sexual orientation. In 2018, 503 respondents who identified as transgender also identified as lesbian, gay, bisexual, or as another sexual orientation. In 2019, 205 respondents who identified as transgender also identified as lesbian, gay, bisexual, or as another sexual orientation.

CHAPTER 3

1. Thank you to Lydia Gomez de la Vega and the California Polytechnic State University BEACoN Research Mentorship program, Samantha Sukhram, and Angel Powell for assisting in the design and construction of the survey instruments and helping to analyze data and prepare conference presentations.

The first survey was approved by California Polytechnic State University Institutional Review Board (IRB) on April 7, 2021. IRB #2021-075-OL. The second survey was approved by California Polytechnic State University IRB on November 14, 2021. IRB #2021-221-OL.

2. Funding to conduct this survey was awarded through the California Polytechnic State University Research Scholarly and Creative Activities (RSCA) Grant Program administered by the Cal Poly division of Research, Economic Development and Graduate Education. In accordance with the provisions of the grant application, survey data collected from the quota sample of LGBT people is available for public download through Dataverse. See Cravens (2022b).

3. The reasons for this difficulty constitute what I characterize as a cycle of marginalization within social scientific research that perpetually excludes LGBT people. The process begins when LGBT people are excluded from social scientific research designs. Heterosexism and cisnormativity in the social sciences contribute to characterizations of LGBT people as non-normative, a mere minority of the population, an aberration that, for many, does not warrant independent study (Herek 2007; Mucciaroni 2011; Novkov and Barclay 2010). Exclusion of LGBT experiences from research designs feeds a data gap about LGBT people in social scientific research. For example, the General Social Survey, the longest-running survey of American social and political experiences, has measured respondents' attitudes about homosexuality since 1973; however, the survey instrument was not designed to actually ask respondents' sexual orientation until 2008. Not only in research designs but bias in funding opportunities, too, limits the ability of survey researchers to recruit probability samples of LGBT people (see Coulter et al. 2014; Gates 2017).

The lack of funding means random sampling can be employed to recruit LGBT people for survey research, but the cost associated with recruiting a large enough sample to make statistically meaningful observations is prohibitive for most academic researchers. Because data about the experiences of LGBT people are, therefore, limited, their experiences can be easily dismissed as unimportant or marginal compared to the sociopolitical experiences of heterosexuals. Their reified marginality, then, makes them unworthy of inclusion in research designs and the cycle begins anew.

4. Panel data would be ideal—that is, survey data from the same individuals tracking the same behaviors over a long period of time. However, such a design that focuses explicitly on religious and political experiences over a time horizon that would track LGBT people from youth through adulthood has never been undertaken. Furthermore, because a panel study of that magnitude is beyond the financial resources of the author, it is necessary to rely on retrospective survey questions to ascertain past behavior (Magnusson and Bergman 1990).

CHAPTER 4

1. I asked the two samples of survey participants in this study to describe how their religious beliefs changed after coming out as LGBT. Of the 1,100 responses, six in ten said they experienced no change in their religious beliefs, while about three in ten, slightly more than what Egan, Edelman, and Sherrill (2008) found more than fourteen years ago, said they became less religious. About 6% of the people I surveyed said they became more religious after coming out.

2. Since about 60% of the survey participants reported becoming no more or less religious after coming out, this lends evidence to the point in the preceding paragraphs that being "religious" means more than simply identifying with a faith tradition and likely has more to do with how the people I interviewed changed their public and private religious devotion after coming out as LGBT.

CHAPTER 5

1. The analysis was greatly improved by the work of two research assistants, Angel Powell and Lydia Gomez de la Vega, and by helpful comments from Dr. Kylie Parrotta.

CHAPTER 6

1. In both contemporary and historical accounts of SOS-SF activism during this period, SOS-SF mentions its intention to remain apolitical and that was and is not affiliated with the Moral Majority. In the O'Laughlin (1981) story, Michael Brodeur, who is cited as the "coordinator for SOS," is quoted saying as much. Brodeur is also listed on the SOS Ministries website as a "Founding Father" of the group and as pastor of Promised Land Fellowship in San Francisco (https://www.sosmin.com/?page_id=51). The same organization has been the subject of protests by San Francisco's LGBT community for promoting "conversion therapy" programs. A 2007 SFGate.com story about one of the protests notes that Brodeur and his wife "do weekly outreach in the Castro to encourage gay people to re-evaluate their sexual orientation" (https://www.sfgate.com/bayarea/article/SAN-FRANCISCO-Demonstrators-protest-ex-gay-2616741.php).

CHAPTER 7

1. The alternate regression models use a binary racial identity variable for Black or Latinx. The appropriate binary variable is interacted with the other independent variables of interest. The models are calculated with robust standard errors; however, the small sample size of Black and Latinx respondents results in low cell counts in certain situations (i.e., for Black LGBT people who identified as Roman Catholic, non-Christians, or atheist before coming out and for Latinx LGBT people who identified as anything other than Roman Catholic before coming out) that make it all but impossible to confidently infer relationships from the data. I, therefore, do not make any representations about statistical relationships based on these data points.

2. While it could be argued that the results reflect an artifact or anomaly in the data, relationship between the "born again" dummy variable and support for sexual orientation–based and gender identity–based protections in law is also positive (as shown in Online Statistical Appendix XIV). However, in these cases, the level of statistical significance is $p \leq .1$, which is greater than the traditional value of $p \leq .05$. So, although the relationship achieves statistical significance, it is not at traditional levels of significance; therefore, I cannot reject the null hypotheses in these cases.

References

Adamczyk, Amy, and Cassady Pitt. 2009. "Shaping Attitudes about Homosexuality: The Role of Religion and Cultural Context." *Social Science Research* 38(2): 338–351.

Adibi, Ida. 2020. "Voting While Trans: How to Combat Voter ID Laws and Disenfranchisement of the Transgender Community." *Georgetown Journal of Gender and the Law* 22(1): Online. https://www.law.georgetown.edu/gender-journal/voting-while-trans-how-to-combat-voter-id-laws-and-disenfranchisement-of-the-transgender-community/. Accessed 9/5/2022.

Alwin, Duane F., and Jon A. Krosnick. 1991. "Aging, Cohorts, and the Stability of Sociopolitical Orientations over the Life Span." *American Journal of Sociology* 97(1): 169–95.

American Council of Christian Churches. 2019. "Resolution on Religious Freedom and 'The Equality Act.'" Orwell, OH: ACCC. https://accc4truth.org/2019/11/20/religious-freedom-and-the-equality-act/. Accessed 10/14/2020.

Ammerman, Nancy Tatom. 1987. *Bible Believers: Fundamentalists in the Modern World.* New Brunswick, NJ: Rutgers University Press.

Anderson, Joel R., and Yasin Koc. 2020. "Identity Integration as a Protective Factor against Guilt and Shame for Religious Gay Men." *Journal of Sex Research* 57(8): 1059–68.

Anderson, Meg. 2020. "United Methodist Church Announces Proposal to Split Over Gay Marriage." *NPR*, January 4, 2020. https://www.npr.org/2020/01/04/793614135/united-methodist-church-announces-proposal-to-split-over-gay-marriage. Accessed 9/23/2020.

Ansolabehere, Stephen, and Brian F. Schaffner. 2017. "CCES Common Content, 2016." *Harvard Dataverse.* https://dataverse.harvard.edu/api/access/datafile/3047286. Accessed August 1, 2020.

Ansolabehere, Stephen, Brian F. Schaffner, and Samantha Luks. 2020. "CCES Common Content, 2019." *Harvard Dataverse.* https://doi.org/10.7910/DVN/WOT7O8. Accessed August 1, 2020.

Ayers, John W., and C. Richard Hofstetter. 2008. "American Muslim Political Participation Following 9/11: Religious Beliefs, Political Resources, Social Structures, and Political Awareness." *Politics and Religion* 1(1): 3–26.

Baca Zinn, Maxine, and Bonnie Thornton Dill. 1996. "Theorizing Difference from Multiracial Feminism." *Feminist Studies* 22(2): 321–31.

Baptiste, Nathalie. 2014. "It's Not Just Uganda: Behind the Christian Right's Onslaught in Africa." *The Nation*, April 4, 2014. https://www.thenation.com/article/archive/its -not-just-uganda-behind-christian-rights-onslaught-africa/. Accessed 10/11/2020.

Barringer, M. N. 2019. "Lesbian, Gay, and Bisexual Individuals' Perceptions of American Religious Traditions." *Journal of Homosexuality* 67(9): 1173–96.

Barton, Bernadette. 2010. "'Abomination'—Life as a Bible Belt Gay." *Journal of Homosexuality* 57(4): 465–84.

———. 2011. "1CROSS + 3NAILS = 4GVN: Compulsory Christianity and Homosexuality in the Bible Belt Panopticon." *Feminist Formations* 23(1): 70–93.

———. 2012. *Pray the Gay Away: The Extraordinary Lives of Bible Belt Gays*. New York: NYU Press.

Bates, Aryana. 2005. "Liberation in Truth: African American Lesbians Reflect on Religion, Spirituality, and Their Church." In Scott Thumma and Edward R. Gray (Eds.), *Gay Religion*, pp. 221–37. Lanham, MD: AltaMira Press.

Battle, Juan, Antonio Jay Pastrana, and Jessie Daniels. 2010. "Social Justice Survey Project: 2010 National Survey, Including Puerto Rico." Ann Arbor, MI: Inter-University Consortium for Political and Social Research.

Battle, Juan, Antonio Pastrana Jr., and Angelique Harris. 2017. *An Examination of Black LGBT Populations Across the United States: Intersections of race and sexuality*. New York: Palgrave Macmillan.

Bennet, Allen, Ken Kammann, Jim N. Dykes, and Jane Adams Sphar. 1981. "The 'Moral Majority'—A Response." *More Light Update*, June 1981, pp. 1, 9. Shepard Family Papers (Box 9 MS 2988–15), Oregon Historical Society Research Library, Portland, OR, United States.

Bennett, Matthew R., and Christopher J. Einolf. 2017. "Religion, Altruism, and Helping Strangers: A Multilevel Analysis of 126 Countries." *Journal for the Scientific Study of Religion* 56(2): 323–41.

Berger, Peter L., and Thomas Luckman. 1966. *The Social Construction of Reality: A Treaties in the Sociology of Knowledge*. New York: Anchor Books.

Bernstein, Mary. 1997. "Celebration and Suppression: The Strategic Uses of Identity by the Lesbian and Gay Movement." *American Journal of Sociology* 103(3): 531–65.

Bérubé, Allan. 1990. *Coming Out Under Fire: The History of Gay Men and Women in World War Two*. New York: The Free Press.

———. 2001. "How Gay Stays White and What Kind of White It Stays." In Birgit Brander Rasmussen, Eric Klinenberg, Irene J. Nexica, and Matt Wray (Eds.), *The Making and Unmaking of Whiteness*, pp. 234–65. Durham, NC: Duke University Press.

Beyerlein, Kraig, and Mark Chaves. 2003. "The Political Activities of Religious Congregations in the United States." *Journal for the Scientific Study of Religion* 42(2): 229–46.

Bonilla-Silva, Eduardo. 2018. *Racism without Racists: Color-Blind Racism and the Persistence of Racial Inequality in America*, 5th ed. Lanham, MD: Rowman & Littlefield.

Boykin, Keith. 1998. *One More River to Cross: Black and Gay in America*. New York: Anchor.

Brady, Henry E., Sidney Verba, and Kay Lehman Schlozman. 1995. "Beyond SES: A Resource Model of Political Participation." *The American Political Science Review* 89(2): 271–94.

Brega, Angela G., and Lerita M. Coleman. 1999. "Effects of Religiosity and Racial Social-ization on Subjective Stigmatization in African American Adolescents." *Journal of Adolescence* 22: 223–42.

Brown, R. Khari, and Ronald E. Brown. 2003. "Faith and Works: Church-Based Social Capital Resources and African American Political Activism." *Social Forces* 82(2): 617–41.

Browne, Kath, Sally R. Munt, and Andrew K. T. Yip. 2010. *Queer Spiritual Spaces: Sexuality and Sacred Spaces*. Burlington, VT: Ashgate.

Bull, Chris, and John Gallagher. 2001. *Perfect Enemies: The Battle between the Religious Right and the Gay Movement*. Lanham, MA: Madison Books.

Bullock, III, Charles S., and John Christopher Grant. 1995. "Georgia: The Christian Right and Grass Roots Power." In Mark J. Rozell and Clyde Wilcox (Eds.), *God at the Grass Roots: The Christian Right and the 1994 Elections*, pp. 47–65. New York: Rowman & Littlefield.

Burdette, Amy M., Christopher G. Ellison, and Terrence D. Hill. 2005. "Conservative Prot-estantism and Tolerance toward Homosexuals: An Examination of Potential Mecha-nisms." *Sociological Inquiry* 75(2): 177–96.

Burge, Ryan P. 2021. "What's Up with Born-Again Muslims? And What Does That Tell Us about American Religion?" *Religion in Public*, March 2, 2021. https://religionin public.blog/2021/03/02/whats-up-with-born-again-muslims-and-what-does-that-tells -us-about-american-religion/. Accessed 3/4/2021.

Burgess, Susan, and Anna Sampaio. 2017. "Power, Politics, and Difference in the Amer-ican Political Science Association: An Intersectional Analysis of the New Orleans Sit-ing Controversy." In Marla Brettschneider, Susan Burgess, and Christine Keating (Eds.), *LGBTQ Politics: A Critical Reader*, pp. 198–211. New York: NYU Press.

Cadge, Wendy. 2005. "Reconciling Congregations Bridging Gay and Straight Communi-ties." In Scott Thumma and Edward R. Gray (Eds.), *Gay Religion*, pp. 31–45. Lanham, MD: AltaMira Press.

Calhoun-Brown, Allison. 1996. "African American Churches and Political Mobilization: The Psychological Impact of Organizational Resources." *The Journal of Politics* 58(4): 935–53.

———. 1999. "The Image of God: Black Theology and Racial Empowerment in the Afri-can American Community." *Review of Religious Research* 40(3): 197–212.

Call Me Troy. Dir. Scott Bloom. Frameline, 2007. Film.

Calvillo, Jonathan, and Stanley R. Bailey. 2015. "Latino Religious Affiliation and Ethnic Identity." *Journal for the Scientific Study of Religion* 54(1): 57–78.

Cassel, Carol A. 1999. "Voluntary Associations, Churches, and Social Participation The-ories of Turnout." *Social Science Quarterly* 80(3): 504–17.

Castle, Jeremiah. 2019. "New Fronts in the Culture Wars? Religion, Partisanship, and Po-larization on Religious Liberty and Transgender Rights in the United States." *Amer-ican Politics Research* 47(3): 650–79.

Cavendish, James C. 2002. "Church-Based Community Activism: A Comparison of Black and White Catholic Churches." *Journal for the Scientific Study of Religion* 39(3): 371–84.

Chappell, Bill. 2019. "United Methodist Church Votes to Keep Bans on Same-Sex Wed-dings, LGBTQ Clergy." *NPR*, February 26, 2019. https://www.npr.org/2019/02/26/698 188343/united-methodist-church-votes-to-keep-bans-on-same-sex-weddings-lgbtq -clergy. Accessed 9/23/2020.

Chaves, Mark. 2004. *Congregations in America*. Cambridge, MA: Harvard University Press.

———. 2011. *American Religion: Contemporary Trends*. Princeton: Princeton University Press.

Chen, C., and Jeung, R. (Eds.). 2012. *Sustaining Faith Traditions: Race, Ethnicity, and Religion among the Latino and Asian American Second Generation*. New York: NYU Press.

Cherry, Kittredge. 2012. "Rainbow Christ Prayer Honors LGBT Spirituality." *Huffington Post*, June 25, 2012. https://www.huffpost.com/entry/rainbow-christ-prayer-hon_b_1616193. Accessed 3/10/2021.

Claassen, Ryan L., and Andrew Povtak. 2010. "The Christian Right Thesis: Explaining Longitudinal Change in Participation among Evangelical Christians." *The Journal of Politics* 72(1): 2–15.

Coley, Jonathan S. 2020. "Reframing, Reconciling, and Individualizing: How LGBTQ Activist Groups Shape Approaches to Religion and Sexuality." *Sociology of Religion* 81(1): 45–67.

Coley, Jonathan S., and R. G. Cravens. 2022. "Record Numbers of Americans Identify as LGBTQ. What Does That Mean for Christianity?" *Religion News Service*, February 23, 2022. https://religionnews.com/2022/02/23/record-numbers-of-americans-identify-as-lgbtq-what-does-that-mean-for-christianity/. Accessed 7/1/2022.

Comstock, Gary David. 1996. *Unrepentant, Self-Affirming, Practicing: Lesbian/Bisexual/Gay People within Organized Religion*. New York: Continuum.

Conron, Kerith J., Shoshana K. Goldberg, and Kathryn O'Neill. 2020. "Religiosity Among LGBT Adults in the US." Los Angeles, CA: Williams Institute.

Converse, Philip. 1964. "The Nature of Belief Systems in Mass Publics." In David Apter (Ed.), *Ideology and Discontent*, pp. 206–61. New York: Free Press.

Cook, Timothy E. 1979. "Legislature vs. Legislator: A Note on the Paradox of Congressional Support." *Legislative Studies Quarterly* 4: 43–52.

Coulter, Robert W. S., Karey S. Kenst, Deborah J. Bowen, and Scout. 2014. "Research Funded by the National Institutes of Health on the Health of Lesbian, Gay, Bisexual, and Transgender Populations." *American Journal of Public Health* 104(2): e105–e112.

Council on Religion and the Homosexual. n.d. "CRH Formed." *LGBT Religious Archives Network*. https://lgbtqreligiousarchives.org/exhibits/crh/R. Accessed 2/1/2021.

Cox, Daniel, and Robert P. Jones. 2010. "Less Than 1-in-5 Give America's Places of Worship High Marks on Handling Issue of Homosexuality." Washington, DC: Public Religion Research Institute. https://www.prri.org/research/less-than-1-in-5-give-americas-places-of-worship-high-marks-on-handling-issue-of-homosexuality/. Accessed 10/14/2020.

———. 2011. "Generations at Odds: The Millennial Generation and the Future of Gay and Lesbian Rights." Washington, DC: Public Religion Research Institute. https://www.prri.org/research/generations-at-odds/. Accessed 10/16/2020.

Cox, Daniel, Juhem Navarro-Rivera, and Robert P. Jones. 2014. "A Shifting Landscape: A Decade of Change in American Attitudes about Same-Sex Marriage and LGBT Issues." Washington, DC: Public Religion Research Institute. https://www.prri.org/research/2014-lgbt-survey/. Accessed 10/20/2020.

Cragun, Ryan T., and J. E. Sumerau. 2015. "The Last Bastion of Sexual and Gender Prejudice? Sexualities, Race, Gender, Religiosity, and Spirituality in the Examination of Prejudice toward Sexual and Gender Minorities." *Journal of Sex Research* 52(7): 821–34.

———. 2017. "No One Expects a Transgender Jew: Religious, Sexual and Gendered Intersections in the Evaluation of Religious and Nonreligious Others." *Secularism and Nonreligion* 6(1): 1–16.

Crary, David. 2021. "Southern Baptists Oust 2 Churches over LGBTQ Inclusion." *AP News*, February 23, 2021. https://apnews.com/article/race-and-ethnicity-baptist-south ern-baptist-convention-kentucky-louisville-3d117834c18621f0af125f192d4a194c. Accessed 2/24/2021.

Cravens, Royal Gene. 2017. "Politics at the Intersection of Sexuality: Examining Political Attitudes and Behaviors of Sexual Minorities in the United States." PhD diss., University of Tennessee. http://trace.tennessee.edu/utk_graddiss/4453.

———. 2018. "The Politics of Queer Religion." *Politics and Religion* 11(3): 576–623.

———. 2019. "Same-Sex Marriage and the Policy Process." *Sexuality, Gender and Policy Journal* 2(1): 43–85.

———. 2020. "The Tipping Point: Examining the Effects of Heterosexist and Racist Stigma on Political Participation." *Social Politics*. Online First: https://doi.org/10.1093/sp /jxaa009.

———. 2021. "The View from the Top: Social Acceptance and Ideological Conservatism among Sexual Minorities." *Politics, Groups, and Identities* 9(5): 975–96.

———. 2022a. "Christian Nationalism: A Stained-Glass Ceiling for LGBT Candidates?" *Politics, Groups, and Identities*. Online First: https://www.tandfonline.com/doi/abs /10.1080/21565503.2022.2070076.

———. 2022b. "Yes Gawd! How Faith Shapes LGBT Identity and Politics Data and Appendices." *Harvard Dataverse*. https://doi.org/10.7910/DVN/M87Q1V.

Dana, Karam, Matt A. Barreto, and Kassra A. R. Oskooii. 2011. "Mosques as American Institutions: Mosque Attendance, Religiosity and Integration into the Political System among American Muslims." *Religions* 2(4): 504–24.

Davenport, Lauren D. 2016. "The Role of Gender, Class, and Religion in Biracial Americans' Racial Labeling Decisions." *American Sociological Review* 81(1): 57–84.

DeFilippis, Joseph N., and Ben Anderson-Nathe. 2017. "Embodying Margin to Center: Intersectional Activism among Queer Liberation Organizations." In Marla Brettschneider, Susan Burgess, and Cricket Keating (Eds.), *LGBTQ Politics: A Critical Reader*, pp. 110–33. New York: New York University Press.

Delli Carpini, Michael X., and Scott Keeter. 1996. *What Americans Know about Politics and Why It Matters*. New Haven, CT: Yale University Press.

D'Emilio, John. 1998. *Sexual Politics, Sexual Communities*, 2nd ed. Chicago: University of Chicago Press.

Diaz, Jaclyn. 2022. "GLAAD Gives Social Media Giants Poor Grades over Lack of Protections for LGBTQ Users." *NPR*, July 13, 2022. https://www.npr.org/2022/07/13/1111 113396/glaad-social-media-report-lgbtq-online-harassment. Accessed 9/8/2022.

Diner, Hasia R. 2004. *The Jews of the United States, 1654 to 2000*. Berkeley: University of California Press.

Djupe, Paul A., and Christopher P. Gilbert. 2006. "The Resourceful Believer: Generating Civic Skills in Church." *The Journal of Politics* 68(1): 116–27.

———. 2009. *The Political Influence of Churches*. New York: Cambridge University Press.

Djupe, Paul A., and J. Tobin Grant. 2001. "Religious Institutions and Political Participation in America." *Journal for the Scientific Study of Religion* 40(2): 303–14.

Djupe, Paul A., and Jacob R. Neiheisel. 2012. "How Religious Communities Affect Political Participation among Latinos." *Social Science Quarterly* 93(2): 333–55.

Djupe, Paul A., Jacob R. Neiheisel, and Anand E. Sokhey. 2018. "Reconsidering the Role of Politics in Leaving Religion: The Importance of Affiliation." *American Journal of Political Science* 62(1): 161–75.

Djupe, Paul A., Anand E. Sokhey, and Christopher P. Gilbert. 2007. "Present but Not Accounted For? Gender Differences in Civic Resource Acquisition." *American Journal of Political Science* 51(4): 906–20.

Domke, David, and Kevin Coe. 2008. *The God Strategy: How Religion Became a Political Weapon in America*. New York: Oxford University Press.

Donovan, Mark C. 1997. "The Problem with Making AIDS Comfortable." *Journal of Homosexuality* 32(3–4): 115–44.

Driskell, Robyn, Elizabeth Embry, and Larry Lyon. 2008. "Faith and Politics: The Influence of Religious Beliefs on Political Participation." *Social Science Quarterly* 89(2): 294–314.

Duberman, Martin Bauml, Martha Vicinus, and George Chauncey Jr. (Eds.). 1989. *Hidden from History: Reclaiming the Gay and Lesbian Past*. New York: Penguin.

Duncan, Lauren, E., Elizabeth Mincer, and Sarah R. Dunn. 2017. "Assessing Politicized Sexual Orientation Identity: Validating the Queer Consciousness Scale." *Journal of Homosexuality* 64(8): 1069–91.

Eck, Diana. 2001. *A New Religious America: How a "Christian Country" Has Become the World's Most Religiously Diverse Nation*. San Francisco: HarperCollins.

Egan, Patrick J. 2012. "Group Cohesion without Group Mobilization: The Case of Lesbians, Gays and Bisexuals." *British Journal of Political Science* 42: 597–616.

———. 2020. "Identity as Dependent Variable: How Americans Shift Their Identities to Align with Their Politics." *American Journal of Political Science* 64(3): 699–716.

Egan, Patrick J., Murray S. Edelman, and Kenneth Sherrill. 2008. *Findings from the Hunter College Poll of Lesbians, Gays, and Bisexuals: New Discoveries about Identity, Political Attitudes, and Civic Engagement*. New York: Hunter: The City University of New York.

Ellison, Christopher G., Gabriel A. Acevedo, and Aida I. Ramos-Wada. 2011. "Religion and Attitudes toward Same-Sex Marriage among U.S. Latinos." *Social Science Quarterly* 92(1): 35–56.

Erikson, Robert S., and Kent L. Tedin. 2015. *American Public Opinion: Its Origins, Content and Impact*, 9th ed. New York: Routledge.

Erzen, Tanya. 2006. *Straight to Jesus: Sexual and Christian Conversions in the Ex-Gay Movement*. Berkeley: University of California Press.

Faderman, Lilian. 2015. *The Gay Revolution: The Story of the Struggle*. New York: Simon & Schuster.

Family Acceptance Project. n.d. "Overview." San Francisco State University. https://familyproject.sfsu.edu/overview. Accessed 3/24/2022.

Fassinger, Ruth E., and Julie R. Arseneau. 2007. "I'd Rather Get Wet Than Be Under That Umbrella: Differentiating the Experiences and Identities of Lesbian, Gay, Bisexual, and Transgender People." In Kathleen J. Bieschke, Ruperto M. Perez, and Kurt A. DeBord (Eds.), *Handbook of Counseling and Psychotherapy with Lesbian, Gay, Bisexual, and Transgender Clients*, pp. 19–49. Washington, DC: American Psychological Association.

Federman, Adam. 2014. "How US Evangelicals Fueled the Rise of Russia's 'Pro-Family' Right." *The Nation*, January 7, 2014. https://www.thenation.com/article/archive/how-us-evangelicals-fueled-rise-russias-pro-family-right/. Accessed 10/11/2020.

Fetner, Tina. 2008. *How the Religious Right Shaped Lesbian and Gay Activism*. Minneapolis: University of Minnesota Press.

Finke, Roger, and Amy Adamczyk. 2008. "Cross-National Moral Beliefs: The Influence of National Religious Context." *The Sociological Quarterly* 46(4): 617–52.

Finke, Roger, and Rodney Stark. 1992. *The Churching of America, 1776–1990: Winners and Losers in Our Religious Economy.* New Brunswick, NJ: Rutgers University Press.

Fiorina, Morris P., Samuel J. Abrams, and Jeremy C. Pope. 2011. *Culture War? The Myth of a Polarized America,* 3rd ed. Boston: Longman.

FitzGerald, Frances. 2017. *The Evangelicals: The Struggle to Shape America.* New York: Simon & Schuster.

Flores, Andrew, Donald P. Haider-Markle, Daniel Lewis, Patrick Miller, Barry Tadlock, and Jami Taylor. 2018. "Challenged Expectations: Mere Exposure Effects on Attitudes about Transgender People and Rights." *Political Psychology* 39(1): 197–216.

For the Bible Tells Me So. Dir. Daniel G. Karslake. First Run Features, 2007. Film.

Friesen, Amanda J., and Paul A. Djupe. 2017. "Conscientious Women Under the Stained Glass Ceiling: The Dispositional Conditions of Institutional Treatment on Civic Engagement." *Politics and Gender* 13(1): 57–80.

Frontline. 2000. "Reverend Jerry Falwell." Boston: WGBH Educational Foundation. https:// www.pbs.org/wgbh/pages/frontline/shows/assault/interviews/falwell.html#4. Accessed 10/9/2020.

Fuist, Todd Nicholas. 2016. "It Just Always Seemed Like It Wasn't a Big Deal, Yet I Know for Some People They Really Struggle with It: LGBT Religious Identities in Context." *Journal for the Scientific Study of Religion* 55(4): 770–86.

Gabriel, Richard A. 1972. "A New Theory of Ethnic Voting." *Polity* 4(4): 405–28.

Gamson, William A. 1992. *Talking Politics.* New York: Cambridge University Press.

Garcia, Bernardo. 1998. *The Development of A Latino Gay Identity.* New York: Garland.

Garretson, Jeremiah J. 2018. *The Path to Gay Rights: How Activism and Coming Out Changed Public Opinion.* New York: NYU Press.

Gates, Gary J. 2017. "LGBT Data Collection amid Social and Demographic Shifts of the US LGBT Community." *American Journal of Public Health* 107(8): 1220–22.

Gay, David A., and Christopher G. Ellison. 1993. "Religious Subcultures and Political Tolerance: Do Denominations Still Matter?" *Review of Religious Research* 34(4): 311–32.

Gay Atheist League of America. 1978. "Flyer from Gay Atheist League of America." *LGBTQ Religious Archives Network.* https://lgbtqreligiousarchives.org/exhibits/sam pler/View.aspx?ID=GAL&Page=1. Accessed 2/11/21.

Gerber, Lynne. 2008. "The Opposite of Gay: Nature, Creation, and Queerish Ex-Gay Experiments." *Nova Religio: The Journal of Alternative and Emergent Religions* 11(4): 8–30.

Glazier, Rebecca A. 2013. "Divine Direction: How Providential Religious Beliefs Shape Foreign Policy Attitudes." *Foreign Policy Analysis* 9(2): 127–42.

Gleason, Philip. 1983. "Identifying Identity: A Semantic History." *Journal of American History* 69: 910–31.

Goffman, Erving. 1974. *Frame Analysis: An Essay on the Organization of Experience.* Cambridge, MA: Harvard University Press.

Goldberg, Michelle. 2006. *Kingdom Coming: The Rise of Christian Nationalism.* New York: W. W. Norton.

Goodstein, Laurie. 2008. "Episcopal Split as Conservatives form new Group." *New York Times.* December 3, 2008. https://www.nytimes.com/2008/12/04/us/04episcopal.html. Accessed 8/1/2020.

———. 2017. "Methodist High Court Rejects First Openly Gay Bishop's Consecration." *New York Times (Online),* April 28, 2017. https://www.nytimes.com/2017/04/28/us /methodist-high-court-rejects-first-gay-bishops-consecration.html#:~:text=Methodist %20Court%20Declares%20Gay%20Bishop's,law%20on%20marriage%20and%20 homosexuality.

Gray, Mary L. 2009. *Out in the Country: Youth, Media, and Queer Visibility in Rural America*. New York: NYU Press.

Greeley, Andrew M. 1972. *The Denominational Society: A Sociological Approach to Religion in America*. Glenview, IL: Scott, Foresman.

Green, B. 1998. "Family Ethnic Identity and Sexual Orientation: African American Lesbians and Gay Men." In C. Patterson and A. D'Augelli (Eds.), *Lesbian, Gay, and Bisexual Identities in Families: Psychological Perspectives*, pp. 40–52. London: Oxford University Press.

Green, John C., James L. Guth, Corwin E. Smidt, and Lyman A. Kellstedt (Eds.). 1996. *Religion and the Culture Wars: Dispatches from the Front*. New York: Rowman & Littlefield.

Greenberg, Daniel, Maxine Najle, Natalie Jackson, Oyindamola Bola, and Robert P. Jones. 2019. "America's Growing Support for Transgender Rights." Washington, DC: Public Religion Research Institute. https://www.prri.org/research/americas-growing-support-for-transgender-rights/. Accessed 10/14/2020.

Greene, Steven. 2002. "The Social-Psychological Measurement of Partisanship." *Political Behavior* 24(3): 171–97.

Griffin, Horace L. 2006. *Their Own Received Them Not: African American Lesbians and Gays in Black Churches*. Cleveland, OH: Pilgrim Press.

Guittar, Nicholas A., and Rachel L. Rayburn. 2016. "Coming Out: The Career Management of One's Sexuality." *Sexuality and Culture* 20: 336–57.

Guth, James L. 1996. "The Bully Pulpit: Southern Baptist Clergy and Political Activism 1980–92." In John C. Green, James L. Guth, Corwin E. Smidt, and Lyman A. Kellstedt (Eds.), *Religion and the Culture Wars: Dispatches from the Front*, pp. 146–73. New York: Rowman & Littlefield.

Haider-Markel, D. P. 2010. *Out and Running: Gay and Lesbian Candidates, Elections, and Policy Representation*. Washington, DC: Georgetown University Press.

Haider-Markel, Donald, Jami Taylor, Andrew Flores, Daniel Lewis, Patrick Miller, and Barry Tadlock. 2019. "Morality Politics and New Research on Transgender Politics and Public Policy." *The Forum* 17(1): 159–81.

Harris, Fredrick C. 1994. "Something Within: Religion as a Mobilizer of African-American Political Activism." *The Journal of Politics* 56(1): 42–68.

———. 1999. *Something Within: Religion in African-American Political Activism*. Oxford: Oxford University Press.

Harrison, Brian F., and Melissa R. Michelson. 2017. *Listen, We Need to Talk: How to Change Attitudes about LGBT Rights*. New York: Oxford University Press.

Hasbrouck, Jay. 2005. "Utopian Imaginaries and Faerie Practice: Mapping Routes of Relational Agency." In Scott Thumma and Edward R. Gray (Eds.), *Gay Religion*, pp. 239–58. Lanham, MD: AltaMira Press.

Herek, Gregory M. 2007. "Confronting Sexual Stigma and Prejudice: Theory and Practice." *Journal of Social Issues* 63(4): 905–25.

Herek, Gregory M., Aaron T. Norton, Thomas J. Allen, and Charles L. Sims. 2010. "Demographic, Psychological, and Social Characteristics of Self-Identified Lesbian, Gay, and Bisexual Adults in a U.S. Probability Sample." *Sexual Research and Social Policy* 7: 176–200.

Heritage Foundation. 2020. "Religious Freedom: What's at Stake if We Lose It." Washington, DC: Heritage Explains. https://www.heritage.org/religious-liberty/heritage-explains/religious-freedom-whats-stake-if-we-lose-it. Accessed 10/14/2020.

Hill, Samuel S. Jr. 1980. *The South and the North in American Religion.* Athens: The University of Georgia Press.

Hinrichs, Donald W., and Pamela J. Rosenberg. 2002. "Attitudes toward Gay, Lesbian, and Bisexual Persons among Heterosexual Liberal Arts College Students." *Journal of Homosexuality* 43(1): 61–84.

Hoffmann, John P., and Sherrie Mills Johnson. 2005. "Attitudes toward Abortion among Religious Traditions in the United States: Change or Continuity?" *Sociology of Religion* 66(2): 161–82.

Holly, David. 2013. "Coming Out under Jesus: Glide Memorial and the Struggle for Gay Civil Rights in San Francisco." *Clio's Scroll* 14(2): 49–72.

Houghland, James G., and James A. Christenson. 1983. "Religion and Politics: The Relationship of Religious Participation to Political Efficacy and Involvement." *Sociology and Social Research* 67(4): 405–20.

Hunt, Stephen (Ed.). 2015. *Religion and LGBTQ Sexualities: Critical Essays.* London: Routledge.

Irizarry, Yasmiyn A., and Ravi K. Perry. 2017. "Challenging the Black Church Narrative: Race, Class, and Homosexual Attitudes." *Journal of Homosexuality* 65(7): 884–911. http://dx.doi.org/10.1080/00918369.2017.1364566.

Jelen, Ted G. 1994. "Religion and Foreign Policy Attitudes: Exploring the Effects of Denomination and Doctrine." *American Politics Research* 22(3): 382–400.

———. 1998. "Research in Religion and Mass Political Behavior in the United States: Looking Both Ways after Two Decades of Scholarship." *American Politics Quarterly* 26(1): 110–34.

Jelen, Ted G., and Marthe A. Chandler. 1996. "Patterns of Religious Socialization: Communalism, Associationalism, and the Politics of Lifestyle." *Review of Religious Research* 38(2): 142–58.

Jelen, Ted G., and Clyde Wilcox. 1993. "Preaching to the Converted: The Causes and Consequences of Viewing Religious Television." In David C. Leege and Lyman A. Kellstedt (Eds.), *Rediscovering the Religious Factor in American Politics*, pp. 255–69. Armonk, NY: M. E. Sharpe.

Johansen, Bruce E. 2016. "Roger Williams, Native Peoples, and 'Soul Liberty.'" In Barbara A. McGraw (Ed.), *The Wiley Companion to Religion and Politics in the U.S.*, pp. 42–50. West Sussex, UK: John Wiley & Sons.

Johnson, E. Patrick, and Mae Henderson (Eds.). 2005. *Black Queer Studies: A Critical Anthology.* Durham, NC: Duke University Press.

Jones, Jeffrey M. 2021. "LGBT Identification Rises to 5.6% in Latest U.S. Estimate." Washington, DC: Gallup. https://news.gallup.com/poll/329708/lgbt-identification-rises-latest-estimate.aspx. Accessed 2/24/2021.

———. 2022. "LGBT Identification in U.S. Ticks Up to 7.1%." Washington, DC: Gallup. https://news.gallup.com/poll/389792/lgbt-identification-ticks-up.aspx. Accessed 2/22/2022.

Jones, Robert P. 2020. *White Too Long: The Legacy of White Supremacy in American Christianity.* New York: Simon & Schuster.

Jones, Robert P., and Daniel Cox. 2008. "Mainline Protestant Clergy Views on Theology and Gay and Lesbian Issues: Findings from the 2008 Clergy Voices Survey." Washington, DC: Public Religion Research Institute. https://www.prri.org/wp-content/uploads/2011/06/2008-Mainline-Protestant-Clergy-LGBT-Issues.pdf. Accessed 9/10/2022.

Jonsen, Albert R., and Jeff Stryker (Eds.). 1993. *The Social Impact of ADIS in the United States*. Washington, DC: National Academies Press.

Kane, Melinda D. 2013. "LGBT Religious Activism: Predicting State Variations in the Number of Metropolitan Community Churches, 1974–2000." *Sociological Forum* 28(1): 135–58.

Katz, Jonathan Ned. 1983. *Gay/Lesbian Almanac*. New York: Harper & Row.

Kellstedt, Lyman A., and John C. Green. 1993. "Knowing God's Many People: Denominational Preference and Political Behavior." In David C. Leege and Lyman A. Kellstedt (Eds.), *Rediscovering the Religious Factor in American Politics*, pp. 53–77. New York: Routledge.

Kellstedt, Lyman A., and Corwin E. Smidt. 1993. "Doctrinal Beliefs and Political Behavior: Views of the Bible." In David C. Leege and Lyman A. Kellstedt (Eds.), *Rediscovering the Religious Factor in American Politics*, pp. 177–98. Armonk, NY: M. E. Sharpe.

Kim David v. David Ermold, et al. 592 U.S. 1 (2020). https://www.supremecourt.gov /opinions/20pdf/19-926_5hdk.pdf. Accessed 10/14/2020.

King, Gary, and Langche Zeng. 1999. "Logistic Regression in Rare Events Data." Department of Government, Harvard University. http://GKing.Harvard.Edu.

Klepser, Mary. 1979. "Pride Day in Portland: A Hymn of Thanks." In *The Chalice* Christmas 1979, Metropolitan Community Church Portland, Oregon. Shepard Family Papers (Box 9 MS 2988–15), Oregon Historical Society Research Library, Portland, OR, United States.

Kramnick, Isaac (Ed.). 2007. *Alexis de Tocqueville Democracy in America: A Norton Critical Edition*. New York: W. W. Norton.

Kuk, John, Zoltan Hajnal, and Nazita Lajevardi. 2022. "A Disproportionate Burden: Strict Voter Identification Laws and Minority Turnout." *Politics, Groups, and Identities* 10(1): 126–34.

Layman, Geoffrey C. 1997. "Religion and Political Behavior in the United States: The Impact of Beliefs, Affiliations, and Commitment from 1980 to 1994." *Public Opinion Quarterly* 61(2): 288–316.

Lease, Suzanne H., Sharon G. Horne, and Nicole Noffsinger-Frazier. 2005. "Affirming Faith Experiences and Psychological Health for Caucasian Lesbian, Gay, and Bisexual Individuals." *Journal of Counseling Psychology* 52(3): 378–88.

Legge, David C., and Lyman A. Kellstedt. (Eds.). 1993. *Rediscovering the Religious Factor in American Politics*. Armonk, NY: M. E. Sharpe.

Levendusky, Matthew S. 2010. "Clearer Cues, More Consistent Voters: A Benefit of Elite Polarization." *Political Behavior* 32: 111–31.

Lewis, Gregory B., Marc A. Rogers, and Kenneth Sherrill. 2011. "Lesbian, Gay and Bisexual Voters in the 2000 U.S. Presidential Election." *Politics and Policy* 39(5): 655–77.

Little, Lyneka. 2012. "Joe Biden Says 'Will and Grace' Helped Change Public Opinion on Gay Rights." *Wall Street Journal*, May 7, 2012. https://www.wsj.com/articles/BL-SEB -69987. Accessed 1/25/2021.

Liu, Baodong, Sharon D. Wright Austin, and Byron D'Andrá Orey. 2009. "Church Attendance, Social Capital, and Black Voting Participation." *Social Science Quarterly* 90(30): 576–92.

Macaluso, Theodore F., and John Wanat. 1979. "Voting Turnout and Religiosity." *Polity* 12:158–69.

Madison, James. 1787. "Federalist No. 10 The Same Subject Continued: The Union as a Safeguard Against Domestic Faction and Insurrection." *New York Packet*, November

23, 1787. https://guides.loc.gov/federalist-papers/text-1-10#s-lg-box-wrapper-25493273. Accessed 10/5/2020.

Magni, G., and Reynolds, A. 2021. "Voter Preferences and the Political Underrepresentation of Minority Groups: Lesbian, Gay, and Transgender Candidates in Advanced Democracies." *Journal of Politics*. Online First. https://doi.org/10.1086/712142.

Magnusson, David, and Lars Bergman (Eds.). 1990. *Data Quality in Longitudinal Research*. New York: Cambridge University Press.

Mahaffy, Kimberly A. 1996. "Cognitive Dissonance and Its Resolution: A Study of Lesbian Christians." *Journal for the Scientific Study of Religion* 35(4): 392–402.

Mann, Barbara Alice. 2016. "Ending the Ban on Indigenous Spiritualties." In Barbara A. McGraw (Ed.), *The Wiley Companion to Religion and Politics in the U.S.*, pp. 291–304. West Sussex, UK: John Wiley & Sons.

Margolis, Michele F. 2018a. *From Politics to the Pews: How Partisanship and the Political Environment Shape Religious Identity*. Chicago: University of Chicago Press.

———. 2018b. "How Politics Affects Religion: Partisanship, Socialization, and Religiosity in America." *Journal of Politics* 80(1): 30–43.

Marsden, George M. 1980. *Fundamentalism and American Culture: The Shaping of Twentieth-Century Evangelicalism, 1870–1925*. New York: Oxford University Press.

Marti, Gerado. 2012. "The Diversity-Affirming Latino: Ethnic Options and the Ethnic Transcendent Expression of American Latino Religious Identity." In Carolyn Chen and Russell Jeung (Eds.), *Sustaining Faith Traditions: Race, Ethnicity, and Religion among the Latino and Asian American Second Generation*, pp. 31–52. New York: NYU Press.

Masters, Jeffrey. 2021. "Brandi Carlile on Faith, Music, and Motherhood: 'OK, Here's the Truth.'" *The Advocate*, April 6, 2021. https://www.advocate.com/books/2021/4/06/brandi-carlile-interview-faith-music-motherhood-broken-horses. Accessed 8/2/2022.

McAdam, Doug, John D. McCarthy, and Mayer N. Zald (Eds.). 1996. *Comparative Perspectives on Social Movements: Political Opportunities, Mobilizing Structures, and Cultural Framings*. New York: Cambridge University Press.

McCarthy, John D., and Mayer N. Zald. 1973. *The Trend of Social Movements in America: Professionalization and Resource Mobilization*. Morristown, NJ: General Learning Press.

———. 1977. "Resource Mobilization and Social Movements: A Partial Theory." *American Journal of Sociology* 82(6): 1212–41.

McClerking, Harwood K., and Eric L. McDaniel. 2005. "Belonging and Doing: Political Churches and Black Political Participation." *Political Psychology* 26(5): 721–33.

McDaniel, Eric L. 2008. *Politics in the Pews: The Political Mobilization of Black Churches*. Ann Arbor: University of Michigan Press.

McPherson, Miller, Lynn Smith-Lovin, and James M. Cook. 2001. "Birds of a Feather: Homophily in Social Networks." *Annual Review of Sociology* 27(1): 415–44.

McQueeney, Krista. 2009. "'We Are All God's Children, Ya'll:' Race, Gender, and Sexuality in Lesbian- and Gay-Affirming Congregations." *Social Problems* 56(1): 151–73.

Mecca, Tommi Avicolli. 2009. "Gay Pagans and Atheists Manifesto." In Tommi Avicolli Mecca (Ed.), *Smash the Church, Smash the State! The Early Years of Gay Liberation*, pp. 242–45. San Francisco: City Lights Books.

Miller, Arthur H., Patricia Gurin, Gerald Gurin, and Oksana Malanchuk. 1981. "Group Consciousness and Political Participation." *American Journal of Political Science* 25(3): 494–511.

Miller, Emily McFarlan. 2022. "What Happened to United Methodists' Proposal to Split the Denomination?" *Religion News Service*, June 29, 2022. https://religionnews.com /2022/06/29/what-happened-to-united-methodists-proposal-to-split-the-denomina tion/. Accessed 06/29/2022.

Miller, Patrick R., Andrew Flores, Donald P. Haider-Markel, Daniel P. Lewis, Barry Tadlock, and Jami Taylor. 2017. "Transgender Politics as Body Politics: The Conditional Effects of Authoritarianism and Disgust on Transgender-Related Policy Attitudes." *Politics, Groups, and Identities* 5(1): 4–24.

Minwalla, Omar, B. R. Simon Rosser, Jamie Feldman, and Christine Varga. 2005. "Identity Experience among Progressive Gay Muslims in North America: A Qualitative Study within Al-Fatiha." *Culture, Health, and Sexuality* 7(2): 113–28.

Moon, Dawne. 2014. "Beyond the Dichotomy: Six Religious Views of Homosexuality." *Journal of Homosexuality* 61(9): 1215–41.

Moon, Dawne, and Theresa W. Tobin. 2018. "Sunsets and Solidarity: Overcoming Sacramental Shame in Conservative Christian Churches to Forge a Queer Vision of Love and Justice." *Hypatia* 33(3): 451–68.

Moon, Dawne, Theresa W. Tobin, and J. E. Sumerau. 2019. "Alpha, Omega, and the Letters in Between: LGBTQI Conservative Christians Undoing Gender." *Gender and Society* 33(4): 583–606.

Morone, James A. 2003. *Hellfire Nation: The Politics of Sin in American History*. New Haven, CT: Yale University Press.

Movement Advancement Project. 2022. "Equality Maps: Conversion Therapy Laws." https:// www.lgbtmap.org/equality-maps/conversion_therapy. Accessed 02/23/2022.

Movement Advancement Project, Center for American Progress, Freedom to Work, Human Rights Campaign, and National Black Justice Coalition. 2013. "A Broken Bargain for LGBT Workers of Color." Denver, CO: Movement Advancement Project. http:// www.lgbtmap.org/workers-of-color.

Mucciaroni, Gary. 2011. "The Study of LGBT Politics and Its Contributions to Political Science." *PS: Political Science and Politics* 44(1): 17–21.

Murphy, Caryle. 2015. "Lesbian, Gay and Bisexual Americans Differ from General Public in Their Religious Affiliations." Washington, DC: Pew Research Center. http://www .pewresearch.org/fact-tank/2015/05/26/lesbian-gay-and-bisexual-americans-differ -from-general-public-in-their-religious-affiliations/. Accessed 09/2016.

National Association of Evangelicals. 2018. "NAE Welcomes Masterpiece Decision." Washington, DC: NAE. https://www.nae.net/nae-welcomes-masterpiece-decision/. Accessed 10/14/2020.

Negy, Charles, and Russell Eisenmann. 2005. "A Comparison of African-American and White College Students Affective and Attitudinal Reactions to Lesbian, Gay, and Bisexual Individuals: An Exploratory Study." *Journal of Sex Research* 42(4): 291–98.

Neitz, Mary Jo. 2005. "Queering the Dragonfest: Changing Sexualities in a Post-Patriarchal Religion." In Scott Thumma and Edward R. Gray (Eds.), *Gay Religion*, pp. 259–80. Lanham, MD: AltaMira Press.

Nelsen, Hart M., and Anne Kusener Nelson. 1975. *Black Church in the Sixties*. Lexington: University of Kentucky Press.

Neundorf, Anja, and Kaat Smets. 2017. "Political Socialization and the Making of Citizens." *Oxford Handbooks Online*. DOI: 10.1093/oxfordhb/9780199935307.013.98.

Newport, Frank. 2018. "In U.S., Estimate of LGBT Population Rises to 4.5%." *Gallup*, May 22, 2018. http://news.gallup.com/poll/234863/estimate-lgbt-population-rises.aspx. Accessed 5/24/2018.

Norton, Aaron T., and Gregory M. Herek. 2013. "Heterosexuals' Attitudes toward Transgender People: Findings from a National Probability Sample of U.S. Adults." *Sex Roles* 68:738–53.

Novkov, Julie, and Scott Barclay. 2010. "Lesbians, Gays, Bisexuals, and the Transgendered in Political Science: Report on a Discipline-Wide Survey." *PS: Political Science and Politics* 43(1): 95–106.

O'Brien, Jodi. 2004. "Wrestling the Angel of Contradiction: Queer Christian Identities." *Culture and Religion* 5(2): 179–202.

———. 2014. "Outing Religion in LGBT Studies." In Yvette Taylor and Ria Snowdon (Eds.), *Queering Religion, Religious Queers*, pp. xi–xxii. New York: Routledge.

Oldfield, Duane Murray. 1996. *The Right and the Righteous: The Christian Rights Confronts the Republican Party*. New York: Rowman & Littlefield.

Oliver, Pamela E., and Hank Johnson. 2000. "What a Good Idea! Ideologies and Frames in Social Movement Research." *Mobilization: An International Journal* 47(1): 37–54.

O'Loughlin, Ray. 1981. "S.F. Responds to Evangelists Campaign." *The Sentinel* 8(17): 9.

Olson, Laura R., Wendy Cadge, and James T. Harrison. 2006. "Religion and Public Opinion about Same-Sex Marriage." *Social Science Quarterly* 87(2): 340–60.

Olson, Mancur I. 1965. *The Logic of Collective Action: Public Goods and the Theory of Group*. Cambridge, MA: Harvard University Press.

Page, Benjamin I., Larry M. Bartles, and Jason Seawright. 2013. "Democracy and the Policy Preferences of Wealthy Americans." *Perspectives on Politics* 11(1): 51–73.

Parent, Mike C., Cirleen DeBlaere, and Bonnie Moradi. 2013. "Approaches to Research on Intersectionality: Perspectives on Gender, LGBT, and Racial/Ethnic Identities." *Sex Roles* 68:639–45.

Perry, Samuel L., and Kyle C. Longest. 2019. "Examining the Impact of Religious Initiation Rites on Religiosity and Disaffiliation over Time." *Journal for the Scientific Study of Religion* 58(4): 891–904.

Perry, Troy, interview by Dave Aiken. November 9, 1974. "Radio Interview with Rev. Troy Perry: A Sampler of Early Documents." *LGBTQ Religious Archives Network*. https://lgbtqreligiousarchives.org/exhibits/sampler/friends-radio.aspx. Accessed 2/11/2021.

Perry, Troy D., and Charles L. Lucas. 1987. *The Lord Is My Shepard and He Knows I'm Gay: The Autobiography of the Reverend Troy D. Perry*. Los Angeles: Nash.

Pew Research Center. 2013. "A Survey of LGBT Americans: Attitudes, Experiences and Values in Changing Times." Washington, DC: Pew Research Center.

———. 2015. "America's Changing Religious Landscape." Washington, DC: Pew Research Center.

———. 2022. "Modeling the Future of Religion in America." Washington, DC: Pew Research Center. https://www.pewresearch.org/religion/2022/09/13/modeling-the-future-of-religion-in-america/. Accessed 9/15/2022.

Pierce, Jonathan J., Saba Siddiki, Michael D. Jones, Kristin Schumacher, Andrew Pattinson, and Holly Peterson. 2014. "Social Construction and Policy Design: A Review of Past Applications." *Policy Studies Journal* 42(1): 1–29.

Pollock, Philip H. 1982. "Organizations as Agents of Mobilization: How Does Group Activity Affect Political Participation?" *American Journal of Political Science* 26(3): 485–503.

Popkin, Samuel L. 1991. *The Reasoning Voter, Communication and Persuasion in Presidential Campaigns*. Chicago: University of Chicago Press.

Pottenger, John R. 2016. "The Intellectual Foundation and Political Construction of American Religious Pluralism." In Barbara A. McGraw (Ed.), *The Wiley Blackwell Companion to Religion and Politics in the U.S.*, pp.18–32. West Sussex, UK: John Wiley & Sons.

Primiano, Leonard Norman. 2005. "The Gay God of the City: The Emergence of the Gay and Lesbian Ethnic Parish." In Scott Thumma and Edward R. Gray (Eds.), *Gay Religion*, pp. 7–29. Lanham, MD: AltaMira Press.

Public Religion Research Institute. 2020. "Broad Support for LGBT Rights Across all 50 States: Findings from the 2019 American Values Atlas." Washington, DC: PRRI. https://www.prri.org/research/broad-support-for-lgbt-rights/. Accessed 2/22/2021.

———. 2021. "Is Religious Liberty a Shield or a Sword?" Washington, DC: PRRI. https://www.prri.org/research/is-religious-liberty-a-shield-or-a-sword/. Accessed 3/3/2021.

Putnam, Robert D. 2000. *Bowling Alone: The Collapse and Revival of American Community*. New York: Simon & Schuster.

Putnam, Robert D., and David E. Campbell. 2010. *American Grace: How Religion Divides and Unites Us*. New York: Simon & Schuster.

Rahman, Momin. 2010. "Queer as Intersectionality: Theorizing Gay Muslim Identities." *Sociology* 44(5): 944–61.

Ratcliff, Shawn M., and Trenton M. Haltom. 2021. "The Proverbial Closet: Do Faith and Religiosity Affect Coming Out Patterns?" *Social Currents* 8(3): 249–69.

Read, Jen'nan Ghazal. 2003. "The Sources of Gender Role Attitudes among Christian and Muslim Arab-American Women." *Sociology of Religion* 64(2): 207–22.

Robertson, Pat. 1993. "Religious Broadcasters Must Be Salt and Light." *Christian Broadcasting Network*, February 16, 1993. http://www.patrobertson.com/speeches/Religious BroadcastersSaltand%20Light.asp. Accessed 10/9/2020.

Robinson, Christine M., and Sue E. Spivey. 2007. "The Politics of Masculinity and the Ex-Gay Movement." *Gender and Society* 21(5): 650–75.

Robnett, Belinda, and James A. Bany. 2011. "Gender, Church Involvement, and Africa-American Political Participation." *Sociological Perspectives* 54(4): 689–712.

Rodriguez, Eric M., and Suzanne C. Ouellette. 2000. "Gay and Lesbian Christians: Homosexual and Religious Identity Integration in the Members and Participants of a Gay-Positive Church." *Journal for the Scientific Study of Religion* 39(3): 333–47.

Roof, Wade Clark, and William McKinney. 1987. *American Mainline Religion: Its Changing Shape and Future*. New Brunswick, NJ: Rutgers University Press.

Rozell, Mark J., and Clyde Wilcox (Eds.). 1995. *God at the Grassroots: The Christian Right in the 1994 Elections*. Lanham, MD: Rowman & Littlefield.

Savin-Williams, Ritch C. 2006. *The New Gay Teenager*. Cambridge, MA: Harvard University Press.

Schaffner, Brian, and Stephen Ansolabehere. 2019. "2017 CCES Common Content." *Harvard Dataverse*. https://doi.org/10.7910/DVN/3STEZY.

Schaffner, Brian, Stephen Ansolabehere, and Sam Luks. 2019. "CCES Common Content, 2018." *Harvard Dataverse*. https://doi.org/10.7910/DVN/ZSBZ7K.

Schaffner, Brian, and Nenad Senic. 2006. "Rights or Benefits? Explaining the Sexual Identity Gap in American Political Behavior." *Political Research Quarterly* 59(1): 123–32.

Schnabel, Landon. 2018. "Sexual Orientation and Social Attitudes." *Socius: Sociological Research for a Dynamic World* 4: 1–18. https://doi.org/10.1177%2F2378023118769550.

Schnoor, Randal F. 2006. "Being Gay and Jewish: Negotiating Intersecting Identities." *Sociology of Religion* 67(1): 43–60.

Schwadel, Phillip, Jacob E. Cheadle, Sarah E. Malone, and Michael Stout. 2016. "Social Networks and Civic Participation and Efficacy in Two Evangelical Protestant Churches." *Review of Religious Research* 58: 305–17.

Sears, Brad, and Lee Badgett. 2012. "Beyond Stereotypes: Poverty in the LGBT Community." *TIDES: Momentum*, June. http://williamsinstitute.law.ucla.edu/headlines/beyond-stereotypes-poverty-in-the-lgbt-community/.

Sellers, Robert M., Mia A. Smith, J. Nicole Shelton, Stephanie A. J. Rowley, and Tabbye M. Chavous. 1998. "Multidimensional Model of Racial Identity: A Reconceptualization of African American Racial Identity." *Personality and Social Psychology Review* 2(1): 18–39.

Selzer, Richard. 1992. "The Social Location of Those Holding Antihomosexual Attitudes." *Sex Roles* 26(9/10): 391–98.

Sevelius, Jae M. 2013. "Gender Affirmation: A Framework for Conceptualizing Risk Behavior among Transgender Women of Color." *Sex Roles* 68: 675–89.

Sherkat, Darren E. 2016. "Sexuality and Religious Commitment Revisited: Exploring the Religious Commitments of Sexual Minorities, 1991–2014." *Journal for the Scientific Study of Religion* 55(4): 756–69.

Sherkat, Darren E., Kylan Mattias de Vries, and Stacia Creek. 2010. "Race, Religion, and Opposition to Same-Sex Marriage." *Social Science Quarterly* 91(1): 80–98.

Shokeid, Moshe. 1995. *A Gay Synagogue in New York*. New York: Columbia University Press.

———. 2005. "Why Join a Gay Synagogue?" In Scott Thumma and Edward R. Gray (Eds.), *Gay Religion*, pp. 83–97. Lanham, MD: AltaMira Press.

Slothuus, Rune, and Claes H. de Vreese, 2010. "Political Parties, Motivated Reasoning, and Issue Framing Effects." *The Journal of Politics* 72(3): 630–45.

Smith, Jane I. 2010. *Islam in America*. New York: Columbia University Press.

Smith, Timothy L. 1965. *Revivalism and Social Reform: American Protestantism on the Eve of the Civil War*. New York: Harper & Row.

Smith, Tom W., Peter Marsden, Michael Hout, and Jibum Kim. 2016. "General Social Surveys, 2016." Chicago: National Opinion Research Center. gssdataexplorer.norc.org.

Somerville, Siobhan B. 2000. *Queering the Color Line: Race and the Invention of Homosexuality in American Culture*. Durham, NC: Duke University Press.

Son, Joonmo, and John Wilson. 2021. "Is There a Bidirectional Causal Relationship between Religiosity and Volunteering?" *Journal for the Scientific Study of Religion* 60(4): 749–68.

Sorin, Gerald. 1997. *Tradition Transformed: The Jewish Experience in America*. Baltimore, MD: The Johns Hopkins University Press.

SOS Ministries. n.d. "The Beginning 1980." https://www.sosmin.com/?page_id=47. Accessed 3/27/2022.

Southern Poverty Law Center. n.d. "World Congress of Families, Extremist File." https://www.splcenter.org/fighting-hate/extremist-files/group/world-congress-families. Accessed 2/1/2023.

Starke, Rodney, and Roger Finke. 1988. "American Religion in 1776: A Statistical Portrait." *Sociological Analysis* 49(1): 39–51.

Stewart, Katherine. 2020. *The Power Worshipers: Inside the Dangerous Rise of Religious Nationalism*. New York: Bloomsbury.

Stone, Amy L. 2012. *Gay Rights at the Ballot Box*. Minneapolis: University of Minnesota Press.

Strolovitch, Dara Z. 2007. *Affirmative Advocacy: Race, Class, and Gender in Interest Group Politics*. Chicago: University of Chicago Press.

Sumerau, J. E., and Lain A. B. Mathers. 2019. *America through Transgender Eyes*. Lanham, MA: Rowman & Littlefield.

Swank, Eric, and Breanne Fahs. 2013. "Predicting Electoral Activism among Gays and Lesbians in the United States." *Journal of Applied Social Psychology* 43:1382–93.

Swartz, David R. 2012. *Moral Minority: The Evangelical Left in an Age of Conservatism*. Philadelphia: University of Pennsylvania Press.

Tajfel, Henri. 1978. *Differentiation between Social Groups*. London: Academic Press.

Tarrow, Sidney. 1998. *Power in Movement: Social Movements and Contentious Politics*. Cambridge: Cambridge University Press.

Taylor, J. Benjamin, Sarah Allen Gershon, and Adrian D. Pantoja. 2014. "Christian American? Understanding the Link between Churches, Attitudes, and 'Being American' among Latino Immigrants." *Politics and Religion* 7(2): 339–65.

Taylor, Y., and Snowdon, R. (Eds.). 2014. *Queering Religion, Religious Queers*. New York: Routledge.

Thomas, Emma F., Lisa Rathmann, and Craig McGarty, C. 2017. "From 'I' to 'We': Different forms of Identity, Emotion, and Belief Predict Victim Support Volunteerism among Nominal and Active Supporters." *Journal of Applied Social Psychology* 47:213–23.

Thumma, Scott, and Gray, Edward R. (Eds). 2005. *Gay Religion*. Lanham, MD: AltaMira Press.

Tilly, Charles. 1978. *From Mobilization to Revolution*. Reading, MA: Addison-Wesley.

Trammell, Jim Y. 2015. "'Homosexuality Is Bad for Me': An Analysis of Homosexual Christian Testimonies in *Christianity Today* Magazine." *Journal of Media and Religion* 14(1): 1–15.

Twain, Shania. (Host). *Let's Celebrate*. [Audio Podcast]. August 19, 2021. Retrieved from https://music.apple.com/us/station/lets-celebrate/ra.1569220526.

Twenge, Jean M., Ryne A. Sherman, and Brooke E. Wells. 2016. "Changes in American Adults' Reported Same-Sex Experiences and Attitudes, 1973–2014." *Archives of Sexual Behavior* 45:1713–30.

United Methodist Church. 2019. "Protocol of Reconciliation and Grace Through Separation." https://cdnsc.umc.org/-/media/umc-media/2020/01/03/15/48/Protocol-of-Reconciliation-and-Grace-through-Separation. Accessed 9/23/2020.

United States Secular Survey. 2022. "Nonreligious LGBTQ People in America." https://www.secularsurvey.org/lgbtq. Accessed 9/5/2022.

Vaid, Urvashi. 1995. *Virtual Equality: The Mainstreaming of Gay and Lesbian Liberation*. New York: Anchor Books.

Vandermaas-Peeler, Alex, Daniel Cox, Molly Fisch-Friedman, Rob Griffin, and Robert P. Jones. 2018b. "Wedding Cakes, Same-Sex Marriage, and the Future of LGBT Rights in America." Washington, DC: Public Religion Research Institute. https://www.prri.org/research/wedding-cakes-same-sex-lgbt-marriage/. Accessed 10/14/2020.

Vegter, Abigail, and Donald P. Haider-Markel. 2020. "The Special Role of Religion in LGBT-Related Attitudes." *Oxford Research Encyclopedia of LGBTQ Politics and Policy*. https://doi.org/10.1093/acrefore/9780190228637.013.1254.

Verba, Sidney, and Norman H. Nie. 1972. *Participation in America: Political Democracy and Social Equality*. Chicago, IL: University of Chicago Press.

Verba, Sidney, Kay Lehman Schlozman, and Henry Brady. 1995. *Voice and Equality: Civic Voluntarism in American Politics*. Cambridge, MA: Harvard University Press.

Wald, Kenneth D., Lyman A. Kellstedt, and David C. Leege. 1993. "Church Involvement and Political Behavior." In David C. Leege and Lyman A. Kellstedt, *Rediscovering the Religious Factor in American Politics*, pp. 121–38. Amonk, NY: M. E. Sharpe.

Wald, Kenneth D., Dennis E. Owen, and Samuel S. Hill. 1988. "Churches as Political Communities." *American Political Science Review* 82(2): 531–48.

Wald, Kenneth D., and Samuel Shye. 1995. "Religious Influence in Electoral Behavior: The Role of Institutional and Social Forces in Israel." *The Journal of Politics* 57(2): 495–507.

Wald, Kenneth D., Adam L. Silverman, and Kevil S. Fridy. 2005. "Making Sense of Religion in Political Life." *Annual Review of Political Science* 8:121–43.

Wald, Kenneth D., and Clyde Wilcox. 2006. "Has Political Science Rediscovered the Faith Factor?" *The American Political Science Review* 100(4): 523–29.

Walton, Gerald. 2006. "Fag Church." *Journal of Homosexuality* 51(2): 1–17.

Ward, Jane. 2008. "White Normativity: The Cultural Dimensions of Whiteness in a Racially Diverse LGBT Organization." *Sociological Perspectives* 51(3): 563–86.

Warner, Michael. 1999. *The Trouble with Normal: Sex, Politics, and the Ethics of Queer Life*. Cambridge, MA: Harvard University Press.

Warner, R. Stephen. 1998. "Immigration and Religious Communities in the United States." In R. Stephen Warner, and Judith G. Wittner (Eds.), *Gatherings in Diaspora: Religious Communities and the New Immigration*, pp. 3–34. Philadelphia, PA: Temple University Press.

Warner, R. Stephen, and Judith G. Wittner (Eds.). 1998. *Gatherings in Diaspora: Religious Communities and the New Immigration*. Philadelphia, PA: Temple University Press.

White, Heather R. 2015. *Reforming Sodom: Protestants and the Rise of Gay Rights*. Chapel Hill: The University of North Carolina Press.

Whitehead, Andrew L. 2010. "Sacred Rites and Civil Rights: Religion's Effect on Attitudes toward Same-Sex Unions and the Perceived Cause of Homosexuality." *Social Science Quarterly* 91(1): 63–79.

———. 2012. "Gender Ideology and Religion: Does a Masculine Image of God Matter?" *Review of Religious Research* 54(2): 139–56.

Whitehead, Andrew L., and Joseph O. Baker. 2012. "Homosexuality, Religion, and Science: Moral Authority and the Persistence of Negative Attitudes." *Sociological Inquiry* 82(4): 487–509.

Whitehead, Andrew L., and Samuel L. Perry. 2020. *Taking America Back for God: Christian Nationalism in the United States*. New York: Oxford University Press.

Whitley, Bernard E. 2009. "Religiosity and Attitudes toward Lesbians and Gay Men: A Meta-Analysis." *The International Journal for the Psychology of Religion* 19(1): 21–38.

Wilcox, Clyde, and Leopoldo Gomez. 1990. "Religion, Group Identification, and Politics among American Blacks." *Sociological Analysis* 51(3): 271–85.

Wilcox, Clyde, and Lee Sigelman. 2001. "Political Mobilization in the Pew: Religious Contacting and Electoral Turnout." *Social Science Quarterly* 82(3): 524–35.

Wilcox, Melissa M. 2003. *Coming Out in Christianity: Religion, Identity, and Community*. Bloomington: Indiana University Press.

———. 2009. *Queer Women and Religious Individualism*. Bloomington: Indiana University Press.

———. 2012. "Sexuality, Gender, and Religious Attendance." *Fieldwork in Religion* 7(2): 102–16.

Williams, Dave. 1981. "San Francisco Statement Provokes Comment from PLGC'ers." *More Light Update*, August 1981, pp. 2–3. Shepard Family Papers (Box 9 MS 2988-15), Oregon Historical Society Research Library, Portland, OR, United States.

Williams, Rhys H., and N. J. Demerath III. 1991. "Religion and Political Process in an American City." *American Sociological Review* 56(4): 417–31.

Wolkomir, Michelle. 2006. *Be Not Deceived: The Sacred and Sexual Struggles of Gay and Ex-Gay Christian Men*. New Brunswick, NJ: Rutgers University Press.

Woodberry, R. D., and C. S. Smith. 1998. "Fundamentalism et al: Conservative Protestants in America." *Annual Review of Sociology* 24:25–56. https://doi.org/10.1146/annurev.soc.24.1.25.

Yip, Andrew K. 1997. "Attacking the Attacker: Gay Christians Talk Back." *British Journal of Sociology* 48(1): 113–27.

Index

Royal G. Cravens III is a Senior Research Analyst at the Southern Poverty Law Center. He is a previous recipient of the Bailey and Cynthia Weber Awards from the American Political Science Association and has held fellowships with the Social Science Research Council and Public Religion Research Institute.

www.ingramcontent.com/pod-product-compliance
Lightning Source LLC
Chambersburg PA
CBHW070404270326
41926CB00014B/2690